UNSOLVED MYSTERIES

OF SOUTHERN AFRICA

UNSOLVED MYSTERIES

OF SOUTHERN AFRICA

Rob Marsh

STRUIK

ACKNOWLEDGEMENTS

Writing this book would not have been possible without the assistance of a number of people, and it is gratifying to say that my requests for help were always received most kindly and acted upon with both efficiency and speed. To the following people, I am particularly grateful:

Emlyn Brown; Peter Humphries; The Argus Library; the staff at the South African Library, Cape Town; ML Wilson and WJJ van Rijssen at the South African Museum; Pam Wormser at the Hout Bay Museum; the staff of Hout Bay Library; Cynthia Hind; Janie M van Vuuren, SAA Western Cape; Piet de Klerk, Department of Civil Aviation; Nan Rice, the Dolphin Action & Protection Group; the staff of the State Archives, Cape Town; Sergeant SC Stadler, SAP Cape Town; Bernard O'Sullivan; Reinhold Rau; A Botes and Major G Everts at Southern Air Force Commandpost, Silvermine; Trish Gordon; Lindy Nauta; Mrs Rattan; Professor D Scott-Macnab; Professor JC Poynton; M O'Brien; William Barker; Lara Geffen; Professor MN Bruton, JLB Smith Institute of Ichthyology, Grahamstown; Mrs MF Way-Jones, 1820 Settlers Memorial Museum; Joy Redelinghuys; and Karen Korte for her photographic research. A special debt of gratitude is due to Hilda Hermann, my editor at Struik Publishers. Without her unstinting help and encouragement, this book would never have been completed.

AUTHOR'S PREFACE

There are more things in heaven and earth, Horatio
Than are dreamt of in your philosophy.

(Hamlet I v 166-7)

When I was first approached by Struik Publishers to write *Unsolved Mysteries of southern Africa*, I have to admit I had little enthusiasm for the task. As far as I was concerned, the concept was a 'non-starter'. The reason for my reluctance was two-fold. Firstly, I didn't think southern Africa had mysteries worth writing about and, secondly, I wasn't very keen on writing about mysteries. On both accounts I couldn't have been more mistaken.

This book has been the most fascinating project I have ever undertaken. It has involved a considerable amount of research and, despite my efforts, areas of controversy will undoubtedly remain. In a book of this nature, it cannot be avoided.

If *Unsolved Mysteries of southern Africa* is as stimulating to read as it was to research and compile, then I shall feel my efforts to have been worthwhile. In the final analysis, *you*, the reader, will have to be the judge.

Rob Marsh

DEDICATION
To Mom and Dad, with love.

Struik Publishers (Pty) Ltd
(a member of the Struik Publishing Group (Pty) Ltd)
Cornelis Struik House
80 McKenzie Street
Cape Town
8001

Reg. No.: 54/00965/07

First published in 1994
© Struik Publishers 1994
Text © Rob Marsh 1994

Editor: Hilda Hermann
Designer: Alix Gracie
Editorial assistant: Wenda Pace
Proofreader: Sean Fraser
Picture researcher: Karen Korte
Cover marbling: Ann Muir

DTP: Suzanne Fortescue
Reproduction: Hirt & Carter (Pty) Ltd, Cape Town
Printing and binding: Tien Wah (Pty) Ltd, Singapore

ISBN 1 86825 406 2

CONTENTS

THE MYSTIFYING DEATH OF BARNEY BARNATO

Suicide or murder?

In appearance Mr Barnato was of medium height, fair of complexion and with a remarkably broad expanse of forehead, indicating – if his speech did not already – a very keen intellect ...

(Obituary in the *Cape Argus Weekly*, 16 June 1897.)

On 14 June 1897, Barney Barnato was travelling with his family from Cape Town to Southampton on the Union Line mail ship, *Scot*, when he disappeared overboard near the island of Madeira. His nephew, Solly Joel, remarked at the subsequent inquest that Barnato had seemed agitated shortly before his death. According to Joel, he had sat down in a deck chair and his uncle had asked him about the time. He pulled out his watch and said, 'By my watch it is thirteen minutes past three'. He then put his watch back in his pocket and when he looked up he saw 'a flash' just before Barnato vanished over the side of the ship.

Joel shouted 'Murder!' and tried, unsuccessfully, to reach his uncle.

By this time, the commotion had alerted the *Scot*'s fourth officer, William Clifford, who bravely jumped into the sea after Barnato but, despite his efforts, Barnato drowned.

The verdict of the jury at the official inquest into Barnato's death was that he had committed suicide while temporarily insane, a conclusion based on the fact that in the months preceding his death he had been prone to fits of mental instability. But was the verdict correct, or could Barnato have been murdered?

The flamboyant Barney Barnato, performer, diamond magnate and Randlord.

It was not established exactly what the 'flash' was that Joel had seen, nor why he should cry 'Murder!' as his uncle went over the side.

The death of Barnato was, in some respects, as controversial as his life.

FROM RAGS TO RICHES

Barney Barnato, whose real name was Barnett Isaacs, was born in the East End of London on 5 July 1852 – the same area of slum tenements and alleyways where one of London's famous characters, Jack the Ripper, would make a name for himself some thirty years later. Barnato was the son of a Jewish tailor who owned a tiny shop on the corner of Petticoat Lane, Whitechapel, an area long associated with the clothing trade. He left school at the age of thirteen and along with his elder brother, Harry, began his working life by helping his parents in the business. In their spare time the two boys tried to make a little extra money by collecting old clothes and selling them at the local market.

The Isaacs brothers were extroverts and born showmen. Barney in particular had a penchant for the theatre and at one time had the ambition of becoming a serious actor, but his stature – he was short and stocky – ruled against him. Leading roles were inevitably given to taller, more commanding actors. When Barney was twenty years old, he and Harry put together a comic act, involving juggling and acrobatics, and toured the local music halls under the name 'Barnato Brothers'. But professional entertainment was never destined to be more than a sideline for the two young men born into the rag trade. However, Barney would never lose his love for the stage.

A turning point in the lives of both Barney and Harry occurred in 1871, when they learnt of the diamond boom in Kimberley, South Africa, from their cousin, David Harris. Harris had already booked a passage on a Royal Mail steamer when he declared his intention of 'going to South Africa for the diamonds'. A few weeks after his departure Harry followed him, and for the next two years Barney remained in London where he worked as a part-time barman, odd-jobs man and occasional entertainer until, in 1873, he sailed from the port of Southampton to Cape Town on the maiden voyage of the steamship *Anglican*.

Barney arrived in Cape Town with thirty pounds and forty boxes of mildewed cigars supplied to him by his brother-in-law, Joel, who had heard that luxuries of any kind were in short supply in the Cape and had ambitions of starting an export business. He had not let his brother know that he was coming to South Africa, and paid an ox-wagon driver five pounds to take him the 600 kilometres north to Kimberley – a journey which took two months.

In Kimberley, Barney turned his hand to a number of 'jobs' including that of prize-fighter, labourer, juggler and clown, but in 1875 he set up business with Harry who, by this time, had some experience of the diamond business which he had gained while working for a diamond dealer, Van Praagh. In 1875, they became *kopje-wallopers*, going from mining claim to mining claim and buying any newly found stones. Shortly afterwards, 'Barnato Brothers (Dealers in Diamonds – Brokers in Mining Property)' was established. Barney, who had the more flamboyant character, was always destined to be the better known of the two brothers.

The Barnato brothers proved to have a tremendous flair for buying and selling diamonds, and within three short years became a force to be reckoned with in the volatile diamond market. This brought them into direct competition with Cecil Rhodes who, by 1888, was attempting to exert his own control over the market and in the process of establishing the De Beers Consolidated Mines Company. Eventually, a somewhat uneasy alliance was formed between Rhodes and the Barnato brothers.

In exchange for Barney's compliance with his schemes, Rhodes had to make a number of concessions: he agreed to procure Barney's election to the influential Diamond Buyer's Club from which he had been excluded because of his working-class background, and he also agreed to make Barney one of the four life governors of De Beers upon flotation of the company.

An advert for the Scot, *the Royal Mail twin screw steamer which had the fastest passage on record between England and Cape Town, both outwards and homewards.*

During September 1895, signs of an impending slump had appeared in the South African stock market and there had been fears within the financial community that the market would collapse completely. This situation was eventually averted by Barnato, at a cost of £3 million, and tremendous mental and physical effort. The strain took its toll in April 1896, when he fell ill with a slight fever and delirium. At the time he had been advised to leave Johannesburg and return to Cape Town to recuperate. He had stayed at the Sea Point Hotel in Cape Town and taken his place in parlia-

ment to keep his mind off business. But he had a relapse, and hallucinated that he was counting banknotes which crumbled to dust between his fingers; he also had to be prevented from clawing at diamonds which he thought lay embedded in cracks in walls.

Before long, the bouts of delirium were so serious that his nephew, Solly Joel, who had emigrated to help his uncle in his business, came to Cape Town from Johannesburg and arranged to accompany him to England, where it was hoped he would recover away from the intense pressures of work.

Barnato, along with his wife and family and Solly Joel, sailed on the *Scot* for England on 2 June 1897.

THE LAST DAYS

On board the ship, Barnato's health began to improve and, although he was watched discreetly all the time, the ship's doctor did not have to be called. However, on the day before he died he displayed great concern about the fate of the stock market, which was once more under pressure because of the volatile political position in the Transvaal with Kruger, the Boers and the British government, following the abortive Jameson Raid and its subsequent trial. War clouds were beginning to gather over South Africa.

After lunch the next day – the 14th – Barnato played chess with Solly, then insisted that the two of them walk together on the promenade deck. After about an hour Solly sat down on a deck chair but Barnato continued to walk.

'What time is it?' he asked a few moments later.

'Thirteen minutes past three,' came the reply.

Just seconds later Barnato was seen to go overboard.

The *Scot*'s fourth officer, William Clifford, who was dozing on deck, was startled into action by Solly's cry …

'Murder! For God's sake save him!'

When Clifford opened his eyes he thought he saw Solly grasping at Barnato's leg before he went over the side. Without hesitating, Clifford threw off his jacket and jumped overboard after him, but by the time the *Scot* had turned around and lowered a boat into the water, Barnato had drowned. Clifford, who had been unable to reach him in the rough sea, was pulled out of the water exhausted.

THE INQUEST

The *Scot* arrived at Southampton, England, on Friday, 18 June, and an inquest into Barnato's death was immediately held at the South Western Hotel in Southampton.

Solly Joel was the first witness to be called to give evidence ...

'I was a fellow-passenger with the deceased, my uncle, on board the *Scot*. About a quarter-to-three last Monday afternoon we were walking up and down together. I was tired and wanted to rest, but he declined to go below, and we kept walking to and fro. I sat down, and said to him, "Come and sit down". He said, "What time is it?" I pulled out my watch and replied, "By my watch it is thirteen minutes past three".

Above: Was Barney Barnato pushed over the side of the Scot, *or did he commit suicide?*

Below: Barney Barnato, with members of the Legislative Assembly and several reformers on board the RMS Norman, *15 July 1896.*

I had closed my watch and was putting it back in my pocket, when my uncle jumped overboard. I cried out "Murder!" and tried to catch hold of him. I did touch the bottom of his trousers, but could not hold. Mr Clifford was near, and hearing my call, rushed up, saying, "What is it?" I pointed to my uncle in the water and cried, "For God's sake, save him!" Mr Clifford at once slipped off his coat and jumped into the water. He was then perhaps fifty or sixty yards from my uncle. Several life buoys were thrown, the ship was stopped, a boat was lowered and the ship was turned round. The officer was seen first, and Mr Barnato was picked up. Every effort was made to restore him.'[1]

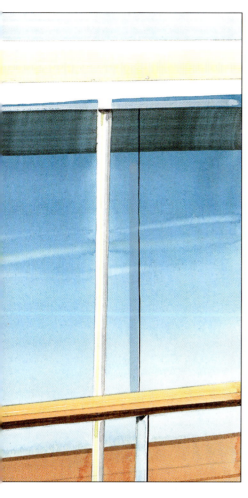

When the Coroner enquired as to Barnato's state of mind, Joel told him how he had been summoned to Cape Town by Mrs Barnato because her husband was in a very bad state of mind and how, when he arrived in the Cape, Barnato was very 'queer' in his actions and had paced restlessly for three days without sleeping.

'The deceased's mind used to wander. One hour he would be well, another ill. He was always brooding and thinking.'

Joel also added that he would sometimes have to shake him to bring him back to his senses and believed that he was not in his right mind at the time of his death.

This assessment was also supported by Barnato's physician in Cape Town. Two days after his death, and even before the official inquest had been convened, the following interview with Barnato's physician was published in the *Cape Argus Weekly*:

Mr Barnato's medical adviser on his last visit to Cape Town, was Doctor Marius Wilson of Mill Street, who was seen shortly after noon today by one of our representatives at his consulting rooms, Hofmeyer's Gardens. Dr Wilson had not heard the news and was naturally very much distressed upon hearing of the tragic death of his patient. He said that a fortnight before Mr Barnato left, the latter's condition was such as to cause extreme anxiety to his friends; but a few days before the Scot *sailed he seemed to have greatly recuperated, though somewhat weak and excitable. On the Wednesday he left these shores (Dr Wilson continued) he had apparently recovered and such an idea as future mental trouble was quite remote.*

At the inquest the jury delivered their verdict – death by drowning while temporarily insane.

Unfortunately, the jury's verdict left a number of unanswered questions. Although Barnato had a history of alcoholism, was clearly under a great deal of stress and had lapsed into periods of mental derangement, there had been nothing in his behaviour to indicate a suicidal state of mind. Furthermore, his wife, Fanny, refused to accept that her husband had committed suicide.

Malicious gossips who saw that Solly Joel had much to gain financially from Barnato's demise, hinted that he had a hand in the death, but these suggestions were completely without foundation. Could Barnato have been threatened in some way and, in an attempt to escape, rushed to the rail? And what was the 'flash' Solly remarked that he had seen? Could it have been a gun? And why did Solly cry 'Murder!'? Could it have been Barnato himself who cried out and that Clifford, in a moment of confusion,

assumed it was Solly? There is no evidence to suggest foul play, although one can argue, as does Stanley Jackson in his biography *The Great Barnato*, that 'accidental death' rather than suicide might have been a more appropriate verdict. Certainly Barnato's history of obsessive hard work, bouts of disequilibrium in Cape Town, insomnia and hyperactivity on board the ship were consistent with that of potential suicide. Unless, of course, there was a genuine reason for his paranoia ...

THE PERPLEXING AFFAIR OF BARON VON VELTHEIM

In February 1898, seven months after Barnato's death, Solly Joel began to receive a number of threatening letters from someone using the name 'Kismet'. The writer, who made a number of veiled threats in his communications, declared that he was in dire need of £12 000, and that he would kill himself – taking Solly and his brother, Woolf, with him – rather than face the disgrace of bankruptcy. 'Kismet' demanded that, as a sign of Solly's willingness to negotiate, he place an advert in the Johannesburg *Star*.

Solly found the contents of the letters, although vague, extremely alarming and approached the police who advised him to go along with mysterious 'Kismet' by placing the advert. In this way they hoped to draw him out into the open, make him state his grievances and apprehend him. Solly did as the police suggested and contact with 'Kismet' was established, but the blackmailer later realized that he was being set up. Nevertheless, the letters continued to arrive. Initially threatening and abusive, their tone changed and 'Kismet' began to hint that he was in possession of valuable political information which could be damaging to Barnato Brothers. Although the threats were no longer personal, Solly was more alarmed as he knew that public confidence in the company was shaky following Barnato's death and that a scandal of any sort could have disastrous consequences.

Woolf Joel then took over negotiations with 'Kismet', and again the tone of the letters changed. This time the writer began to suggest 'loans' and started signing a name to his letters – Baron von Veltheim. Eventually, Woolf, in the company of Harold Strange, the manager of the Johannesburg Consolidated Investment Company met the Baron. He confessed that he had met Barney Barnato on a number of occasions and had been advanced considerable sums of money to arrange the kidnapping of President Kruger and create division among his supporters. Apparently, in the process he had incurred considerable debts which remained unpaid because of Barnato's untimely death. Furthermore, he had a great deal of information specifically relating to a secret plan to remove Kruger and thus avoid the impending war, which would save the company 'millions'.

Woolf, who knew nothing of the meetings to which the Baron referred, believed that he could be bought off with a few pounds. Unfortunately, he completely underestimated the ruthlessness of his adversary ...

Von Veltheim's real name was Karl Kurtze, a 43-year-old German-born confidence trickster, embezzler and bigamist who had come to South Africa in 1897 via England. It was possible that Kurtze, or the 'Baron' as he came to be known, conceived the idea of extorting money from the Joels while staying at a boarding house in Johannesburg. It was here that he met a solicitor, AE Caldecott, who had been a director of one or two of the less successful Barnato companies and held a grudge against the family. Indeed, it is probable that Caldecott's daughter, a woman who had manifested a pathological hatred for Solly Joel and

blamed him for her father's misfortunes, suggested writing the letters in an attempt to 'get back' at Solly.

On 13 March 1898, the Baron went to see Woolf at his office.

This is the cheque given to Barney Barnato by Cecil Rhodes as payment for his interests in the Big Hole. The deal gave Rhodes sole control of the greatest diamond mine in the world.

Strange, who was also present at this meeting, had taken the precaution of bringing along a single-shot Deringer. During the meeting Von Veltheim became angry because the money he demanded was not forthcoming and an argument occurred.

Three shots were fired, leaving Woolf dead. The Baron was holding a gun to Strange's head when staff burst into the room and overpowered him. Kurtze was accused of murder.

At the trial Kurtze pleaded 'not guilty', claiming in his defence that he had been lured into Woolf's office with the promise that he would be paid £12 000, that he had been threatened with a gun and, in self-defence, had been forced to protect himself.

The jury found him 'not guilty' – a verdict which the judge strongly disagreed with – and he was set free, although he was subsequently expelled from the Transvaal as a 'public danger'.

A story told by Kurtze emerged, however, that he had been secretly in the pay of Barnato and was working under-

cover to depose Kruger. Although there was no evidence to support his claims, and despite the fact that his story was riddled with inconsistencies, it was not possible to prove that he was lying.

Shortly after the murder trial, Karl Kurtze vanished from the story. But ten years later, in 1907, he reappeared.

Still claiming that Woolf Joel had promised to pay him £12 000, he attempted once more to blackmail Solly Joel. He was arrested in Antwerp on charges of blackmail and extradited to England where he was tried at the Old Bailey in February 1908. He was sentenced to twenty years in prison but was released after seven years when he saved a warder's life.

He returned to South Africa, this time seeking supporters for his plan to uncover Kruger's Gold and was eventually deported to Germany where he died penniless in 1930.

A WILD SUPPOSITION?

There remains the remote possibility that Kurtze, who was known to be a master of disguise (or an accomplice) was on the *Scot* when Barnato died. If this was the case and the two men had been in secret negotiation and had arranged to meet, then Barnato's death takes on an entirely new aspect. Not only would this explain Barnato's fixation with time, but it would also help to explain a number of other inconsistencies. If Kurtze had threatened Barnato with a gun, a glint of light on the gun-barrel would explain Joel's reference to the 'flash' and his cry of 'Murder!'. And if Barnato *had* been involved with Kurtze, there is every possibility that Solly Joel would want to keep it quiet.

Speculation aside, the only thing that is certain is that we will never know exactly what happened on the deck of the *Scot* on the afternoon of 14 June 1897 ...

THE FLYING DUTCHMAN
The phantom ship destined to sail forever

During the middle watch the so-called Flying Dutchman *came across our bows. She first appeared as a strange red light, as of a ship all aglow, in the midst of which light her masts, spars and sails, seemingly those of a normal brig, some two hundred yards distant from us, stood out in strong relief as she came up. Our lookout man on the forecastle reported her as close to our port bow, where also the officer of the watch from the bridge clearly saw her, as did our quarterdeck midshipman, who was sent forward at once to the forecastle to report back. But on reaching there, no vestige nor any sign of any material ship was to be seen either near or away to the horizon ... the night being clear and the sea calm.*

This extract, dated 11 July 1881, came from the log of HMS *Bacchante* and was written by a young midshipman – a man who later became King George V of England. HMS *Bacchante* was accompanied by two other warships – HMS *Cleopatra* and HMS *Tourmaline* – both of which also sighted the phantom ship. Seven hours later, a further entry was made in the log of HMS *Bacchante*:

The ordinary seaman who had reported the Flying Dutchman *fell from the topmast cross-trees, and was smashed to atoms. His body was committed to the deep with full naval honours, and his messmates were left certain that Van der Decken had gained another member of his ghostly crew.*

Painting by W Daniell from the Fehr Collection.

THE LEGEND OF THE FLYING DUTCHMAN

The *Flying Dutchman*, a spectre ship doomed to sail the waters of the Cape of Good Hope for eternity, and the appearance of which is believed to warn of imminent disaster, has been retold generation after generation. The legend's origin, however, is obscure. Some say it dates back to 1490, when the Portuguese navigator, Bartholomeu Dias, was drowned when his ship sank off the Cape, barely two years after he had made history by being the first European to round the most southern tip of Africa. But the most oft-repeated version dates back to the early seventeenth century ...

Darkness fell upon the *Flying Dutchman* as she sailed around the Cape of Good Hope; a mighty wind began to blow and a restless sea began to toss and move around the tiny vessel.

When the storm was at its height a deputation of passengers and crew approached the captain, begging him to steer the ship towards the safety of the nearest port. But even in the teeth of the gale their pleas fell on deaf ears.

'We will continue. Nothing shall stop us. Neither wind nor weather, nor God himself!' Van der Decken declared, and cursed them for their weakness.

At that moment, a wall of water swept up from the dark depths below and threw itself upon the stricken craft. As the vessel began to flounder in the sea, Van der Decken called out to his men to double their efforts. Even as the water began to pour into his ship he cried out to them:

'Damn you all! I shall complete this journey or sail the same course until doomsday!'

It was then that an apparition of the Almighty is said to have appeared before him on the deck of the ship, but in his madness, Van der Decken withdrew his pistol and fired upon the shape shouting, 'Come not for me now!' and, with this, gambled his salvation.

From that instant, Van der Decken was destined to sail the oceans of the world forever in the *Flying Dutchman*, and be a torment to sailors until the Day of Judgment, or until he could find another vessel willing to carry a letter back to Holland begging his forgiveness for having put so many innocent souls at risk. The appearance of the ghost ship, however, strikes terror into everyone who see her, and no-one has been prepared to help.

OTHER SIGHTINGS

Sightings of a ghost ship have been reported on a number of occasions. In 1899, the captain of the steamship *Hannah Regan*, which was sailing in the Pacific off the coast of Okinawa, made the following entry in the ship's log:

George V, who saw the Flying Dutchman *in 1881.*

It was a fine, calm and clear night when my attention was drawn to what I at first thought was a peculiar shadow some half a mile distant from my ship. I watched it closely for some time and then, to my astonishment, the shadow assumed the shape and appearance of a sailing vessel, clearly distinguishable but of a type which had not sailed the seas for at least two hundred years. There could be no mistaking it. She was headed in our direction, and driving along as if in the grip of violent winds, yet she carried no sail. I stood spellbound and was about to shout, to summon help, for it looked as if she could not help running us down, but then it flashed in my mind that this was a phantom and no material vessel. The spectral ship came on, her starboard quarter almost awash and with masses of heavy water pouring over her. She came right alongside, and then I doubted my own shocked senses, for I could see right through her, though every detail of her deck work and her rigging stood out, clearly. Two of her boats were hanging from their falls and dragged alongside. So she passed us by, still lower at the stern and in such a way disappeared beneath the sea. [1]

Admiral Karl Doenitz, Commander-in-Chief of Germany's U-boat fleet during the Second World War, recorded the following report in 1944:

Certain of my U-boat crew claimed that they saw the Flying Dutchman or some other so-called phantom ship on their tours of duty east of Suez. When they returned to their base, the men said they preferred facing the combined strength of Allied warships in the North Atlantic than know the terror a second time of being confronted by a phantom vessel. [2]

During the summer of 1939, a group of holiday-makers at Glencairn, near Muizenberg in the Cape, claim to have seen the *Flying Dutchman* materialize out of the thin mist and vanish just as mysteriously. The sea lay dead calm at the time making the ghost ship clearly visible as she moved majestically across the horizon.

A report in the *Cape Times* the following day said that the ship,

> ... with all her sails drawing well, although there was not a breath of wind at the time, appeared to be standing in towards Muizenberg. The ship then sailed steadily on until it seemed certain to run aground on the sands of Strandfontein beach and then vanished into thin air.

There was reportedly an attempt to explain the Muizenberg 'mystery ship' sighting as a mirage created by a process of light refraction and that the ship seen was actually hundreds of miles away.

But those who saw the vessel thought this to be an unlikely explanation for what they had seen.

·THE LEGEND IN LITERATURE

The tale of the *Flying Dutchman* has been the inspiration for a number of books and poems. The popular novel, *The Mystery Ship*, by Captain Frederick Marryat (1839), relates Phillip van der Decken's successful, but disastrous, search for his father – the captain of the *Flying Dutchman*.

Richard Wagner's famous opera, *Der Fliegende Hollander* (1843), is also based on the story of the *Flying Dutchman*. The composer's 'Flying Dutchman' is a sea captain who has been condemned by the devil to sail the seven seas until the Day of Judgment, unless he can find a girl who will love him faithfully until his death. Every seven years he is allowed to leave his ship to seek such a woman.

The legend of the *Flying Dutchman* gained further acceptance after the publication in 1798 of Samuel Taylor Coleridge's *Rime of the Ancient Mariner*. In the poem, the ancient mariner accosts three young gallants who are on their way to a marriage feast, and recounts the story of his ship which was driven into the ice of the South Pole by a storm, where disaster befalls them and where they encounter a ghost ship on which Death and Life play dice to win his soul.

Is the existence of a ghost ship, destined to sail the oceans of the world for eternity, fact or fiction? Most people would claim that the tale is merely a romantic notion or superstition, or the product of elaborate imaginations. And perhaps they're right.

The legend of the *Flying Dutchman*, however, has been told for generations, and not everyone who claims to have seen her can have their accounts dismissed as fantasy.

LIGHT REFRACTION AND MIRAGE

T*he Flying Dutchman may be nothing more sinister than an optical illusion of light refraction. The refraction or 'bending' of light waves occurs when they pass from one medium to another. A pencil in a glass of water, for example, looks broken at the water-line. This phenomenon occurs because light waves travel at different velocities in different media. Light refraction also takes place when light waves pass through layers of warm and cool air. Light rays from a distant ship, for example, may bend as they pass from the cool, heavy air near the surface, to the upper warm, light air. This can make the ship appear closer than it really is. Light refraction frequently causes mirages, which are fairly common optical illusions. Possibly the most common mirage is the pool of water one seems to see lying on a hot, paved road – the 'water' disappears as one approaches. Some mirages may cause an object, such as a mountain or a ship, to appear to float in the sky. Another type of mirage, called Fata Morgana, occurs when a layer of hot air traps rays of light from distant objects. Objects such as rocks or chunks of ice then appear to be the towers of a fairy-tale castle. Fata Morganas, Italian for 'Morgan the Fairy', are often seen in the Straits of Messina, and are traditionally attributed to the sorcery of Morgan le Fay, an enchantress believed to reside in Calabria, in southern Italy. According to English legend, Morgan le Fay was the ruler of Avalon and sister of King Arthur.*

SAA HELDERBERG
The air disaster which left no clues

The SAA *Helderberg* crashed into the sea about 160 miles from the coast of Mauritius on 27 November 1987. The aircraft, a Boeing 747, one of two 'combi' aircraft in the SAA fleet, was carrying passengers and a cargo of general goods contained in six pallets loaded in the tail. A partition or false wall of honeycomb-type material separated the cargo bay from the passenger compartment. All of the passengers and crew, numbering 160, died in the crash, making it the worst disaster in South African Airways history.

Flight SA295 left Taipei's Chiang Kai-shek Airport at 14h23, climbed to a cruising altitude of 35 000 feet and was en route to Johannesburg. Just before midnight, forty minutes flying time from Mauritius, Captain Dawie Uys contacted Mauritian air traffic control (MRU) at Mauritius' Plaisance Airport ...

23:48:51 (Uys) Eh, Mauritius, Mauritius, Springbok two nine five.

23:49:00 (MRU) Springbok two nine five, eh, Mauritius, eh good morning, eh, go ahead.

23:49:07 (Uys) Eh, good morning, we have, eh, a smoke eh, eh, problem and we're doing emergency descent to level one five, eh, one four zero.

23:49:18 (MRU) Confirm you wish to descend to level one four zero.

23:49:20 (Uys) Ja, we have already commenced, eh, due to a smoke problem in the aeroplane.

23:49:25 (MRU) Eh, roger, you are clear to descend immediately to flight level one four zero.

23:49:30 (Uys) Roger, we will appreciate if you can alert, eh, fire, ehy, ehp, eh, eh...

23:49:40 (MRU) Do you wish to, eh, do

The SAA Helderberg *crashed into the sea off the coast of Mauritius.*

you request a full emergency?

23:49:48 (Uys) Okay Joe, (the chief flight engineer) *kan jy ... vir ons ...*

23:49:51 (MRU) Springbok two nine five, Plaisance.

23:49:54 (Uys) Sorry, go ahead.

23:49:56 (MRU) Do you, eh, request a full emergency please a full emergency?

23:50:00 (Uys) Affirmative, that's charlie charlie.

23:50:02 (MRU) Roger, I declare a full emergency, roger.

23:50:04 (Uys) Thank you

23:50:40 (MRU) Springbok two nine five, Plaisance.

23:50:44 (Uys) Eh, go ahead.

23:50:46 (MRU) Request your actual position please and your DME distance.

23:50:51 (Uys) Eh, we haven't got the DME yet.

23:50:55 (MRU) Eh, your actual position please.
23:51:00 (Uys) Eh, say again?
23:51:02 (MRU) Your actual position?
23:51:08 (Uys) Now we have lost a lot of electrics, we haven't got anything on the aircraft now.

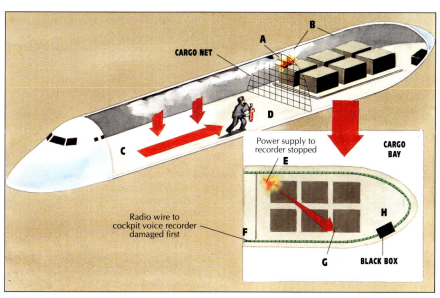

Above: Cross-section of the Helderberg. *(A) Fire starts in pallet in main cargo bay, (B) Fire detectors set off alarm in cockpit, (C) Crew member gets extinguisher, (D) Extinguisher recovered, empty, with melted cargo net, (E) Temperature: 1 000 °C, (F) Power cables to black box burnt through, (G) Fire spreads, (H) FDR and CVR damaged.*

Below: Piet de Klerk among the recovered wreckage in the debris centre, Jan Smuts Airport.

23:51:12 (MRU) Eh, roger, I declare a full emergency immediately.
23:51:15 (Uys) Affirmative.
23:51:18 (MRU) Roger.
23:52:19 (MRU) Eh, Springbok two nine five, do you have an echo tango alpha Plaisance?
23:52:30 (Uys) Ja, Plaisance.
23:52:33 (MRU) Do you have an echo tango alpha Plaisance please?
23:52:36 (Uys) Ya, eh, zero zero eh eh eh three zero.

23:52:40 (MRU) Roger zero zero three zero, thank you.
23:52:50 (Uys) Hey, Joe, shut down the oxygen left.
23:52:52 (MRU) Sorry, say again please.
00:01:34 (295) Unintelligible transmission.
00:01:36 (295) Unintelligible.

00:01:45 (295) Unintelligible transmission.
00:01:57 (295) Unintelligible transmission.
00:02:10 (295) Unintelligible transmission.
00:02:14 (295) Unintelligible transmission.
00:02:25 (295) (Carrier wave only.)
00:02:38 (Uys) Eh Plaisance, Springbok two nine five, do you copy?
00:02:41 (MRU) Eh, negative, two nine five, say again please, say again.
00:02:43 (Uys) We're now sixty-five miles.
00:02:45 (MRU) Confirm sixty-five miles.
00:02:47 (Uys) Ja, affirmative charlie charlie.
00:02:50 (MRU) Eh, roger, Springbok eh two nine five, eh, you're recleared flight level five zero. Recleared flight level five zero.

Air traffic control at Plaisance airport cleared Captain Uys to descend to 5 000 feet, and then relayed information regarding wind speed, air temperature and cloud cover, and declared runway 14 clear for landing. Captain Uys confirmed that he was tracking in on runway 'one four'. Five minutes later the aircraft crashed into the sea.

In evidence given before the Board of Inquiry into the *Helderberg* disaster, Mr Khodacabus, the air-traffic controller who had had the last radio contact with the doomed aircraft, said that he had first received a call from the captain of the aircraft at 23h48.

'He [Captain Uys] told me he was making an emergency descent to flight level 140 as he had a smoke problem. He requested me to alert emergency services at the airport and I cleared him for descent.'

After Khodacabus had done as Captain Uys requested, he twice tried to contact the aircraft.

'There was no reply. There was a radio silence of eight minutes, but I did not interpret this as a loss of communication as they could have been very busy dealing with the problem.

'Then the pilot called again and said he was 65 miles north-east of us. I then cleared him to descend to flight level 50 and gave him full instructions on landing. We expected the aircraft to land at runway 14, but we watched both landing routes intensely. Our emergency services were already in place.'

The *Helderberg* which plummeted into the water at high speed, had broken up and its scattered wreckage was strewn over an area of four and a half square kilometres. There was a suggestion, which was strongly denied by Boeing, the manufacturers of the aircraft, that the *Helderberg* had broken up in mid-air as a result of the fire on board. This scenario was suggested by the fact that parts of the aircraft were found in two distinct debris fields lying some 600 metres apart. Experts at Boeing maintained that the aircraft broke up *only* on impact with the sea. There had been no mayday, no position given and no indication that the crew were preparing to ditch the aircraft. The air-traffic control personnel at Plaisance airport

were under the impression that the situation was under control.

So why did the *Helderberg* go down? And what catastrophe happened in the few minutes following Captain Uys' last recorded words?

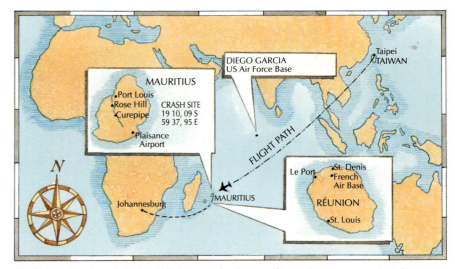

The flight path and crash site in which the search for the aircraft's wreckage was concentrated.

THE SEARCH

The International Civil Aviation Organization has three stages laid down for handling an air disaster. The first stage is called ALERFA, which is a declaration of warning of disaster, the second stage is UNCERFA, which is declared as soon as uncertainty exists about the safety of a flight, and the third stage is DETRESFA, declared when it is clearly evident that a flight is in distress.

The controller at Plaisance airport declared DETRESFA at 00:40:00 on 28 November 1987 when the *Helderberg* failed to arrive within the time estimated by Captain Uys. Thirty-five minutes later, the search and rescue co-ordinators at Plaisance informed the Mauritian Search and Rescue Centre that the aircraft was missing and that a search was to be initiated. At the same time the South African Department of Civil Aviation was informed that an ALERFA-DETRESFA had been declared. The South African authorities enquired

whether assistance was necessary and informed Plaisance Airport that a Lockheed 382 would be ready to leave Jan Smuts Airport at 08h00 South African time. The search for survivors continued unabated for two days, then the search for bodies and wreckage began on 30 November 1987 after the decision had been taken to abandon the search for survivors. The South African Department of Transport's Directorate of Civil Aviation, in collaboration with South African Airways undertook the investigation to determine the cause of the disaster and the country in which the aircraft was built – the USA – was asked to assist. A member of the United States National Transport Safety Board, accompanied by representatives of the Federal Aviation Administration (also from the USA), and the Boeing Aircraft Company joined the investigating team.

Following a month-long exhaustive search of the ocean floor, the *Helderberg*'s debris fields were finally located on the sea bed. At this point it was decided by the board of investigation to appoint Eastport International, an American company with an impressive record for deep sea salvage, to recover selected items from the wreckage. Eastport International's surface vessel

Stena Workhorse was commissioned to use its remotely piloted submersible, *Gemini*, to photograph and recover the *Helderberg*'s two 'black boxes' – a digital flight recorder (DFR) and a cockpit voice recorder (CVR) – both of which contain magnetic tape recorders that record the aircraft's speed, direction and altitude and the words spoken by the cockpit crew during the flight. These, it was hoped, would have recorded the details that the accident investigators needed in order to piece together what had happened on the ill-fated flight. It was also considered essential to bring to the surface as much of the aircraft as possible. The *Gemini* made its first successful dive on 22 November 1988.

The operation to uncover the secrets of the *Helderberg* was plagued by bad weather, but during the months that followed the *Stena Workhorse* taking up its station above the debris site, *Gemini* repeatedly made the two and a half hour descent of 4 000 metres to the darkness of the sea bed to map out the site.

Vital sections of the aircraft, including parts of the internal structure on which the black boxes were mounted and parts of the tail section with SAA's colours clearly visible, were spotted within days and a detailed photographic mapping of the site commenced. Some sections of the aircraft had remained remarkably intact – from nose to tail and wing to wing – but debris was strewn over an area of almost five square kilometres. Numerous pieces of wreckage were later identified and included the tail section, landing gear, parts of the engines, a tail-mounted auxiliary power unit, pieces of the galley, several computer parts (which had formed part of the cargo), undercarriage, floor structure, fuselage structure, wings and the cargo compartment floor. The first part of the aircraft raised from the sea bed was a chunk of metal from one of the engines, one of the first pieces of wreckage to be seen.

At 09h00 on the morning on Friday, 6 January 1989, and nine hours into a twelve-hour shift, Frik Corneelsen, an employee of SAA, and an observer on the *Gemini,* who was monitoring the search operation, spotted the black box they had been looking for for seven months. It had been lying on the sea bed for almost 14 months.

'First I went hot, then cold,' Corneelsen admitted. 'I turned to my assistant, Gys Lucas and said, "Heck, man, I think I've got the real thing on the screen".'

Word that the cockpit voice recorder had been found spread through the *Stena Workhorse* like wildfire. The first thing that had to be done was to establish whether what Frik Corneelsen had seen was indeed the CVR, and to do this a high-quality zoom camera on board the ship was lowered over the side. The recorder which is usually red, not black, and has crosses of reflective tape on every side was identified – but it had been heat-blackened. It was grasped in the *Gemini*'s remote-controlled extendible arms and then the box began its long journey to the surface.

'This was a worrying time, because if the box had slipped it might have been lost forever. Would the box come unstuck? Would *Gemini* make it? In the meantime we lowered a cage on a rope into the sea.

'At fifteen metres below the surface, divers went down and clamped a safety line to the recorder. The recorder was also put inside a transportation container and slowly lifted to the surface.'

Once on board the ship, the CVR was handled with great care to ensure that no further deterioration of the tape occurred. It was essential that any air bubbles were prevented from getting to the tape and that it did not dry out. Any deposits of salt or chemicals that found their way on to the tape would damage the recorded information. For a similar reason, it was important that the tape be kept at a constant temperature.

'The tapes must stay wet and cold,' explained Wally Staffetius, a representative of the Department of Civil Aviation.

Debris recovered from the sea bed.
From top to bottom: engine fan blade;
a passenger's suitcase; part of the fuselage
structure; and the main cargo compartment.

'The sea water in the container had to be flushed out and replaced with de-ionized water. The entire box then had to be kept on ice.'

Once the box arrived at Jan Smuts Airport, technicians from the SAA laboratory cleaned the tape by winding it from reel to reel, still immersed in water. Later it was carefully dried in a vacuum chamber, then sent to the laboratory of the American National Transportation Safety Board where the recorded data was recovered. Meanwhile, out at sea, the *Stena Workhorse* continued its salvage operation with the *Gemini*, recovering pieces of wreckage for analysis, some of which had been subject to soot and fire damage. The digital flight data recorder was never recovered, despite the fact that it was mounted in the aircraft next to the CVR.

THE REVELATIONS OF THE CVR

After all the effort expended in retrieving the CVR, it was found to contain only 72 seconds of cockpit crew dialogue – its power-supply wires had been destroyed in the fire.

When the emergency was discovered most of the passengers would have been asleep. The recording begins with an alarm bell alerting the crew to a problem on board. A voice, probably that of the captain, asks what the source of the alarm is, and is told by the flight engineer that it is from the main cargo compartment. Then there is a second alarm. (The evidence suggests that the *Helderberg* was then grappling with an inferno in the cargo hold, although it was unlikely that any of the crew would have been aware of this.)

On the recording, the intercom chime sounded four seconds after the first alarm bell started ringing. (It is thought that this chime was the cabin crew putting emergency procedures into operation. The captain then asks for the checklist to be read. The intercom chimes again and activity in the cockpit becomes hectic as emergency procedures are carried out. At this stage the crew of the aircraft appear to be in control of the situation as there is no mention of ditching in the sea. Shortly afterwards the captain asks '*Wat de donner gaan nou aan?*' (What the hell is going on now?)

The tape, which lasts for thirty minutes, is on a continuous loop and automatically erases the previous recording before starting to re-record. It did not include the last thirty minutes of the flight. The tape ended in a warble after 29 minutes and 52 seconds.

THE BOARD OF INQUIRY – AUGUST 1988 TO MAY 1990

Based upon all available evidence, the Board of Inquiry, chaired by the Honourable Justice Margo, established that at the time of take-off from Taipei, the *Helderberg* was serviceable and defect-free. The flight had proceeded normally until a fire which had developed on the right front pallet in the main deck cargo hold became out of control. Flight SA 295 was carrying seven pallets, of which six were full of goods and the seventh, the one at the back, empty. Substances involved in the combustion included plastic and cardboard packing material, but the actual source of ignition could not be determined. Two senior Department of Transport crash investigators, Piet de Klerk and Martin Venter, went through the recovered debris in an attempt to discover the actual source of ignition, but there was insufficient evidence to determine the cause of the fire. It was established that smoke and carbon dioxide penetrated the passenger compartment and possibly the cockpit – this was based on the fact that blood tests conducted on the bodies of some of the victims recovered, contained extremely high levels of carbon dioxide and soot. The tremendous heat from the fire would have prevented the crew from getting close enough to use a fire extinguisher effectively. The fire damaged the aircraft's systems and structure and it was out of control when it crashed into the sea. There was also the likelihood that some or all of the passengers and crew had been overcome by fumes and were unconscious or dead before the *Helderberg* hit the sea.

It was the view of the Board of Inquiry that the chances of sabotage were virtu-

The cockpit voice recorder, held in the clamps of the Gemini.

ally nil, and, in conclusion, it stated that there was no basis on which to attribute blame for the loss of the *Helderberg* to any person or body. The Board of Inquiry also found that the fire-detection and fire-fighting equipment and procedures on the *Helderberg* were inadequate and recommended that the 'combi' system should not be used in aircraft until 'present shortcomings' in fire detection and equipment had been overcome – for example, in the event of a fire, a crew member would have had to fight a blaze with a hand-held fire extinguisher 'of limited capacity'.

Fire detection and control systems on all aircraft, particularly those with a 'combi' configuration, have been upgraded internationally since the *Helderberg* disaster. However, during the course of the investigation by the Board of Inquiry, it was to become apparent that the 'combi' system, whereby passengers and cargo were carried on the same deck, which had been employed in over 200 Boeing 747s world-wide since 1979, had been a source of controversy for some time *before* the disaster. No 'live fire' test had ever been conducted by Boeing in the upper deck of a 747 'combi' prior to the *Helderberg* disaster, and within some quarters of the aviation community it was felt that the fire-fighting equipment kept on board was inadequate. SAA resorted to a passenger-only configuration in its other 'combi' aircraft shortly after the disaster.

On 12 May 1990, the Board of Inquiry under the chairmanship of Justice Cecil Margo made its report public.

DID THE *HELDERBERG* CARRY DANGEROUS CARGO?

Although the findings of the Board of Inquiry were inconclusive, several rumours persist regarding the nature of the *Helderberg*'s cargo.

There was the suggestion that Captain Uys had been concerned about part of the cargo. This claim, however, was

THE PROPHECIES OF NONGQAWUSE

And the nation that committed suicide

Between April 1856 and February 1857, the Xhosa people, acting on the prophecies of Nongqawuse, a 15-year-old orphan living near the Gxarha river in what is now Transkei, slaughtered their cattle and stopped planting crops in the belief that this would lead to the resurrection of their ancestors and a period of idyllic prosperity. The results were truly devastating: tens of thousands of Xhosa died, while others fled their homes. Thousands of cattle were slaughtered. But why did these events occur? Did the Xhosa people truly believe Nongqawuse? Was the whole affair a carefully planned and executed scheme perpetrated by a callous British colonial administrator or is there some other secret behind the story?

THE ANCESTORS SPEAK

Nongqawuse was the niece of Mhlakaza, the head of the homestead where she lived; Nombanda was his sister-in-law. It was while Nongqawuse and Nombanda were at the Gxarha river, where they had gone to scare birds away from the cultivated fields along its bank, that Nongqawuse said she heard her name being called by two strangers.

The strangers, who claimed to speak on behalf of Napakade, a descendant of the god *Sifuba-sibanzi*, asked her to tell her people that their ancestors would rise from the dead - only when all the

cattle had been slaughtered. The cattle had to be killed, they explained, because they had been reared by contaminated

Two prophetesses, Nongqawuse (left) and Nonkosi. The photograph was taken by Major Gawler's wife ca. 1858.

people who associated with those practising witchcraft. The strangers also said that the people had to stop growing crops, but that new grain pits must be dug, and new houses and large cattle pens built in preparation for the great day of resurrection.

According to WW Gqoba, whose narrative of the cattle killing is based on oral traditions collected from believers, Nongqawuse related her experiences to Mhlakaza and he realized that one of the men she described was his younger brother. A few days later, Mhlakaza went to see the strangers for himself, and although they did not reveal themselves to him, they did speak to Nongqawuse. Once again, the strangers told her that they represented *Sifuba-sibanzi*. Their task, they claimed, was to help the Xhosa nation rid itself of the yoke of the white man. But this would be achieved *only* if the people proved themselves worthy, by following their instructions.

Mhlakaza became chief interpreter of Nongqawuse's visions, and lost no time in spreading this message of divine salvation to the Xhosa nation. A deputation of high-ranking officials, representing some of the great chiefs of the Xhosa, was sent to visit the strangers. They returned to their kraals, convinced that the predictions were genuine and the cattle killing began.

That Nongqawuse's predictions were so readily accepted by the vast majority is not so surprising when one realizes that there had been other prophets who had also suggested cattle-killing as a way to rid the Xhosa nation of evil. (At the time of the predictions many of the crops were blighted and a lung-sickness epidemic, which was killing many thousands of cattle, was spreading through the territory.)

Early in July 1856, Chief Sarhili, king of the Xhosa, visited the 'new people' for himself. He was the senior chief of the Gcaleka Xhosa and ruled over a vast territory including British Kaffraria, the area between the Great Kei and Keiskamma rivers.

The strangers spoke to Sarhili and, after determining from Nongqawuse and Mhlakaza that there was no way to avoid the killing of the cattle, he issued a decree ordering his people to start the slaughter. As a sign of his commitment, he returned to his kraal and killed his favourite ox, an animal known throughout the kingdom.

The cattle-killing movement gathered momentum and many people made the pilgrimage to the Gxarha river in the hope of seeing the 'new people' for themselves.

Many claimed that they heard the sound of rocks being broken, and when Nongqawuse ordered them to go to the sea they also 'saw' a great mass of cattle and a crowd of people surging just below the water's surface and heard the bellowing of the bulls. Although this vast army never left the water, and only Nongqawuse is said to have heard them speak, many people came to believe that her prophecies were authentic.

One of the magistrates of the region, Vigne, observed 'large numbers of skeletons lying in the veldt' along the road to East London, and rumours of the extent of the cattle killing soon reached Sir George Grey, then Governor of the Cape.

Towards the end of August 1856, Grey embarked on a month-long tour of the region. In a letter to Henry Labouchere, the Secretary of State for the Colonies, he wrote:

A (Xhosa) prophet who is partially deranged ... has lately given out that he has been favoured with visits from the spirits of the great chiefs and their followers who for several preceding generations have occupied Kaffraria, and that these are all ready to return to earth with a new and improved race of cattle, which can be affected by no sickness, and with all sorts of desirable property, surpassing all that has hitherto been seen by man ... But, as a necessary preliminary to their again taking human form, it is necessary that all existing cattle and property of every kind should be destroyed ...

Portrait of Sir George Grey painted by Charles Gow. During the time of the Xhosa cattle killing and crop destroying (1856-1857), he held the office of Governor of the Cape.

Some people preferred to sell their cattle rather than kill them, but before long there were so many on the market that prices dropped dramatically. Animals, which would normally have sold for three or four pounds, went for less than fifteen shillings (less than one-quarter of the normal price).

THE FIRST DISAPPOINTMENT – AUGUST 1856

Mhlakaza was eventually forced to name the day on which the 'new people' would rise from the dead. The great event, he said, would follow the full moon mid-August when two red suns would rise in the sky and darkness would cover the land. After a great storm, which only the newly built houses and cattle pens would survive, the righteous dead would rise up and the new cattle would emerge from the earth at the mouths of the Kei, Kwenxurtha, Tyhume and Keiskamma rivers. The animals would be wearing white blankets. The English and their collaborators would then retreat into the sea, which would rise up and engulf them.

Despite Mhlakaza's predictions, the day came and went without incident. But this was easily explained: the 'new people' had not arisen because their demands had been ignored – some people were hiding their cattle or selling them and not killing them. On this the prophets were unequivocal. Unless the people followed the words of Nongqawuse to the letter, the prophecy would not come true.

Following the First Disappointment, the cattle-killing movement foundered. During Grey's visit to the region (August to September 1856) he ordered Sarhili to end the killing or face the wrath of the British Government. He had threatened to undermine the traditional power and control of local chiefs by establishing an unpaid police force under the leadership of paid 'headmen'.

Effectively, control in the district would pass from the chief to the magistrates. Sarhili responded by saying that the matter was out of his hands. 'I was ordered to do so,' he said, 'by the thing which speaks in my country.'

Within weeks of the First Disappointment the rains began to fall, and the Xhosa in British Kaffraria turned to Chief Sandile, senior chief of British Kaffraria, for guidance as to whether they should plant crops for the next season. Sandile, however, who was more concerned with maintaining his position among the chiefs, did not respond. His failure to condemn the cattle killing made the situation worse, as his silence was taken as support for the actions.

In mid-October 1856, Governor Grey ordered HMS *Geyser*, which was en route from Natal to Cape Town, to call in at the Kei River mouth as a show of strength. The '*Geyser* incident', as the affair came to be known, turned out to be a fiasco. Watched by a Xhosa war party, the *Geyser* went up the wrong channel as it entered the river mouth, a boat put into the water overturned, and the ship departed as undignified as it had arrived.

News of this 'defeat' was greeted with great enthusiasm by the believers. Many of them saw this event as confirmation of the accuracy of Nongqawuse's predictions and the cattle killing gathered pace once more ...

THE (SECOND) GREAT DAY ARRIVES ...

Nongqawuse and Mhlakaza were reluctant to name the day on which the 'new people' would arise, but after some insistence from Sarhili, Mhlakaza declared that the great day would occur about eight days after the first full moon in January 1857 – if the moon rose blood-

Above: Sarhili, Xhosa paramount chief.

Below: The brass plaque marks the grave of Nongqawuse, the Xhosa prophetess whose visions led to mass destruction of crops and cattle, causing thousands of people to starve to death.

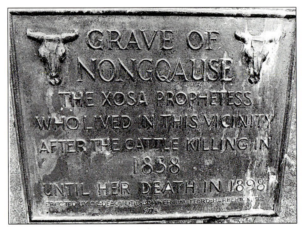

red on that day! If this did not happen, the nation was to wait for the next full moon in February.

Nongqawuse and Mhlakaza advised Sarhili that the 'new people' had ordered the Xhosa to kill immediately all the cattle they possessed except for one cow and one goat. Some eight or nine days later a blood-red sun would rise late in the morning, then set again, after which it would be as black as night. A terrible storm of thunder and lightning would follow and the dead would rise from their graves.

Shortly after this pronouncement, both Mhlakaza and Nongqawuse vanished. January passed without incident.

By this time Sarhili believed that he had been deceived, but the killing had reached epidemic proportions and it was too late to plant crops.

The fateful day of resurrection was 16 February 1857 – but nothing happened. Five days later, there was a tremendous storm and many believers ran terrified to their homes, convinced that the great day had arrived. But that great day never came and, in fact, it never would.

THE KILLING IN PERSPECTIVE

To fully understand the cattle killing, one must look in some detail at the era in which it occurred. When the prophesy was first raised, thousands of cattle were dying from lung-sickness. This had been introduced to the colony in 1853 through a consignment of Friesland bulls from Holland. Xhosa cattle losses to this lingering and painful sickness were around 5 000 animals per month. In addition, the Xhosa were frustrated at the British colonial government which exercised a somewhat less than sympathetic domination of the territory. Given this combination of circumstances, the nation was ripe for the acceptance of prophecies which promised an idyllic future.

A number of prophets, of which Nongqawuse was merely one, blamed witchcraft for the evils affecting the Xhosa nation. Simply put, it was thought that when the cattle were slaughtered in a ritualistic manner there was every chance that the gods would be appeased, and peace and prosperity would come to the land. Nongqawuse's prophecies became prominent with the support of Sarhili.

THE CONSEQUENCES

Estimates, particularly those of Commissioner Charles Brownlee, Sandili's magistrate, suggest that between 35 000 and 50 000 people died of starvation, and a further 150 000 were displaced and forced to leave their homes or face death from starvation. Included in these estimates, however, were the results of subsequent British action against Sarhili, ordered by Grey in 1858, after the Xhosa resisted his attempts to convert them into, what he termed, 'Black Englishmen'.

The region was devastated both physically and culturally by the cattle killing. Two-thirds of the land previously occupied by the Xhosa was effectively annexed by the British, paving the way for white settlement and, as Professor Peires points out, the '... national, cultural and economic integrity (of the Xhosa) long penetrated and undermined by colonial pressure, finally collapsed'. Indeed, the cattle killing proved to be a disaster of untold proportion.

AND NONGQAWUSE?

Mhlakaza, and most of the people who lived at the Gxarha River, died of starvation. Nongqawuse was handed over to Major Gawler, a magistrate, by the Chief of Bomvana. It was Gawler's wife who took the photograph of Nongqawuse and another prophetess, Nonkosi.

In 1858 Nongqawuse was taken to Cape Town and confined in the Pauper's Lodge. But when the lodge closed down a year later, Nongqawuse's name did not appear on the register.

In 1905, Sir Walter Stanford claimed that she had returned to the Port Elizabeth region and, using the name Victoria Regina, settled with relatives on a local farm, married and had two daughters. Both Nongqawuse and her daughters are thought to be buried on the farm 'Glenthorn', near Alexandria, in the Eastern Cape.

THE REAL MYSTERY

Was the Xhosa cattle killing a national suicide of horrendous proportions or a carefully contrived act of genocide, planned and perpetrated by Sir George Grey? Even to this day, many lay the blame for this disaster squarely at the feet of Grey, who they believe tricked the Xhosa people into destroying their crops and cattle.

However, official archival documents which relate to the period paint a different picture. To the British, the cattle killing was a conspiracy among certain Xhosa chiefs to bring about war in the Cape, with the intention of driving them out of the colony.

Although the historical accounts of this terrible period in South African history are riddled with lies, distortions and self-delusion, the fact emerges that the cattle killing was not the result of either of these 'plots' against the Xhosa.

It was *neither* murder *nor* suicide, although Sir George Grey capitalized on the situation once the cattle killing was in full swing, to further what he perceived to be the best interests of the British Government.

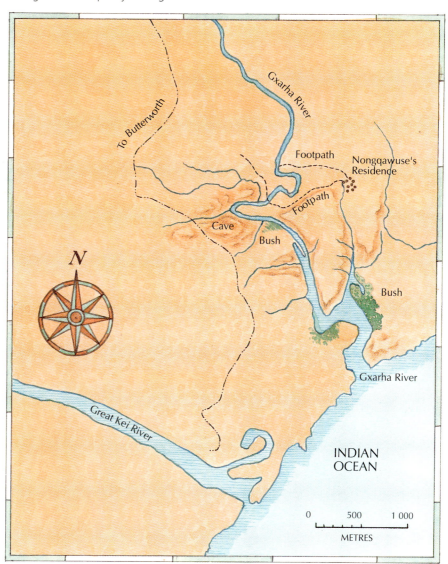

The scene of the prophecies.

THE KRUGER MILLIONS

Gold bullion hidden on the Lowveld?

To this day there are people who believe that a huge treasure chest of gold bullion, buried in the spring of 1900, during the last days of the Transvaal Republic and worth millions of Rands, lies somewhere on the Lowveld. This is the legend of the Kruger Millions.

Most people find the idea of unimaginable wealth just waiting to be unearthed, quite irresistible and, over the years, numerous attempts have been made to discover its location. Even murder has been committed in its name. *Did a huge quantity of gold go missing from the coffers of the Transvaal Republic?*

A MATTER OF FINANCE

On 11 October 1899, the governments of the Transvaal Republic and the Orange Free State declared war on Britain, following a Boer ultimatum directed against the reinforcement of the British garrison in South Africa. The crisis was caused by the refusal of President Kruger to grant rights to 'uitlanders' (foreigners) on the Witwatersrand and the aggressive response to this refusal by the British High Commissioner, Viscount Milner. Within weeks, gold mine owners in and around Johannesburg shut down their mines and left – along with 60 000 other refugees – for safer regions, mainly to the Cape and away from the scene of conflict. Thus began the second of the South African wars, known as the Anglo Boer War, which was to last until 1902.

Although many English people expected the war to be over by Christmas most of the Boer leaders accepted that the ensuing struggle would be long, arduous and costly, which meant it was important to exploit every available source of

revenue. For this reason, the government of the Transvaal Republic, acting according to the instructions of Hendrik Munnik, the state mining engineer, commandeered all the gold mines on the Rand, and took steps to employ enough labour, both black and white, to keep

Paul Kruger, father of the Afrikaner nation.

them operating, to supplement the treasury's depleted war fund.

This proved to be a wise move. A year before the war had been declared, gold production in the Transvaal had overtaken that of Russia, Australia and America, and South Africa had become the greatest gold power in the world. Mining experts expected that the region would produce £20-million worth of gold by 1899, of which over one quarter would be clear profit for the mining companies. The Transvaal also boasted a vast coal-

field around Johannesburg. Indeed, William Waldegrave Palmer, second Earl of Selbourne (and later the High Commissioner for South Africa), accurately described the Transvaal as 'the richest spot on earth'.

PICKING UP THE TRACES

A short time after the Transvaal Government took over from the mining companies, following the declaration of war in October 1899, gold bars were being delivered to the Pretoria Mint. In his article, *The Truth About the Kruger Millions*,[1] Gustav Preller, who (when hostilities began) was attached to the State Artillery near the Tugela River, describes how he was recalled to Pretoria by the chief of the Department of Mines, Mr Kleynhans, to serve in the new administration of the government of the Transvaal.

'It was in this manner [capacity]' Preller claims, 'that the writer took delivery of Mr Munnik's gold bars at the Mint, weighed them and received receipts for them from the head of the Mint, Mr Perrin, who, with his two German assistants, smelted, purified, alloyed, rolled, weighed and ... made money out of them. That finished, the Mint handed the money to Treasurer-General Malherbe who used it to provide the sinews of war and to keep the commandos in action.'

Although the running of the gold mines seemed to be progressing relatively smoothly, the same could not be said for the fortunes of the military. By the end of May 1900, the British had gained the upper hand and were advancing rapidly. Under Lord Kitchener and Field

Marshal Lord Roberts, a number of besieged towns had been relieved and a series of defeats inflicted on the Boer armies in the field. Bloemfontein was occupied in February 1900, and General Louis Botha, at the head of a dispirited army, was retreating to Pretoria. Not only was the Boer rank and file on the brink of total collapse, many of the leaders were convinced that continuing the struggle was futile.

It was against this background that, in June 1900, President Kruger – and most of the Transvaal Government – left Pretoria by train and was taken to the small town of Machadodorp, 230 kilometres down the track towards the Portuguese frontier and away from the advancing enemy. At Machadodorp, Kruger hastily established a 'capital on wheels' – government officials were housed in railway coaches. On sidings nearby stood long rows of covered trucks, guarded both night and day by armed sentries.

Although the gold mines had been abandoned in early May, when British forces began to close in on Pretoria, the manufacture of money at the Pretoria Mint continued until British troops were actually at the gates of the city. Preller picks up the story ...

At Midday on May 28th, the writer was asked by the Chief of the Mines Department to commandeer a vehicle somewhere in the town and at eleven o'clock that night in Church Square, he met a high official of the Republic who was going to manage the transportation of the money and the gold to the railway line. For this was the purpose for which the trolley had to be obtained, namely, to get away the raw gold out of the banks and the minted and smelted gold from the Mint, and to bring it to the Auditor-General whose train was standing ready at the station to depart Eastwards. Gold was stored at three places: in the vaults of the Nederlands

Bank where Mr de Braal, the manager, handed it over to us; in the Mint, a little further on, and in one of the lowest fire-proof chambers of the Palace of Justice. We first emptied the Nederlands Bank and went with our load to the station; then we visited the Mint, and after that the cellars of the Palace of Justice – at that time only half completed. In all we had to make three journeys there and back and by the time we were finished there was not an ounce of gold left

over to which the State had had any claim. In all the value of the gold removed must have been about a million and a half, together with that which was added at Machadodorp, perhaps less – and any way less rather than more.

It consisted for the most part of bars of milled gold, but there was in addition an appreciable amount of cyanide gold which is not so pure and worth almost 20 shillings an ounce less. There were also a number of

THE VELDPOND

Veldponde, *also known as 'siege pieces' or 'money of necessity', are South Africa's most unusual coins. In 1902, only 986 of these hand-made coins were struck, using dies from a heavy fly-press at a gold mine workshop at Pilgrim's Rest in the Eastern Transvaal. They were made of 24 carat gold. The coins are 22,8 mm in diameter, have a milled edge and weigh approximately eight grams. The letters* ZAR *are stamped on one side and* Een Pond *on the other. There have been a number of known forgeries.*

──────── RIMLESS BLANK PONDE ────────

The story goes that in 1900, President Kruger sent the State Attorney, JC Smuts, to the Pretoria Mint to confiscate all the money available, as the city was being evacuated in the face of the advancing British army. It was later discovered that among the completed coins were a number of unstamped discs, although they were the correct weight of a Kruger pound. These 'coins', which comprised 92% gold and 8% copper, are sometimes referred to as Kaal Ponde, *or more commonly,* Rimless Blank Ponde *and were circulated to some extent among the soldiers of the Republican army.*

──────── RIMMED BLANK PONDE ────────

These coins are similar in size, weight and gold content to Rimless Blank Ponde *but are one step nearer completion as they possess a rim. They were issued to the troops but were not favourably received.*

'smooth pounds' which had not yet been stamped with the design, and the plates from which the discs were stamped, with the residue and a little pure alloy ... [2]

Despite the fact that British flying columns, which were galloping ahead of the main force in an attempt to encircle the enemy, had all-but reached the railway line east of Pretoria, the gold was delivered to Machadodorp.

MILLIONS OF TREASURE

In August 1900, Colonel Deneys Reitz, author of the book *Commando*, rode to Machadodorp to visit his father, the then Secretary of State for the Transvaal. He noticed that the freight yards at the railway station were constantly guarded – a fact which a number of his colleagues had also commented upon – and came to share the consensus of opinion that every one of the covered trucks was filled to the brim with gold. Later, however, he would change his mind:

I have since realized that all the bullion in the world, put together, would not have filled those trucks: but, at any rate, we believed the current talk and I well remember with what awe we gazed upon the incalculable wealth that we thought was lying there. And our belief was strengthened when we saw men mysteriously at work at dead of night with dimly lit lanterns, transshipping boxes and cases from the trucks on to mule wagons standing ready, and, as each vehicle was loaded, it was quietly driven off into the dark.
This could only mean that the gold was being taken for storage out of harm's way (as the British Army was once more approaching), and from then onward we were firmly convinced that somewhere below the escarpment lay buried millions of treasure. [3]

Some years later, Reitz would learn from General Botha that the wagons contained war materials which were being secretly distributed to various parts of the Sabie and Lydenburg regions in preparation for a guerrilla campaign against the British. This plan, however, was kept secret. According to Reitz, it became 'common knowledge' among the rank and file that the wagons were not loaded with munitions, but that they

Above: The Transvaal state railway coach. In the foreground are Mr and Mrs WJ Leyds. (Leyds was a state attorney of the South African Republic, and became ambassador for Europe.) There has been much speculation as to whether a large amount of gold, said to be of 'incalculable wealth', was kept on railway trucks in the freight yards of Machadodorp. This gave rise to the rumour that gold bullion was hidden somewhere on the Lowveld.

contained a king's ransom in gold and accumulated spoils which Kruger had brought with him from Pretoria.

In fact, some of the Boer leaders may well have been aware of 'Kruger's millions' but purposefully ignored it knowing that rumours of a vast treasure trove were less harmful to the war effort than the truth itself.

HOW MUCH MONEY?

In Lawrence Green's book *Something Rich and Strange*, [4] he describes how James Gray, a former editor of the *Pretoria News*, once made a detailed study of the Transvaal Government's financial resources and established that in the days leading to the outbreak of the South African War, the Transvaal treasury held only £60 000. One week before war was declared the government commandeered a shipment of gold worth £462 853 from the Rand mines, which was destined for Britain. At the outbreak of hostilities, the Transvaal Republic had just over half a million pounds to fund the war.

To this amount one must add the value of gold production during the period November 1899 to May 1900, which, according to figures provided by the Transvaal Chamber of Mines, amounted to just under £2-million; plus a further £300 000 accrued from official raids on banks and mine safes in the region. All told, the resources available to Kruger's government before and during the war amounted to just under £3-million.

In terms of expenditure, James Gray estimated that the cost of fighting the war was at first a mere £80 000 per month - then it doubled. By the time Kruger abandoned Pretoria, his government had approximately one and a half million pounds at its disposal. Interestingly, this is exactly the same amount estimated by Preller, who organized the evacuation of the gold from the city. It was this amount that formed the basis of the Kruger Millions legend.

WHERE DID THE MONEY GO?

During August 1900, President Steyn, then leader of the Orange Free State, and President Kruger met at Nelspruit, where it was decided that the two states would combine their resources to continue the struggle against the British. Given the desperate shortage of funds, the executive council of the two governments sanctioned an agreement to sell a quantity of unminted or 'raw' gold (which could not be used as currency) to the German firm Wilken and Ackermann of Lourenço Marques, for £3 10s per standard ounce. The agreement stipulated that payment would be received in either British or Transvaal gold currency.

On 11 September 1900, with the British forces swiftly approaching Machadodorp, Kruger crossed the border into Mozambique with thirty cases of unminted gold bullion and made his way to the coast. Some 64 142 ounces of gold was placed on the German ship *Bundesrath* which arrived in Hamburg towards the end of October. Through this transaction, an amount of £224 497 was raised by the Boers.

Around the same time, Kruger and his party set sail for Holland, taking with them £150 000. According to Preller, this money was used to pay for goods such as 'clothing, eatables, matches and similar commodities' which were delivered to the Boer forces in the Transvaal and approximately £25 000 of the gold, later minted in Germany, was also sent to Transvaal commandos via South West Africa (Namibia). But what of the rest?

A vast amount was used to continue the war effort. James Gray's investigation established that around £600 000 was sent to Europe in the form of gold bars for the purchase of munitions, a further £350 000 in notes and coins was given to President Steyn and other Boer leaders for use in the field, and approximately £200 000 was paid to sundry creditors. Gray's figures suggest that roughly £150 000 remained unaccounted for – a considerable sum in those days, but it hardly constituted 'millions'.

Given the fact that the Transvaal government had been forced to abandon Pretoria hastily at the end of May 1900, some weeks earlier than expected, there must have been chaos.

Indeed, Preller remarked that the auditor in charge of getting the gold out of the city had to 'hurry up' those detailed to physically remove the bullion from the banks at which it was stored.

Under these circumstances, it is quite conceivable that *some* money was misappropriated - but not 'millions'. In fact, there weren't 'millions' available to go missing.

What can be said with certainty is that the Transvaal government documents for the period show that a hidden treasure, belonging either to President Kruger personally (the value of his assets during the last four years of his life is known and was divided up amongst his heirs after his death) or to the Transvaal Government, did not exist.

During this period, money was sent to Boer leaders in the field for them to continue the struggle. Bullion was sent to Europe to purchase equipment and given to the charge of President Kruger himself so that he could oversee its shipment out of the country.

One can also surmise that relatively small amounts were entrusted to various individuals for safe-keeping and were subsequently buried to keep them out of British hands.

Of these transactions there is little information.

A MYTH IN THE MAKING

Many people believe that the so-called 'Kruger Millions', in the form of gold coins, is buried somewhere in the Transvaal. Others believe it comprises a large amount of gold bullion which was shipped to Europe. In 1925, a generation after the fighting had stopped, there remained considerable speculation as to how much money was actually involved.

An article in *The South African Nation*, dated 10 October 1925, describes how, after the two Republics pooled their resources, the minted gold was divided. The Transvaal's share came to £20 000 pounds and a shipment of raw gold was sent to Mozambique.

Exactly how many ingots were kept by the two Republics after President Kruger left, exactly how much raw gold was handed to the Lourenço Marques firm, what their share of it was and what they kept in custody for the Transvaal Government are questions which have not as yet, been answered; but this much is certain, that what has been described above were the only financial transactions which took place apart, of course, from the smaller sums handed over to commanders from time to time to enable them to carry on operations. [5]

A number of questions posed by the article were only answered six years later, following the release of documents belonging to Dr WJ Leyds, the last representative of the Transvaal government overseas (in Brussels). In the Leyds papers, details were given of the movement of the 'wagonload' of gold destined for Germany. [6]

Leyds stated, 'I can positively declare that no government gold was buried either before or after the departure of President Kruger for Europe. The President would have spoken to me about it, and moreover all the circumstances were against it'.

LEGENDS AND RUMOURS ...

Despite repeated denials by the Transvaal Government officials and careful public accounting, myths about the 'Kruger Millions' remain.

THE *DOROTHEA*

At the time Kruger was in Lourenço Marques the *Dorothea* set sail for Natal and the Cape with a cargo of cement. It was rumoured that the gold which Kruger had brought eastwards was hidden in her hold and mystery was compounded when, according to legend, the *Dorothea* sank off St Lucia and eleven men lost their lives in various attempts to salvage her.

How this story originated is unclear, but it was claimed that Kruger was in Lourenço Marques at the same time as the *Dorothea* and he did arrange shipment at this time for a cargo of gold bullion to Europe. However, as the *Dorothea* was wrecked in 1898, a year before the Anglo-Boer War broke out, this seems unlikely.

PHILLIPUS SWARTZ

Another famous character from this period, and one whose name continually crops up among talks of buried treasure, is Phillipus Swartz. Swartz, who was eventually incarcerated and hanged for murder, is suspected of having possessed specific knowledge of the whereabouts of the 'Kruger Millions'.

According to Lawrence Green, who interviewed Colonel HF Trew of the South African Police (who issued permits to those wishing to dig for buried treasure), Swartz,

in the company of three companions, including a man named Van Niekerk, went into the Lowveld near Phalaborwa to search for Kruger's gold which Swartz claimed he helped bury during the Anglo-Boer War.

However, shortly after arriving at the spot where the money was allegedly buried, Van Niekerk mysteriously disappeared. Swartz later went back to Van Niekerk's farm, but the story he told Mrs van Niekerk roused suspicion and she contacted the police. Swartz vanished and a patrol sent out to look for him came across a corpse being savaged by a number of jackals. On the corpse was a ring bearing the initials CvN.

The patrol tracked Swartz for a number of days and finally caught up with him – he had been laid low by malaria. He was subsequently transported to Pietersburg jail and allegedly visited by a number of high-ranking British officials seeking to establish, for the Government, the hiding place of Kruger's gold. Swartz said nothing, and he was later tried for murder in Johannesburg, found guilty and hanged. The secret hiding place of the gold – if it ever existed – died with him.

According to Colonel Trew, Swartz did however say something about the gold to one of the warders who guarded him during his time in Pietersburg jail ... 'The money is ours, and no damned British government shall ever have it!'

Of course, this may well have been hearsay, but there is another side to this incredible story.

According to Swartz's attorney, his legal costs were paid in gold coins received in the dead of night in a Pretoria backstreet, handed over by an unknown man. Furthermore, 'A large number of the coins showed traces of having been buried for a long time'.

Another intriguing development was that one of the witnesses to the Swartz/Van Niekerk affair who had visited the spot at which Van Niekerk died, testified that while no gold was found at the place indicated by Swartz, they did discover a small bag of cut diamonds hidden in the riverbank!

It is not known how the diamonds came to be there or who they belonged to. Deneys Reitz, however, speculated that the diamonds belonged to Baron Bentinck of Holland who vanished in the region shortly before the Swartz episode. Reitz suggested that Swartz may well have murdered the Baron while attached to a commando and then hidden the diamonds. He then concocted the story of the 'Kruger Millions' to elicit assistance to return to the area and search for the place where he had hidden his ill-gotten gains.

Even if the account given by Reitz' 'witness' is accurate, this sheds no light on the matter of the Kruger Millions as diamonds did not form part of the 'treasure'. When Swartz returned to the area to reclaim his 'goods' it would appear that he actively promoted the idea that the Kruger Millions existed as it gave credence to his own activities.

As a consequence, his name and the story of the Kruger Millions became inextricably entwined.

But was there ever a Kruger fortune?

THE OWL HOUSE
And the mysterious mind of Helen Martins

Helen Martins was, and remains, something of an enigma. For a quarter of a century she was possessed by the need to create, out of concrete and glass, a world of beauty, colour and movement. Now her small home in Nieu-Bethesda, deep in the heart of the Karoo, is a shrine to her memory and a place of pilgrimage.

But why did she build her statues?

Was she a visionary of insight and imagination? Or someone tormented by invisible demons?

Or was she, perhaps, just a private woman quietly creating her own private paradise?

Helen Martins' legacy of sculptures continues to enthral and mystify almost twenty years after her death. But the questions regarding her motives remain. In the end, we must all make up our own minds about Helen Martins and her Owl House.

BEGINNING AT THE END

One Friday in August 1976, Helen Martins, creator of the Owl House, committed suicide by drinking caustic soda. It was known that she had become increasingly depressed because of her failing eyesight, but whether it was this that drove her to her last fatal act remains uncertain. Her death remains as mysterious as her life.

On the afternoon that she poisoned herself, Koos Malgas, one of the local men she had employed to build her wondrous statues, left her house for less than an hour; when he returned, one of the neighbours was waiting for him on the stoep, looking very worried. Inside the house the dominee, his wife

and the local district nurse were doing what they could to make Miss Helen comfortable, but she was very weak and failing fast.

She was taken to the Graaff-Reinet hospital where she died from her actions three days later. It was, perhaps, a fit-

tingly bizarre end to the life of a most unconventional person.

Helen Martins was an eccentric, an art lover. She lived virtually her entire life in the small town of Nieu-Bethesda, where she created both in and around her small house, a mythical world of birds, animals and people. She lived in River Street in a house she inherited from her parents. Her home, still preserved by 'The Friends of the Owl House', is a typical Karoo dwelling: single-storied, with a tin roof and a front verandah. But this is where the ordinary ends. A cage of cement owls stands on the front stoep and the front windows are frosted suns made from crushed glass glued to the panes. Next to the verandah is the 'Moon Gate', a glass encrusted cement arch, surmounted by a double-faced owl. At the back of the house is the sculpture gar-

A TROUBLED CHILDHOOD

Helen Martins was born just before the turn of the century, and was the youngest of six children. Her parents were unhappily married and there are those who believe that much of their misery spilled over and blighted young Helen's life. But there were also other factors to consider ...

When Helen was a young girl she had to have her two small toes amputated, and she was acutely sensitive of this 'disfigurement'. On one occasion, she was

walking to the post office when some strangers turned into the street. She promptly sat down in the middle of the road and covered her feet with her skirt until they had passed by. Only deep and painful personal embarrassment could have caused such an extreme response. When she was older, children in the neighbourhood thought Helen strange and would sometimes knock at her door and run away. They threw stones into her yard – one of the reasons why she constructed a fence round her property and protected it with tall-growing, thorny, Queen of the Night cactus plants.

Her father also had a reputation as an eccentric. For example, Gertruda Claassen, Nieu-Bethesda's town clerk recalled how he used to sit on the stoep with a hat pulled down over his eyes; his ill-humour was legendary. There was also the occasion when Mr Martins lay prostrate on the ground with an orange box over his head. When someone called to see him he shouted, 'Can't you see I'm busy?' and refused to get up.

Helen Martins left Nieu-Bethesda for three years to train as an English teacher at Graaff-Reinet teacher's training college, where she proved to be an outstanding student. Shortly after her graduation she married a Karoo farmer,

Above: The view from the kitchen window.

Right: What inspired Helen Martin's creations?

den – called the 'Camel Yard' by Helen Martins – crammed with an assortment of statues, both fantastic and real: pilgrims, people, animals and birds, acrobats and buddhas, lions and suns ...

The interior of the Owl House is a sparkling jewel, a place of light, and no less astonishing than the outside. Everywhere are mirrors, lamps, and painted suns and walls that gleam with the glitter of crushed glass. Helen Martins was obsessed with the moon, and the effects of light and the ground glass on the walls is designed to capture the moonlight when it shines into the house.

Beer bottle man and woman.

Johannes Pienaar, but after six months, the marriage ended in divorce. A second marriage also ended in divorce. In the early 1930s, Helen's mother fell ill and it was this that prompted her to return home to nurse her mother until she died. Afterwards she stayed on at the house to look after her father until his death in 1945. For over thirty years Helen hardly ever left Nieu-Bethesda. But if she couldn't go to the world then, perhaps, the world could come to her ...

CREATING THE OWL HOUSE

When Helen was almost 50 years old she began, without fanfare, to create the Owl House, in the process transforming her small home into a place of wonder. What is amazing, however, is that not one of the sculptures in the garden was made by Helen herself. Local craftsmen, such as Jonas Adams, Koos Malgas, and Piet van der Merwe, built the animals, people and birds to Helen's designs, usually working from pictures she had taken from books and cards she kept in the house. Piet van der Merwe suggested that much of the inspiration for the works came out of a large book –

probably an old family Bible – which she kept with her at all times. Unfortunately, Piet van der Merwe couldn't read so he never knew the book's title, and it has since vanished from the house. Helen Martins conceived a masterplan for her house, but she was not a wealthy woman – her income was derived almost solely from a small pension she received. To pay for the materials she needed and the artisans who worked for her, she economized on personal items such as clothing and even food, sometimes living simply on bread and tea. In her pantry, the shelves were lined with bottles of ground glass of varying fineness.

The materials Helen most often worked with were concrete and glass. Many of the statues are built from wire frames filled with stone chips, with concrete poured over these frames and smoothed by hand. Most of them are embellished with pieces of glass, and shards of broken glass are strewn underfoot throughout the yard.

Although Helen was not a church-goer, religion was important to her – even if her views on the subject were somewhat unorthodox. The sculpture garden, for example, contains a model of a church with a spire, nativity scenes, tall pillars topped with glittering stars and shrines composed of bottles which she called her Meccas. She was not a convert to Islam but she had an interest in the Muslim religion.

Helen's interest in birds was also well known, especially owls which she regarded as symbols of wisdom, and local people used to bring to her birds caught in the veld. When she died, there were a number of pigeons and Egyptian geese at her house.

Helen Martins was also regarded as a woman prone to sudden bouts of enthusiasm. If she liked someone, she would go up to them, put her arms around their neck and stare intently into their eyes. She was an eccentric, although some would say she was disturbed. To others she was viewed as someone who knew clearly what she wanted, namely to devote herself to her works of art. Everything else took second place.

Clearly, Helen Martins was a unique person blessed, some would say, with a unique vision of the world. Perhaps she was exorcising her own ghosts or speaking to us, not with words but through her sculptures.

NIEU-BETHESDA

Nieu-Bethesda – named after a healing pool in Jerusalem – is situated at the foot of the Sneeuberg, 54 km north of Graaff-Reinet. It was established as a mission station in 1875 and became a municipality approximately eleven years later. The old watermill, situated in Pienaar Street, was built in 1860 and is reached by going past the cemetery which dates back to 1786.

Nieu-Bethesda's original church, which once served as a wagon-house, has now been abandoned. In recent years, the town has provided a home for South Africa's only Zen Buddhist centre.

31

WARATAH
The ship that vanished without a trace

On the night of 28 July 1909, the 'unsinkable' steamship, *Waratah*, with 211 passengers and crew, vanished without a trace en route from Durban to Cape Town.

What happened to the *Waratah* that stormy night so many years ago? No trace of the vessel has ever been found – at least, not until recently. There is evidence to suggest that the final resting place of this vessel *has* been discovered and, if this is indeed the case, then there was at least one witness to the tragedy.

She was so comfortable and luxurious. I was a little girl of about six at the time but I still remember things so vividly.

I recollect one storm that was bad, very bad.

The plates on our dinner table were sliding and even bouncing up and down so much they had to be tied down somehow.

The lifeboat drill caused a lot of excitement. We had to put on our life belts and report to certain lifeboats, each with its own person in command.

And I remember the drama when my younger sister's big straw hat blew overboard in the wind.

She was so upset that she tried to climb over the rails to jump in after the hat, and I clung to her legs, crying and screaming until a member of the crew ran to help me.

The voyage took five weeks and it was lovely.

We landed in Durban then went by train to Johannesburg. We were all so upset when we heard later that she

What happened to the Waratah?

had just vanished like that, with all her passengers and crew.

Oh, yes, and I remember how we met Captain Ilbery and he shook my hand. He was a big man with a big beard. But then I suppose all men look big when you are a tiny little thing, don't they?'

(Recollections of the maiden voyage of the *Waratah* by Mrs Alice Katz of Muizenberg, in an interview with the *Argus* in June 1989.)

BEFORE THE DISAPPEARANCE

At 6 p.m. on the evening of Monday, 26 July 1909, the steamship *Waratah*, pride of Lund's Blue Anchor Line, left Durban harbour and sailed in a south-westerly direction for Cape Town, where she was scheduled to arrive on the morning of Thursday 29 July. After a short stop-over in Cape Town, the ship was to continue its voyage to London. Early on Tuesday morning, about twelve hours after the *Waratah* had left Durban, she was spotted coming up astern by the officers-on-watch of the much slower *Clan MacIntyre*. The *Clan MacIntyre*, which had left Durban a few hours before the *Waratah*, was also en route to London. Around 8.30 a.m., when the two ships were alongside one another,

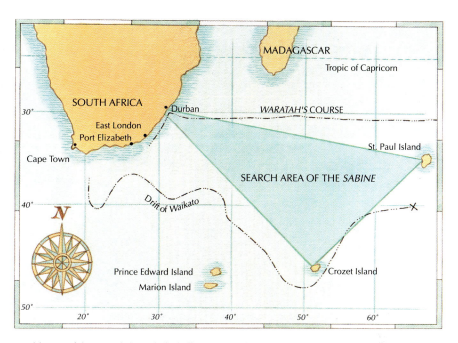

courtesy flag signals were exchanged – neither vessel carried radio – then the *Waratah* crossed over to the *Clan MacIntyre*'s starboard side and steamed slowly ahead. By the time the *Waratah* finally disappeared over the horizon, the seas were rough and there was a heavy swell building. Cape Town maritime historian, Peter Humphries, has estimated the *Waratah*'s position as being approximately 17 miles south-west of the Mbashe River mouth.

That was the last definite sighting of the *Waratah*, although shortly before 10 p.m. that same night, another vessel,

Could parts of the Waratah *have drifted off course like the* Waikato?

the Union Castle liner, *Guelph*, signalled a ship near East London. The identity of this ship has never been established, however, and the officers of the *Guelph* could only make out the last three letters of her name – 'T', 'A' and 'H'.

THE SEARCH COMMENCES

For the first twenty-four hours after the *Waratah* failed to arrive according to schedule in Cape Town, no-one was unduly worried by the fact that the vessel was overdue because it was assumed that she had been delayed by the extremely bad weather. Although all lookout stations and ports along the coast were placed on alert, it wasn't until she was a full two days late that the alarm was raised.

On 1 August, the Table Bay Harbour Board's tug *TE Fuller* was sent to look for the *Waratah* along the Agulhas bank; if the ship had suffered engine trouble a tug would be able to tow her to port. The *Harry Escombe* also left Port Natal on a similar mission. But neither the *TE Fuller* nor the *Harry Escombe* found any trace of the missing vessel.

At the time of the disappearance there

were several unsubstantiated rumours regarding the fate of the *Waratah*. The master of the Rennie liner, *Insizwa*, for example, reported seeing what he thought were bodies floating in the Bashee River mouth region. The tug, *Buffalo*, which was based in East London, was sent to investigate. The crew found pieces of meat floating in the water, but this was believed to be whale meat from a Durban whaling station.

The Royal Navy based in Port Natal then joined in the search and sent two cruisers, HMS *Pandora* and HMS *Forte*, into the waters of the Indian Ocean off the east coast. Although joined at a later stage by HMS *Hermes*, they found no clues as to the fate of the missing ship.

By September 1909, when hope of finding the *Waratah* had all but evaporated, the Blue Anchor Line in collaboration with the Australian government chartered the Union Castle ship, *Sabine*, to conduct a thorough search of the area.

The *Sabine* cruised South African coastal waters and beyond for three months but found nothing which could be identified as having come from the missing ship. In 1910, Australian relatives of the missing passengers and crew chartered the steamer *Wakefield* to conduct their own search.

The *Wakefield*, which sailed from Melbourne on 10 February 1910, called at Durban, then followed a zig-zag passage of some 30 000 kilometres over a period of six months searching across the Indian Ocean and into the Antarctic including the Crozets and Heard islands and Kerguelen, in what ended up as a fruitless search for evidence of the missing ship.

THE OFFICIAL INQUIRY

In December 1910, seventeen months after the ship had vanished, an official inquiry into the fate of the *Waratah* was held at Caxton Hall in London.

After hearing evidence from several witnesses, including former crew members and passengers, naval architects, representatives of the owners and the builders, the court handed down its findings on 22 February 1911.

The conclusion reached was that the *Waratah* had foundered in a gale of exceptional violence on 28 July 1909, and that she had capsized as a result of a 'chain of events that must remain undetermined'. The court further declared that it considered the *Waratah* to be both seaworthy and properly manned but noted that there was insufficient evidence to indicate whether all proper safety precautions had been taken after her departure from Durban, namely that all hatches were correctly battened down and that her lifeboats were ready to be launched in the event of the ship having to be abandoned at short notice.

The *Waratah* inquiry had reached its conclusion, but that was far from the end of the story ...

THE SHIP

The *Waratah*, a coal-fired, twin-screw passenger and cargo steamship of 9 339 tonnes, was constructed in the shipyards of Barclay, Curle & Co. on the Clyde in

Top: The Waratah, *launched in 1908.*
Above: Joe Conquer, who saw the Waratah *sink.*

Scotland. Less than a year old, she was built around eight watertight compartments running the length of the hull and was reputed to be unsinkable. She possessed the most up-to-date equipment and machinery (apart from radio), carried a crew of 119, had above standard accommodation for 100 passengers, including a separate dining room and lounge for first-class passengers, and could boast a speed of over 13,5 knots.

Her maiden voyage from London to Adelaide, Australia, passed without incident and her Captain, Josiah Ilbery, a man who had commanded nearly every one of Lund's vessels and had sailed from Great Britain to Australia for almost thirty years declared himself well satisfied with his new charge.

The *Waratah* left London for her second voyage on 27 April 1909. She began the return leg from Melbourne on 1 July and reached Durban twenty-five days later. When she left Durban for Cape Town she was carrying, in addition to her crew, 92 passengers and a cargo of farm produce, mainly flour and frozen meat, and 1 100 tonnes of lead tailings.

WHY DID THE *WARATAH* SINK?

No-one knows for certain why the *Waratah* went down, but there are a number of theories. The most popular, although it attracted little official notice, is that she suddenly turned turtle in the heavy weather.

Martin Leendertz, the shipping correspondent for the *Cape Times* newspaper in 1909, visited the *Waratah* during her stopover in Cape Town harbour on her maiden voyage. In the account he wrote at the time he described the vessel as 'an extremely lofty ship'.

'I can confess now,' he said in an article published in *The South African Shipping News* almost fifty years later, 'that that was my ultra-cautious way of saying I thought she was top heavy ...'.

However, Leendertz was not the only one who held this opinion.

Claud Sawyer, one of the passengers who had booked a berth from Australia to London, was so convinced that the ship was heading for disaster that he forfeited his passage money and disembarked in Durban. The readon he gave, which was later recalled at the official enquiry, was that the *Waratah* appeared to hang at each roll and was slow in recovering. He had had a succession of dreams during the voyage involving a sword and a blood-stained cloth which he regarded as an ill-omen. In the wire he later sent to his wife to explain his action, he said that he thought the ship was unstable.

Not everyone agreed with Sawyer. Fellow passengers, including Moerien Morgan, who had also left the ship at Durban, maintained that in very heavy weather encountered during the journey from Australia, the *Waratah* had behaved impeccably.

Yet another passenger who had travelled on the *Waratah*'s maiden voyage, sang the praises of the ship. However, he had observed that the ship was coaled through a chute from the extreme top of the boat deck, and speculated that if the chute itself was filled to capacity it could increase the top-heaviness of the ship. In fact, he had discussed the matter with the *Waratah*'s

chief engineer, Mr Hodder, and was told that it was unlikely that the ship would ever coal that high.

Perhaps the *Waratah* suffered engine or steering failure and, while labouring in heavy seas, a giant wave stoved in her forehatch. Or did she catch fire and sink before there was time to launch the lifeboats? (though this is unlikely on such

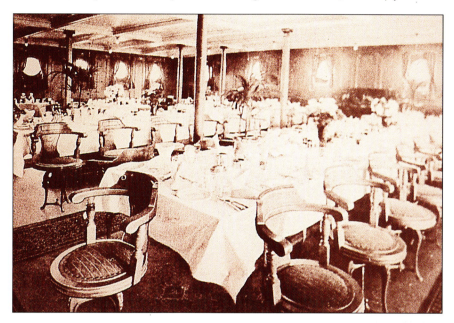

Above: The second-class dining room. The Waratah *had above standard accommodation for 100 passengers,*

Below: The smoking room.

a well-frequented shipping route). Was she engulfed by a tremendous mid-ocean vortex or whirlpool caused by an underwater earthquake? Had she steamed head-on into a gigantic wave and been buried by thousands of tons of water? If this did occur, the *Waratah* may well have slid into the trough, a huge hole in the sea, and simply been

engulfed. Experienced sailors have also remarked that on some occasions a freak wave can be preceded by two large companions. If the *Waratah* experienced this while labouring heavily and was slow to respond, she may have heeled over at the first wave, been driven further over by the second and completely overturned by the third. Should the *Waratah*'s cargo have shifted during the storm, she would have been made all the more unstable.

Despite the fact that the *Waratah* was labelled 'unsinkable', no vessel would survive such a pounding. Of course, one may speculate that any ship that was struck with a wave of such force would have its decks 'swept clean'.

Perhaps the most curious factor of all is not that the *Waratah* went down, but that no evidence of the sinking was left at the water's surface.

The suggestion that a fire caused the *Waratah* to sink is also problematic. If a fire had occurred, then why was the smoke not seen by other vessels in the area? And why were no lifeboats launched? There is nothing to suggest that the lifeboats were anything but serviceable. If there had been a fire that had led to an explosion, why was no debris from the stricken vessel ever found?

GONE BUT NOT FORGOTTEN

For a number of years after the *Waratah* disappearance there were reports of wreckage washed-up along the Southern Cape coast of South Africa and the coast of Australia, but none of the items supposedly originating from the *Waratah* could be reliably identified as coming from the ill-fated ship.

In 1910, for example, there was a report that a life belt from the *Waratah* had washed-up on the Australian coast to the north of Freemantle. But when the man who made this claim returned to the scene, the life belt had vanished. In March of the same year, trooper Dan Marais reported his find of a number of items along the Great Brak River, including boxes marked 'Andrew Lusk and Co' and 'Lunham Brothers' but these could not be tied to the *Waratah*.

Also in 1910, the *Star of Scotland* reported that it had seen floating wreckage, although it had not stopped to investigate. The *Star of Scotland* claimed in a belated report to have passed an upturned lifeboat which the crew suspected may have come from the *Waratah*. The ship had not stopped to investigate, however, for fear of becoming entangled in the mess of wreckage that surrounded it. The position given by the *Star of Scotland* was also some way south-east of the *Waratah*'s last known position and, as a result, this report was treated with some caution. A year later the steamship *Palatina* struck an object while entering East London harbour and then limped into port where she had to be beached because of the serious damage to her hull. At the subsequent inquiry, the *Palatina*'s master suggested that he might have struck the *Waratah*.

The TE Fuller *searched for the* Waratah *along the Agulhas bank, while HMS* Forte *checked the Indian Ocean off the east coast. They found no clues as to the fate of the missing ship.*

WHY WAS NO WRECKAGE FOUND?

The loss of the *Waratah* is one mystery, but the fact that not one piece of wreckage has ever been found, is quite another. Or is it? On many occasions it seems that fact is stranger than fiction where the sea is concerned. For example, in May 1860, the *Snake*, a small schooner which plied the south-east coast, began to sink in heavy seas after leaving Mossel Bay en route to Cape Town. The ship was eventually abandoned and her crew took to the safety of a passing French vessel. Nothing further was heard of the *Snake* until 30 November when the British vessel *Peerless* happened upon her north of Mauritius and took her in tow to Batavia where, in January 1861, the boat and her cargo were sold.

On 7 October 1925, the Greek steamer *Margarita* left East London with a cargo of maize and turned south. Early the next morning she sent out a distress signal. At that time, she reported her position as south of the mouth of the Great Fish River.

'Ship almost unmanageable with 20 degrees list. Heavy seas breaking through.'

Those were the last words ever heard from the *Margerita*. Within hours of the report three vessels had gone to her aid but, like the *Waratah*, she had vanished without a trace. According to accounts in the *Eastern Province Herald*

'... (the affair) recalls the dramatic disappearance of the *Waratah* not so very many miles from the same spot'.

In 1971, another incident occurred which may shed some light on the reason why no wreckage from the *Waratah* was ever discovered. The incident involved a cargo vessel, the *Heythrop*, which suffered an explosion in her engine room while travelling between East London and Port Elizabeth.

Apart from causing considerable damage, the force of the explosion blew one of the lifeboats overboard. Most of the crew and their wives were put aboard a passing vessel, the *Showa Venture*, for safety, after which the *Heythrop* was towed to Algoa Bay. The lifeboat was written-off until it was found fifteen months later in a small harbour in Western Australia. Apart from a bent propeller blade, the boat was in near perfect condition.

WHERE DID THE *WARATAH* GO DOWN?

The search for the *Waratah* has continued to the present day, but opinion as to her final resting place remains divided.

When the ship was last seen from the *Clan MacIntyre* on 10 July 1909, she was about 17 miles south-west of the Mbashe River mouth, situated to the north of East London. At the time, the *Waratah*, which was estimated to have been travelling at a speed of 17 knots (13 knots plus the four knot Mozambique Current) and would, therefore, have been a considerable distance further south.

Peter Humphries, believes the ship went down in the vicinity of the mouth of the Great Fish River which is south of East London. He reasons that she may have been heading for shelter at Port Elizabeth at the time, steamed further inshore than intended, ripped her hull open on submerged rocks and sank like a stone.

This view is supported by Professor JK Mallory, Emeritus Professor of Oceanology at the University of Cape Town. He believes that the *Waratah* probably foundered between East London and the Great Fish River, and theorises that an abnormal wave may have capsized or engulfed the vessel.

Another Cape Town researcher, however, Emlyn Brown, who to date has organized four expeditions in search of the elusive ship is convinced that the *Waratah* lies much further north, about ten kilometres off the Xora River mouth

Top: The JAGO submarine, used on one of the expeditions to discover the resting place of the Waratah.

Above and Right: The diving bell on board Deep Salvage 1, *used during the July 1989 expedition.*

which is approximately 100 kilometres north of East London. He bases this belief on both geophysical survey of the ocean bed and circumstantial evidence, most notably the accounts of Joe Conquer and Brigadier Roos …

Joe Conquer, a member of the Cape Mounted Rifles in 1909, came forward twenty years later and claimed to have seen the ship go down while managing a heliograph station on the Transkei

coast. In 1930, Brigadier Roos claimed to have seen a wreck off the Xora River mouth from his aeroplane.

Peter Humphries dismisses these claims as conjecture. He is convinced that the wreck referred to by Roos was in fact that of the German ship *Khedive* which went down in 1910. He also questions why Joe Conquer was never called to give evidence at the official inquiry, even though witnesses were called from all over the world, and why his evidence only 'surfaced' after Roos had made his claim.

Emlyn Brown, however, argues that this was simply because the official investigation was held in Britain and that Joe Conquer's report to his superiors of the incident went missing, resulting in his not being called. His view that the *Waratah* disappeared further north than many people believe is supported by Captain George Foulis, master of the survey ship *Meiring Naude*. A sonar survey of the sea bed along the east coast of South Africa was conducted in 1977 and Foulis claims to have come across what he believes may be the wreck of the *Waratah*.

'It is definitely a wreck and not a sea mountain, and we're pretty certain she is the *Waratah*,' Foulis told the *Argus* in a report published in July 1989. (A sea mountain is a ridge of land rising from the sea bed.) 'During our geophysical survey we covered thousands of kilometres and we saw absolutely nothing else. We have been convinced for years that she is the *Waratah*.

'It is true she would have been much further south when she ran into heavy weather. It would then have made all the sense in the world for Captain Ilbery to turn around and run with the weather for the comfort of the passengers.' [1]

THE MYSTERY REMAINS ...

Over the years there have been a number of expeditions to locate the *Waratah*, the most recent of which took place in 1989. Emlyn Brown commissioned a geophysical survey company to conduct an investigation which laboriously 'painted' a 100 square mile stretch of ocean floor with sonar (sound navigation and ranging), an echo-sounding device, in exactly the same way as was used to locate the *Titanic*. Using this method, comput-

ers interpret the information gathered to produce an accurate 'picture' of the sea bed, and microwave links (in this case with the Transkei coast) provide accurate computer-guided navigation.

He is convinced he has located the *Waratah*, lying in 120 metres of water about 10 km from the Xora River mouth. Unfortunately, on the one occasion when an underwater camera was lowered over the side of the survey vessel to film the wreck, the scaffold holding it collapsed from the weight of water and the force of the current, and the camera was lost.

In 1989, Emlyn Brown returned to the site in the Cape Town-based salvage vessel *Deep Salvage 1*, this time taking with him a sophisticated diving bell. Dogged by bad luck and stormy weather, the

diving bell could only be used on one occasion, although it did provide a view of the section of hull which, given the 'vintage' of the rivets, Brown maintains, confirms the identity of the vessel.

Captain Peter Wilmot, the master of *Deep Salvage 1* descended to the sea bed and videotaped small sections of the wreck before an overheating power pack forced him back to the surface. It was impossible, however, to say if the ship was actually the *Waratah*.

'Granted, it could be any other ship down there, but its highly likely that it is the *Waratah* – the evidence is far too overwhelming to say it's not,' says Emlyn Brown. There are others, of course, who would disagree.

For the time being, however, the fate of the *Waratah* remains a mystery.

FREAK WAVE PHENOMENON

In 1973, Professor JK Mallory, Emeritus Professor of Oceanography at the University of Cape Town, published a paper entitled *Abnormal Waves on the South East Coast of South Africa*. It was distributed to a number of ships that navigated the section of coastline in question and received international publicity. Professor Mallory deduced that abnormal waves occurred in a very narrow belt off the south-east coast, between Durban and the Great Fish River, in the area immediately outside the edge of the continental shelf. These abnormal waves, which could be experienced any time after a well-defined cold front (and thus generally occurred during the winter months), could reach up to twenty metres in height and only lasted a few minutes. Abnormal waves are caused by a coincidence of smaller waves of varying wave lengths, which are themselves the result of a confluence of two or three wind systems.

Abnormal, gigantic waves, which rise up without warning, are characterized by extremely deep troughs and all-but sheer wave fronts. Any vessel unfortunate enough to encounter such an abnormal wave while moving in a south-westerly direction, would have no time to take avoiding action. The vessel would steam into the trough and, while nose-down, be engulfed by a tremendous weight of water, with catastrophic results.

The photograph is of a freak wave engulfing a 250 000 ton oil tanker passing the Cape.

THE LOST CITY OF THE KALAHARI
Home of an ancient civilization?

For over a hundred years, academics and explorers alike have been casting doubt upon the existence of a 'lost city' of the ancients, allegedly discovered in 1885 by the American showman and adventurer, Gilarmi A Farini, while journeying through the Kalahari. Over the years, a number of expeditions have set out to find this fabled 'lost city', but all without success. So did Farini's 'lost city' really exist thousands of years ago, or was it simply a figment of the music-hall star's overwrought imagination? Or could the whole story merely have been a born performer's last attempt to draw attention to himself and his enterprise to be in the limelight once more?

Early in January 1885, would-be explorer, Gilarmi A Farini, accompanied by his son Lulu, and a companion, Gert 'Kert' Louw, sailed from London to South Africa on the SS *Roslin Castle*. This was Farini's first trip to Africa. The stories he had heard of Africa had fired his imagination and his objective, it seemed, was to mix business with pleasure.

They docked in Cape Town, spent some time there, and then headed north for the Kalahari Desert early in February.

From the coast the three intrepid travellers took the weekly 'mail express' across the Karoo to Hope Town, at that time the nearest railway station to the newly-opened diamond fields of Kimberley. They provisioned a light wagon and a team of mules, and then embarked on a journey of discovery into the interior. On his return to Europe some months later, Farini recounted how he and his companions had discovered, in the forbidding wastes of the desert, the abandoned ruins of a 'city ... of a great nation' that had existed, he speculated, 'perhaps thousands of years ago'. And so the story of 'the lost city of the Kalahari' became one of southern Africa's most popular legends ...

Gilarmi Farini and his companions claimed to have found extensive ruins of the Lost City of the Kalahari. However, subsequent expeditions, of which there have been several, have not succeeded in relocating the site. This poses the question of whether in fact there was a Lost City?

GILARMI FARINI: GREAT EXPLORER

Farini, whose real name was William Leonard Hunt, was a colourful and flamboyant character. He was born in New York in 1839 and at the age of 25 had been the second man to cross the Niagara Falls by tightrope (Blondini being the first in 1864).

Not long afterwards, he bettered this achievement by crossing the more dangerous Chaudriere Falls in Canada. Through this and similar feats he assumed the name 'Farini the Great'.

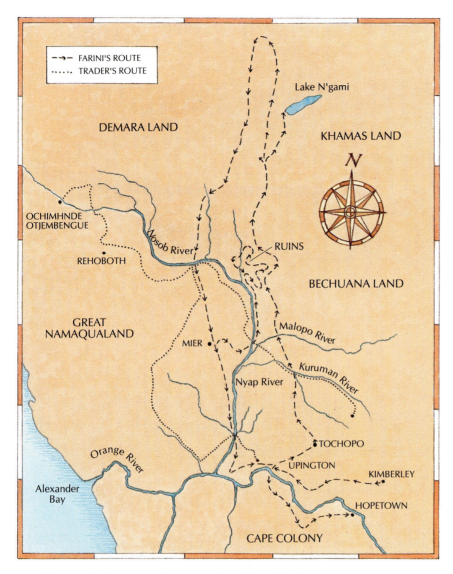

Map of the route taken by Farini on his journey through the Kalahari.

According to Farini's book *Through the Kalahari Desert,* which was published shortly after his return to Europe, Farini, his son and 'Kert' Louw left Kimberley, travelled by wagon westwards along the north bank of the Orange River to within fifty miles of Upington, then turned north-eastwards at Wilkerhouts Drift. At Tehepo, which was about two hundred miles further on, they changed direction again – this time heading almost due north.

They entered the Kalahari Desert proper in Bechuanaland after crossing the dry bed of the Molopo River.

The explorers continued northwards as far as Lake N'gami via Lehutitung (now Lehututu in present-day Botswana), eventually circled eastwards and then turned south in the direction of the Cape.

The homeward leg of the adventurers' trip skirted the area of Damaraland in Great Namaqualand (present-day Namibia), crossed the Nossob River and eventually reached the small settlement of Mier (Rietfontein).

Mier, which Farini described as 'a collection of huts formed of bent sticks, covered with anything that came handy, pitched on a bare stony patch ...' [2] was the headquarters of Dirk Verlander, the self-appointed chief of the Basters or Bastards, descendants of a group of ex-slaves who had been held in bondage by the Dutch, but who later escaped and subsequently intermarried with the Namaqua Hottentots.

Under Verlander, a small kingdom, completely free of European influence had been established.

A group of Baster hunters from the settlement was about to set off on a hunting trip just as the three travellers arrived at Mier, and Farini, who was impressed by Verlander's account of the wealth of game to be found along the Nossob River, swiftly arranged for his party to go along.

During the 1880s, once his performing days were over, Farini became an impresario, leased the famous Royal Westminster Aquarium in London and staged a number of spectacular shows and exhibitions of exotic animals and people. Believing firmly that the 'pygmies and dwarf earthmen' of southern Africa would be of more than passing interest to Europeans, Farini sent his secretary, WA Healey, to the Kalahari Desert in 1883 to collect a group of Bushmen and their artifacts for display. In the meantime, Farini had returned to America, which is where Healey joined him with six Bushmen and an interpreter, 'an old half-breed hunter, Kert (Louw)' who, according to Farini, had acquired 'a smattering of their language'. [1] The Bushman exhibition first went to a Coney Island, New York, amusement park early in 1884, and then moved to London in September the same year.

In England, Louw's accounts of the grass-covered plains, fertile savannas and forests teeming with game, gave the impression that the Kalahari was in fact a hunter's paradise and Farini, who needed a change of climate because his health was troubling him, decided to go on his own expedition.

THE LOST CITY DISCOVERED

The hunting party headed eastwards and probably travelled almost as far as Lehututu before turning back towards Mier. On the return journey they camped at the foot of 'Ki Ki Mountain on the Nosob (sic) River' and it was here, Farini claimed in *A Recent Journey in the Kalahari*, that they came across the ruins of a lost city. (Confusingly, later in the same chapter of the book, Farini contradicts himself and states that the party only reached the 'Ki Ki Mountain' three days after leaving the ruins.)

We camped ... beside a long line of stone which looked like the Chinese Wall after an earthquake, and which, on examination, proved to be the ruins of quite an extensive structure, in some places buried beneath the sand, but in others fully exposed to view. We traced the remains for nearly a mile, mostly a heap of huge stones, but all flat-sided, and here and there with the cement perfect and plainly visible in layers. The top row of stones were worn away by the weather and the drifting sands, some of the uppermost ones curiously rubbed on the underside and standing out like a centre table on one short leg.
The general outline of this wall was in the form of an arc, inside which lay at intervals of about forty feet apart a series of heaps of masonry in the shape of an oval or an obtuse ellipse, about a foot and a half deep, and with a flat bottom, but hollowed out at the sides for about a foot from the edge. Some of the steps were cut out of solid rock, others were formed of more than one piece of stone, fitted together very accurately. As they were all more or less buried beneath the sand, we made the men help uncover the largest of them with the shovels – a kind of work they did not much like – and found that where the

sand had protected the joints they were quite perfect. This took nearly all one day, greatly to Jan's disgust: he could not understand wasting time uncovering old stones; to him it was labour thrown away. I told him that here must have been either a city or a place of worship, or the burial ground of a great nation, perhaps thousands of years ago. [3]

Determined to investigate the 'lost city' more thoroughly, Farini, along with his two companions spent some time excavating the site.

Gilarmi Farini, the great explorer, adventurer and author.

So the next day we had it all to ourselves, and the discoveries we made amply repaid us for our labours.
On digging down nearly in the middle of the arc, we came upon a pavement about twenty feet wide, made of large stones. The outer stones were long ones, and lay at right angles to the inner ones. This pavement was intersected by another similar one at right angles, forming a Maltese cross, in the centre of which at one time must have stood an altar, column, or some sort of monument, for the base

was quite distinct, composed of loose pieces of fluted masonry.
Having searched for hieroglyphics or inscriptions, and finding none, Lulu took several photographs and sketches, from which I must leave others more learned on the subject than I to judge as to when and by whom this place was occupied.

After this one-day archaeological sojourn the three explorers returned to Mier and then continued their journey southwards, arriving back in Cape Town on 21 July 1885. Strangely, the inhabitants of Mier seemed unaware of Farini's momentous discovery since there is no record of subsequent expeditions to the site. Indeed, it would seem that as far as the people of Mier were concerned, there had been no 'find'. However, what is all the more surprising is that Farini did not mention this 'lost city' to anyone on his return to Cape Town. Surely if Farini had discovered a lost city, he would have returned to Cape Town, organized a second, better-equipped expedition and returned to the site to conduct a more comprehensive investigation? In this way his fame would have been assured. He would, after all, have rewritten the history books. But, he returned to London and it is here that the story surfaced.

One cannot help suspecting that the whole affair was a carefully worked-out ploy, designed to gain Farini maximum publicity, while at the same time running the minimum risk of being revealed as a fraud. In fact, there has always been a measure of uncertainty as to whether he *did* discover anything vaguely resembling a lost city, which is why a number of expeditions have since attempted to prove or disprove his claim.

SEARCH FOR THE LOST CITY

In March 1886, Farini delivered a lecture on his travels through the Kalahari to the members of the Royal Geographical Society in London, and it was during this lecture that he spoke of his discovery of what he described as a 'lost city' of 'cyclopean' proportions. He also spoke of some of its ruin features, including 'a kind of pavement of long narrow square blocks neatly fitted together, forming a cross, in the centre of which was what seemed to be a base for either a pedestal or monument' and 'a broken column, a part of which was in a fair state of preservation, the four flat sides being fluted ...'.

Farini aroused much interest among his audience but, surprisingly, the discussion that followed this startling revelation did not question the *authenticity* of his claims, but centred upon the problems of water supply which the inhabitants of such a lost city would have encountered, being situated in such an arid region.

THROUGH THE KALAHARI

In 1886, Farini published *Through the Kalahari Desert*, documenting his African adventure, and the book, which proved very popular, was later translated into German and French.

In 1887, however, the book received an extremely critical review in Petermann's *Geographische Mitteilungen* by Dr Hans Schinz, a highly respected German scientist-explorer who had extensive first-hand knowledge of the Kalahari. Schinz pointed to a number of discrepancies in Farini's account of the journey, not least of which were the dates given for the venture.

Through the Kalahari Desert begins with the words, 'The evening of Friday 2nd June, 1885, found a crowd of people, travellers with heaps of friends to see them off ... on the platform of Cape Town station'. This is the date on which Farini had set out. What is known for certain, however, is that seven weeks later he was back in Cape Town – an interview with the *Cape Argus* about his journey was published on 22 July 1885.

If both dates are correct, this means that Farini and his party covered a

distance of close on 3 000 miles, much of it by ox-wagon in the sandy terrain of the desert, in less than fifty days.

Farini arrived in Cape Town on 29 January 1885, and left on 20 July – a total of 175 days. If one deducts from this the time he spent in Cape Town, the two rail journeys, the time spent equipping for the expedition, rest periods and hunting trips, one is left with around 50 days for the actual expedition. To average over 400 miles per week by ox-wagon was simply not possible.

Lulu, the artist.

Casting further doubt over the time period was the fact that Farini, in his lecture to the Royal Geographical Society, said that the expedition had averaged twenty to twenty-five miles per day.

Schinz calculated that Farini left Cape Town on 2 January, *not* 2 June (which did not fall on a Friday), as the evidence indicated that he had started his journey into the desert from the Orange River on 10 February. Why Farini thought it prudent to change the date of departure remains a mystery.

When Schinz investigated Farini's claims more fully, he discovered that the few white farmers who lived in the region of Lake N'gami, had never heard

of Farini, nor, as it turned out, was he known in the territory to the north and west. A careful examination of the expedition, its duration and route, suggested that Farini and his party had travelled directly from Kimberley to Upington and from Upington to Mier (Rietfontein) along well-frequented trading routes, and that the brief excursions into the desert proper, took place in the company of local hunters.

Although Farini claimed he had discovered a 'lost city', it is significant that he did not mention this momentous discovery in the interview with the *Cape Argus* on his return to Cape Town. According to the reporter who interviewed him, he was willing 'to discuss with perfect frankness his objects in going up to the western side of the Protectorate and on up into Lake N'Gami ...'.

A further pointer of suspicion is the fact that although his son, Lulu, returned with superb photographs of such places as the Augrabies Falls, there is not one photograph of the 'lost city', although there is a somewhat elaborate sketch of the site in *Through the Kalahari Desert*.

SEEKING THE TRUTH

Farini's account of the fabled 'lost city' went largely ignored until the early 1920s when it was investigated for the first time by Professor EHL Schwarz. He subsequently came to regard the entire story with great suspicion. In 1923, it was reported that a man named Tasker, an old Kalahari hunter and trader, claimed that Farini was a fraud and that he had never been further north on his journey than Khuis, on the Molopo.

In the early 1930s the matter was investigated once again, this time more scientifically, by Dr WM Borcherds and FR Paver, then editor of the *Johannesburg Star*. They looked closely into the details of Farini's alleged journey, and went to passenger lists of the Union Castle shipping line to establish exactly when he arrived in and left South

ELDORADO – CITY OF GOLD

Eldorado (Spanish for 'the gilded one') became the name of a legendary kingdom located in the Amazon Basin. The name was first used by the Spanish and referred to a legendary Indian ruler. During festivals, this ruler reportedly plastered his body with gold dust in the morning and washed it off in a lake in the evening. Before 1530, one of the Spanish Conquistadores reported that he had visited Eldorado himself and that he was to be found in a city called Omagua.

In the decades that followed this revelation, a number of foreign adventurers converged on what is now Colombia and unsuccessfully scoured the Bogotá highlands in search of 'the gilded one'. Although the legendary kingdom of Eldorado was never found, it was indicated on maps of Brazil and the Guianas for years thereafter.

The site was promising. It was located more or less in the area we [his father and two companions] expected and in most details closely resembled Farini's description. The outline of a large, oval-shaped amphitheatre, perhaps a third of a mile in breadth and a mile in length, could hardly be mistaken. In numerous places there was a striking resemblance to a double wall constructed from large, glistening black rocks; it required little imagination to see how many of the individual boulders could be confused with square building blocks. There were several examples of flat slabs of rock perched precariously like tabletops on underlying rocks, and one of them closely matched the one appearing in Farini's illustration. One or two rocks showed a kind of fluting, several were encrusted with a mortar-like substance, and one or two were shaped like a basin.

Significantly, when Clement entered Rietfontein and showed the picture of the 'lost city' taken from Farini's book to the town's oldest resident, the man immediately declared,
'Yes, I know the place,' and directed them to Eierdopkoppies.

Did Farini's 'lost city' ever exist? All the evidence points to the simple conclusion that the 'lost city' was a fabrication – intentional or otherwise – offered to a willing public by a born showman. One must not forget that Farini was first and foremost an entertainer, and, no doubt, a good one at that. But he may have genuinely believed that he had discovered a lost civilization – he was, after all, not the first person to suggest such a thing. In 1885, Rider Haggard published *King Solomon's Mines*, which suggests that it was fashionable to believe outposts of ancient European civilizations had been established deep in the African continent. Could they be linked?

What is certain is that the 'lost city' of the Kalahari will remain a legend.

Africa. Since then, there have been at least 25 expeditions, including one by *The Automobile*, which attempted to establish, among other things, the origin of a porcelain statue of Buddha, found in a Kimberley mine, reputed to have been brought there by Bechuana workmen and picked up in the Kalahari.

THE SITE OF THE LOST CITY

In 1964, AJ Clement, an authority on the subject of the lost city and author of the book *The Kalahari and its Lost City*, visited the area where Farini claimed to have made his find and returned convinced that the 'lost city' was a 'flight of fancy' and merely a product of Farini's imagination. Clement also made the

point that there would not have been adequate supplies of water to sustain the type of settlement Farini described, as the climate had not changed appreciably for many thousands of years.

Clement believed Farini's 'lost city' may have been at the southern end of the Hakskeenpan in the shadow of the Eierdopkoppies, a few miles south-east of Rietfontein and near the road which links the town with Upington. The effect of weathering on the dolerite rock in the area resulted in cracks, joints and staining, which to the untrained eye could be misconstrued as the result of human action. In an article for *Geographical Magazine*, which subsequently appeared in the *Journal of South African Science*, Clement wrote,

PHOENICIAN GALLEY AT THE CAPE?

Perhaps the history books are wrong

In 1419, a school for navigators was established in Portugal by Prince Henry, later known as Prince Henry the Navigator, the fourth son of King John I of Portugal. Under Prince Henry's patronage, Portuguese seamen began to explore and colonise the unknown coastline of Africa, and within half a century Portugal had become the most prominent seafaring nation in the world. Thus began the 'voyages of discovery'.

According to the history books, the Portuguese explorer, Bartholomeu Dias,
was the first European to round the southern tip of Africa in 1488, but there is evidence to suggest that the Phoenicians, a seafaring nation of Mediterranean origin, visited southern Africa 2 000 years earlier. Even more astounding, is the fact that these ancient mariners may well have been forced to abandon one of their ships in what is now the suburb of Maitland in Cape Town. If this can be proven true, the history books as we know them will have to be re-written ...

PHOENICIA

The Phoenicians were based in what we now call Lebanon. The major cities of Tyre, Sidon, Byblos and Berot (Beirut) were independent city-states ruled by hereditary kings, but dominated by a ruling class of traders and merchants.

Although it remains uncertain what the Phoenicians called themselves, it is thought they were known as the Kena'ani or Canaanites; the word Kena'ani is Hebrew for 'merchant'.

The Phoenicians probably left Canaan and settled on the eastern seaboard of the Mediterranean around 3 000 BC. From early histories of the region, it is known they did brisk trade with Egypt and many of the other nations dotted along the coastline. Over time they established their own settlements throughout the region and by the second millennium BC had built up a vast commercial empire stretching from Phoenicia in the east, to the mineral-rich kingdom of Iberia (Spain) in the west.

Phoenician exports included Tyrian purple dye, cedar and pine wood, furniture, fine linens and jewellery, but they also traded embroideries, wine, metalwork, glass, salt and dried fish. Their most lasting contribution to western civilization, however, was the 22-letter alphabet, which was later adopted by the Greeks and eventually became the precursor of the modern alphabet.

The decline of Phoenicia began with the conquest of Tyre by Alexander the Great from Macedonia, in what is now northern Greece. After this epic siege, they were faced with commercial competition from the colonies and then attacks by the Sea Peoples, the Assyrians and the Greeks, all of which led to their demise as a trading nation.

PHARAOH NECHO

Pharaoh Psammetichus I restored Egypt's independence and unity after the kingdom had been divided by attacks from the Assyrians and Nubians. His son, Necho II, continued this process of consolidation by turning his attention to the lands to the north. Necho first won back Syria, then regained Media, Chaldea and, finally, Nineveh, creating a huge

and powerful empire. Realizing that trade would provide the basis for the nation's long-term prosperity, Necho began excavating a canal from the Red Sea to the Nile River, anticipating the Suez Canal by over two thousand years. However, he discontinued this project when he was warned by soothsayers that he was 'labouring for the barbar-

ians' – possibly a reference to the growing power of Nebuchadnezzar II, king of Babylonia, who subsequently invaded Egypt in 604 BC.

It seems that, at this point in Egyptian history, Necho began to look to the unexplored territories of Africa for new lands to conquer. As the Phoenicians were the acknowledged expert seafarers, it would have been logical for him to approach this nation if he wished to mount a naval expedition into the uncharted regions of the south. According to the Greek historian, Herodotus, Necho supported an expedition to circumnavigate Libya (Africa) at the end of the sixth century BC.

In his book *History*, Herodotus made the following remarks:

I wonder then at those who have mapped out and divided the world into Libya, Asia and Europe; for the difference between them is great ... Libya shows clearly it is encompassed by the sea, save only where it borders on Asia; and this was proved first (as far as we know) by Necos, King of Egypt. He ... sent Phoenicians in ships charging them to sail on their return voyage past the pillars of Heracles [the Straits of Gibraltar] till they should come into the northern sea and so to Egypt. And so the Phoenicians set out from the Red Sea and sailed the southern seas; whenever autumn came they would put in and sow the land, to whatever part of Libya they might come and there await the harvest; then, having gathered in the crop, they sailed on so that after two years ... they rounded the pillars of Heracles and came to Egypt. There they said (what some may believe though I do not) that in sailing around Libya they had the sun on their right hand. [1]

This story by Herodotus is astounding – not only because it implies that at the time of writing it was common knowledge that Libya (Africa) was surrounded on three sides by water, (a fact which most historians would argue only became apparent after the voyages of discovery almost 25 centuries later), but also because of the claim made by the mariners that they had sailed with 'the sun on their right hand'. No person would have known at that time that, below the equator the sun is not in the south but in the north, unless he had

I n March 1989, a remarkable vessel, the Pount, which means 'Land of the Gods', briefly took up berth in Table Bay harbour, Cape Town. Nine months earlier, the ship had sailed from the South of France. Its journey had taken it across the Mediterranean, down the Suez Canal, and along the east coast of Africa. The vessel, which was a replica of Egyptian sea-going trading ships of around 1500 BC, had been built by its captain, André Gil-Artagan, using blueprints provided by a naval architect, based on centuries-old relief carvings from the temple of Queen Hatshepsut in Egypt. The Pount eventually reached Alexandria, Egypt, in November 1991. The circumnavigation of Africa had taken two-and-a-half years.

sailed westwards in the southern hemisphere! It is also interesting to note that in the next chapter of *History*, Herodotus remarks that, 'according to their own account the Carthaginians also made the voyage', although he gives no details.

There is, therefore, historical evidence to suggest that seamen from Phoenicia circumnavigated Africa long before Dias, but the story does not end here ...

THE SEARCH FOR A GALLEY

Following the British occupation of the Cape in 1795, an attempt was made to ascertain whether any coal deposits were present in the region. In 1797, British soldiers with coal-mining experience were used to sink boring rods into the soil at various places in the Cape and, eventually, minor coal deposits were

found on the banks of the Klaasjagers River on the edge of the Cape Flats. Sir John Barrow, who visited this excavation site in 1798, later recorded what he had seen:

... in some places were dug out large ligneous blocks in which the traces of the bark, knots and grain were actually visible; and in the very middle of these were embedded pieces of iron pyrites, running through them in crooked veins, or lying in irregular lumps. [2]

In 1852, it was suggested by the Surveyor General, Charles Bell, that what had been described as having 'ligneous blocks' and 'iron pyrites' was a section of decomposed wooden superstructure with iron bolts belonging to an ancient

ship. Around this time a rumour was circulating in the Cape that the wreck of an ancient sailing vessel had been found, and there is speculation that this may have been prompted by Barrow's observations. George Thompson, who later wrote *Travels and Adventures in Southern Africa* visited what was possibly the same site. His observations, however, were more specific:

On the skirts of the Downs, or Flats, which form an isthmus between the Cape Peninsula and the rest of the continent, there was discovered a few years ago, at a considerable distance from the sea, what seemed to be the timbers of a vessel deeply embedded in the sand. This I had myself a cursory view of, but there was too little of the wood visible to enable me to form any clear judgment of its shape, or probable purpose. I found, however, some metallic substance fixed in the wood in a very corroded state. A nautical gentleman, who examined it with more care than I had an opportunity of bestowing, thinks that the wood (which has apparently been buried for ages in the sand) greatly resembles cedar and conceives it possible that this may be the remains of some ancient Phoenician vessel, wrecked here when our present Cape Flats were under water, forming perhaps a shallow strait between Wynberg and Koeberg. This is certainly a rather wild-looking hypothesis – yet, that the land in the southern extremity of Africa might be elevated from the sea without necessarily affecting (as Mr Barrow supposes) the level of the northern extremity, is evident from the effects produced by recent earthquakes in Chili, in elevating the whole extent of coast for some hundred miles. Is it not also possible to account for the formation of a low sandy isthmus like the Cape Downs, from the agency of tides and winds alone collecting a mass of sand in a shallow strait? The formation of the immense sandhills along the southern coast, and on the shores of Table Bay itself, indicates pretty clearly how such an operation would proceed if once commenced. Whatever may be in this, Captain Owen seems to have obtained strong evidence of the commerce of the Phoenicians having extended from the Red Sea, much farther down the eastern coasts of Africa than is generally imagined: and to have pretty clearly ascertained that the celebrated gold mines of ancient Ophir were situated in the vicinity of Inhamban – where it is remarkable that a place of the name Ophir, still rich in gold and ivory exists to the present day. It seems, therefore, not altogether incredible that the Phoenician mariners may have actually doubled the Cape of Good Hope from the Indian Ocean.

Though Thompson was unable to form a 'clear judgment' as to what he had found and seems to have been influenced by 'a nautical gentleman' (presumably Captain Owen), he remained convinced of the very real possibility that he had witnessed the remains of a Phoenician galley. Not surprisingly, the rumour persisted that the ancients had visited southern Africa long before the Portuguese.

In the late 1820s another traveller-adventurer, James Holman, visited the Cape. In *A Voyage Round the World, Including Travels in Africa*, published in 1834, he also refers to a visit to what was presumably the same mysterious wreck on Wednesday, 3 June 1829. His account, however, proved sceptical ...

Soon after breakfast I set off, in company with Messrs. van Reenen and G Thompson in a six horse wagon to visit the spot mentioned by Sir John Barrow, on the sandy flats one hour from Cape Town where are supposed to lie the remains of a Phoenician

wreck; a Mr Joubert having joined us about noon, we proceeded to examine the place, with pickaxes and shovels. We dug up several pieces of wood but were not able to determine what they were, on account of their decayed state. The argument that has been used by some persons in favour of them forming part of a vessel, is supported by the appearance of what they call iron nails and bolts; certain it

is that a substance of a metallic nature is visible enough in some pieces of wood; but may not these be knots of trees, which have undergone some process of mutation, and assumed a metallic character? – for the wood appears to have been felled near the spot, or brought down from the mountain by watercourses, during heavy rains; this supposition is partly upon this situation in which it lies and

Top and above: Exploratory archaeological excavations at the South African Police cricket field, Jan Smuts Drive, Pinelands.

is so low that it resembles a ditch; besides, it is questionable, whether or not the Phoenicians used iron in building vessels. I should suspect that the iron and copper bolts used in marine architecture at the present time, in conjunction with tree nails is a vast improvement on the method of the ancients, who are supposed to have used tree nails only ....

AN OFFICIAL INQUIRY

In 1852, the matter of the Phoenician galley was raised again – this time at official level. On 26 July 1852, Charles Bell (after whom Bellville was named), then Surveyor General of the Cape, wrote the following letter to the Lieutenant Governor, Mr CH Darling:

Sir, I have the honour to report for the information of His Honour the Lieut. Governor the result of my enquiries up to this date with reference to the annexed extract from Barrow's work on the Cape ... respecting coal.

2. I mentioned to his Honour when he drew my attention to the subject, my reasons for supposing that nothing that could be called a coal field would be found in this part of the Cape Colony and pointed out the position of the formation as proved by the researches of Mr AG Bain. I alluded to the vague and contradictory description of the locality and stated that many years ago I had heard of the wreck of an ancient ship at Tygerberg, which I had then disregarded thinking it impossible that the Isthmus could have been so far submerged within Historic Times – but that the description of the carbonized wood and iron bolts was very much like that of Sir John Barrow's Ligneous Blocks with iron pyrites running through them. His Honour requested me to trace my authorities, examine the locality, if it could be found, and

enquire further. I did so, and on Friday I have handed specimens of the wood to his Honour.

3. However extraordinary it may seem, I am compelled to believe that this wood is part of a large vessel upwards of 70 feet in length, wrecked when the sea washed up to some of the ancient sea beaches on the Lion's Head, and now raised hundreds of feet in height above the present highwater mark and left at a distance of at least 10 miles from the shore.

4. This wreck seems to have been washed open by a change in the course of the Hardekraaltjie Stream about 30 years ago. It is embedded in stiff clay about 10 or 12 feet deep and when first seen the ribs and knees stood up above the surface to a height of perhaps five feet, probably connected by the planks of one side. These have, from time to time, been broken off and carried away. About 20 years ago, it is said, that nearly a wagon load was collected and sent to England, from which a reply came that 'no one could tell what wood it was'!

One informant told me that only a short time ago he had carried off a large knee, that there were iron bolts or Tree Nails, but no copper, and that it was not so long ago that he had seen the children of one of his relations playing with one of the Block sheaves found at the wreck. All that I saw was the planking, or what I supposed to be such, shewing itself in the bank for a length of about 70 feet.

5. It would be idle to indulge at present in any archaeological speculations. I would merely allude to the accounts which have reached our times of the early circumnavigation of Africa while the Pyramids were yet new. The Block cannot be taken as being of recent construction, for Blocks are pictured and carved by the

ancient Egyptians and Assyrians, and if, solely from position, I avert to the possibility of this being a relic perhaps of the age of the Pharaoh Necho and to the care with which of later years, the archaeologists of Europe have called and classed all that relates to the prehistoric annals of their country, particularly in Norway and Scotland. I do so, only that the chance of some interesting discovery may not be lost.

6. As the wreck is on Government Ground, I would request permission to disinter it carefully, sifting the clay immediately around and for a short distance in those directions in which the action of the sea or of the stream, may be supposed to have driven anything belonging to it. The remains of the wreck will then be measured, and

Top: Bernard O'Sullivan stands close to wood, dated by the CSIR to be over 44 000 years old.
Above: Archaeological excavations at Pinelands.

position of an extensive coal deposit in the vicinity of Tygerberg, His Honour desires me to state he would be much obliged to you for the trouble you have taken in the matter. With reference to the examination which you propose into the appearance in that locality of a series of ligneous blocks in a state of carbonization and apparently arranged according to some system, His Honour considers the enquiry one of great interest and will readily place at your disposal a sum not exceeding £20 for that purpose. [4]

It is likely that Bell conducted the excavation, but there appears to be neither further record of his findings in the State Archives nor any reference to the use he made of the twenty pounds. We do know, however, that AG Bain, the Geological Surveyor for the Colony visited the site of the 'wreck' himself some time later. In a lecture on 'The Geology of southern Africa', which he delivered in Grahamstown, Bain dismissed the idea of the existence of a Phoenician galley as pure fantasy ...

might be expected to undertake a work of this nature, and that, if entrusted with it, I will engage that the expenses shall not exceed Twenty Pounds. [3]

Just over a week later, Bell received a reply from the Colonial Office:

Sir, having laid before the Lieutenant Governor your letter of the 26 inst. containing the result of investigations made by you with reference to that part of the account of Sir John Barrow's travels which led to the sup-

With regard to the coal mania, I dare say many of you will recollect that in 1853 Lieutenant Governor Darling offered 100 pounds to anyone who would discover coal in the Cape District, or at a certain distance from any of our seaports. This magnificent prize set many good folks digging for coal, and a report soon reached headquarters that it had actually been discovered near Constantia ...
In consequence of this [Bain's appointment as Geological Surveyor of the Colony] Mr Darling, when on a visit to Bain's Kloof, where I then resided, was pleased to request me to come to town for the purpose of examining and reporting on the coal discovery. On our way thither, we drove a little off the road, on the Cape Flats, for the purpose of

such drawings taken as will best describe it.
Before taking any other measure to provide the means, I would respectfully suggest that the Government

examining portions of what was said to be the wreck of one of the Phoenician fleet that first doubled the Cape of Good Hope, and which was buried in a deep ditch ten miles from the nearest sea. I had frequently heard of this wreck, even forty years before, and was happy in having such a good opportunity of examining it. Solomon says 'there is nothing new under the sun'; so that if this was part of a Phoenician vessel, that leviathan steamer now building by Scott, Russel & Co (which is without a name, as they cannot find one large enough for it) is 675 feet long; but by the mighty ribs of this jolly old Phoenician, plainly traceable as she lies buried in the clay ten feet below the surface of the flats, I found she must have been upwards of a mile in length! Let Messrs. Scott, Russel & Co. after this, 'hide their diminished heads', and be content to play second fiddle to the ancient Phoenicians. It does not say much for the love of science in the 'far west' that this wonderful curiosity should have been known for at least forty years to have been buried within twelve miles of the capital, and never properly examined or described; or that they should have allowed the Lieut. Governor of the Colony to visit the spot for the purpose of viewing in situ what was supposed to be a Phoenician wreck, buried in the middle of the Cape Flats, which at a glance I recognized to be merely a bed of lignite or brown coals, which, as will afterwards appear, is found all over the flats. 5

It appears that the subject of the Phoenician galley was effectively laid to rest until the 1920s, when it was resurrected by, among others, the eminent palaeontologist and anthropologist, Professor Raymond Dart.

In an article published in *Nature* in 1925 concerning the suggestion of European influence in certain rock paintings found in the Drakensberg and Lesotho, Professor Dart also referred briefly to the discovery in 1880 of an ancient ship on the Woltemade Flats near Cape Town.

His Honour the Administrator of the Transvaal (Professor Jan H Hofmeyr) has informed me that the remains of what was presumably an ancient galley were discovered during the laying out of Maitland Cemetery on the Woltemade Flats near Cape Town in the nineties. At the time the contact of one end of Africa with the other by navigation was undreamt of, and the significance of finding a boat one hundred and eighty feet in length, buried six feet underground at a distance of three miles from the present coastline, was lost on the workmen, who utilized it for firewood. The event at least indicates that the followers of Prince Henry were not the first to anchor in Table Bay. 6

From this letter, one can deduce that Dart enquired into the matter of the wrecked Phoenician galley, and through the assistance of Colonel Graham Botha, who in turn had been aided by the Secretary of the Board of Trustees of the Maitland Road cemetery, established that the site was 'about two hundred yards on the other side of the railway line, immediately opposite the present stores of Messrs. Spilhaus & Co., on the Maitland side of the cemetery'.

(Note that this 'wreck' which is given as 'a distance of three miles from the present coastline', is clearly not the same as the one 'at least 10 miles from the shore' mentioned by Charles Bell in his letter to Lieutenant Governor Darling.)

Professor Dart then approached Colonel JW Carr, the assistant general manager of the railways, Cape Town, who helped him make contact with two of the men who had worked on the site where the wreck had been unearthed in 1880. On 12 January 1925, Dart interviewed the two men and the following day wrote a letter of thanks to Colonel Carr ...

I wish primarily to thank you for your great courtesy to me yesterday afternoon in the matter of the 'old galley' discovered in 1880 on the Maitland-Woltemade Flats.
You will recollect that I promised before leaving you to send to you the names of the two workmen from whom details of this boat have been learnt. They are:
1. Mr C Milder who was on 'point' duty at the time (1880) when the discovery was first made. In his time Bill Rynold was foreman of the party. Milder left the service before the boat had been completely unearthed, and
2. Mr D Vroy who was in the service in (1896-97 circa.). When he arrived half of the boat had been taken away, many piles of its timbers lay

The Point, *a replica of Egyptian sea-going vessels of around 1500 BC, was built from blueprints based on centuries-old relief carvings found in the temples of Egypt.*

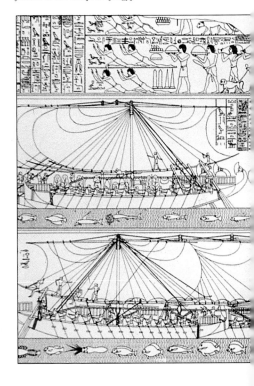

about and about 50 feet length of the more or less intact boat remained. He saw (4-5) truckloads of timber taken to Cape Town. Mr William Bort (or Byrd) was guard of the train and Mr Bolton was foreman of the party while Mr Male (Mail or Meyer) was Inspector of the Railways.
Frankly this evidence is somewhat sketchy as my informants were not worried about niceties of spelling nor orthography, but the details, such as they are, may serve to call to mind certain of the railway officials still living and to whom details of the transactions must be known. My mind is now at rest in knowing that the matter is in such excellent hands. Mr Graham Botha will be eagerly awaiting any details you succeed in discovering both as to individuals concerned with the work (and whose evidence we should gather to make the story complete and reliable) and as to the timbers themselves and their present location and thirdly as to the feasibility of some further excavation on the site with a view to retrieving any remnants of the timbers and

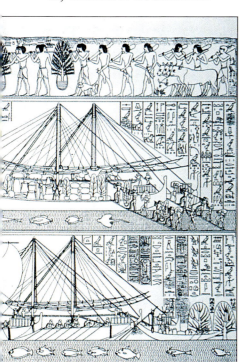

possibly some pieces of metal or weapons and even, as the old workman Milder put it, the 'safe'.
With renewed thanks for your interest and kindness.
Raymond Dart

According to the notes Dart made at the interviews, Milder said that a mast 'at least 3'6" in diameter' and '60 to 70 feet in length' lay 'on top of timbers' under a 'gravel bed'. He also claimed to have seen 'two iron rings and iron bolts fastening portions of the mast' and that he 'tried to burn pieces of the mast but the tarry and mud smell was overpowering and he would not take it away for firewood'.

Vroy remembered that individual timbers 30' to 40' in length and 2' to 2'6" thick were lying in heaps. He thought these were inside timbers and could not remember seeing any of the outside thin planking. Vroy said that he was unable to tell the exact breadth of the ship but he noted it must have been great. Also, the timbers were fairly rotten and could be broken by bars and picks.

Although Dart was unable to get to the bottom of the mystery, he was able to establish that the wreck's position was under a 'gravel surface where there are clay pits used for brick-making by railways [in 1898]'. [7]

It is believed that the site on which the wreck is to be found was once situated on the bank of the Salt River. In the past, seagoing vessels would sail into the tidal estuary of the river, where they would beach themselves to be warped (hauled on to dry land) and then careened (turned on to one side) to remove barnacles from the hull. This could explain the presence of a Phoenician vessel at the location. Furthermore, since Phoenician squadrons normally comprised four ships, there is no reason to believe that, if this was the number of vessels Pharaoh Necho had sent around 'Libya', the loss of one vessel would prevent the others from continuing their journey.

A SCIENTIFIC STUDY

During the mid- and late 1980s the matter was investigated once more – this time, by Cape Town attorney, Bernard O'Sullivan, who had developed an interest in the whereabouts of the Phoenician galley after meeting Professor Dart.

O'Sullivan, working in co-operation with representatives of the South African Cultural History Museum, excavated a number of trenches and drilled five bore holes at the site previously identified by Professor Dart. Wood fragments unearthed during the excavation were sent to the Swiss Federal Institute of Technology in Zurich for radiocarbon dating and to Dr Colin Johnson of the Department of Botany at the University of the Western Cape and Stephanie Dyer of the South African Forestry Research Institute in Pretoria for examination.

In a report by Bernard O'Sullivan, published in the *South African Journal of Science* in November 1990, regarding the drilling and trenching on the Woltemade Flats in 1988 and 1989, he concluded:

Our investigations have shown beyond doubt that two pieces of wood of northern hemisphere, most likely Mediterranean origin, dated to about 1 900 and 500 years ago respectively, have come to rest on the Cape Flats. Professor Dart's enquiries in 1925 provided incontestable evidence that at exactly the same location during the 1880s and 1890s several people had seen the remains of a large boat.
It is hard not to conclude that the site is eminently worthy of further archaeological enquiry. Should Dart's comments turn out to be as inspired as some of his others, although initially discounted, the site may help to rewrite the history of oceanic travel in the southern hemisphere.
A major archaeological investigation is called for. [8]

FURTHER INVESTIGATION

It has neither been proved that a fleet of Phoenician galleys circumnavigated 'Libya', nor whether one of them was abandoned at the tip of southern Africa. Yet for over 300 years, a rumour has persisted that the wreck of such a ship was to be found at the Cape.

A close examination of the evidence, however, suggests that the two sites have been associated with an aban-doned vessel. The first possible wreck site identified was located on the Cape Flats and investigated by Sir John Barrow and Charles Bell amongst others, but this has since been discounted.

The second site, which has come under more recent scrutiny is in Maitland.

A more scientific and systematic study of available evidence relating to the Maitland site by Professor Raymond Dart and, more recently, Bernard O'Sullivan, suggests that a vessel possibly of Phoenician origin, was beached at this site, an ancient backwater of the Salt River, some 2 000 years ago.

This, however, raises further compli-cations. The expedition sponsored by Pharaoh Necho to circumnavigate Africa commenced around 600 BC, but the wood fragments found at the site of the wreck are dated at around 100 AD. Clearly, the wood fragments found at the Maitland site did not come from one of Necho's ships, but this does not inval-idate the hypothesis that ancient sea-farers circumnavigated Africa many centuries before Dias.

In April 1993, a second excavation of the wreck site in Maitland was under-taken and more fragments of timber were uncovered and sent for analysis. A group of archaeologists from the University of Cape Town are cautiously optimistic that these fragments will con-firm finally that an ancient vessel, pos-sibly of Phoenician origin was once located at the site.

There is also speculation that the site was once a ship 'graveyard', but this is still to be confirmed.

In an interview with the *Johannesburg Star* on 3 April 1993, Bernard O'Sullivan was quoted as saying:

> This is very exciting stuff. It could change the course of history if we find what we hope to.
> Strabo, the Greek father of geogra-phy recorded the unearthing of a galley at Dar es Salaam, Tanzania. The evidence so far points to the remnant of a galley also being found here at the tip of Africa ...

If, as Bernard O'Sullivan hopes, further excavations prove that explorers from Europe visited southern Africa approxi-mately two thousand years ago, one mystery will end.

But if ancient seafarers *did*, in fact visit our shores so many years ago, who were they?

And what else did they leave behind?

RADIOCARBON DATING

Radiocarbon dating is the system used in archaeology and other associated fields to establish the age of organic materials, such as bone or wood. The system was developed by Willard F Libby and his associates shortly after 1945 and Libby subsequently earned the Nobel prize for his work. Plants absorb carbon-dioxide gas from the atmosphere, which is then incorporated in their tissue. Some of the absorbed carbon contains the radioactive isotope, carbon-14. As soon as the plant dies, the absorption of carbon-14 ceases and the remaining amount begins to decay at a steady rate. Carbon-14 has a half-life of 5 730 years, which means that it takes 5 730 years for half of the carbon-14 present in the tissue to decay; another 5 730 years for half of the remaining amount to decay; and so on. After 120 000 years, so little carbon-14 is left that it becomes impossible to measure. Radiocarbon-dating works best on samples that are between 500 and 50 000 years old. Consequently, by measuring the amount of carbon-14 that exists, it is possible to establish the number of years that have elapsed since the plant died. Animals absorb carbon-14 by digesting plant tissue, thus their remains can be dated using the same method.

The dating of rock is done by radiometric dating which assesses the amount of radioactive decay of naturally occurring isotopes, for example the decay of uranium into lead. Different elements and isotopes are used, depending on the isotopes present and the age of the rocks to be dated.

ROSALIND BALLINGALL
The girl who simply disappeared

On the morning of 12 August 1969, 20-year-old University of Cape Town student, Rosalind Ballingall, walked out of the house where she was staying with friends on the edge of Knysna forest and vanished without a trace. Over twenty years later, stories and rumours surrounding her mysterious disappearance continue to surface. Who was Rosalind Ballingall? Why is her name so well-remembered? And does anyone know what happened to her?

THE MYSTERY BEGINS

On 11 August 1969, Rosalind Ballingall drove from Cape Town to Knysna in the company of Sasja Sergier, a Ukrainian-born friend and Lara Geffen, a girl whom she had never met before. The three young 'hippies' as the newspaper reports later described them, stayed at the house of sculptor Peter Davis and his wife, Denise.

Rosalind Ballingall, a drama student, had been working hard on the production *Pantagleize* and was allegedly under some pressure. She wanted to have a short break away from the city to relax and recuperate.

After breakfast on the morning following her arrival, Rosalind announced that she was 'going for a walk'. She spoke to the Davis' housemaid before leaving, asked if there was a church in the area and if she could accompany her when next she went. The Davis' gardener saw

Rosalind cross the lawn and leave the property through a grove of trees at the end of the garden, but was unable to say whether she had turned left or right at the dirt road running behind the house, or had cut straight across

Rosalind Ballingall

country, down a valley ahead of her. She was carrying a Bible and was dressed in a jersey, trousers and sandals. Her cloak and bracelet – all that she had brought with her – were left in the house.

Unfortunately, neither Sasja nor Lara knew Rosalind well enough to be concerned when she didn't return after a few hours. They only became alarmed when it became dark, by which time they believed that it was too late to contact the police as a search could not begin until morning.

SEARCH FOR ROSALIND

The next day Denise Davis reported to the police that her guest was missing. On the suspicion of foul play, the CID was immediately called in and began questioning the local residents, but no-one had seen Rosalind pass by. Word that a girl had gone missing soon spread, and a day or so later three people reported seeing a girl resembling Rosalind buying stamps at the George post office on the day after her disappearance. One of the witnesses said that she was sure the girl had joined two men waiting at a parked car outside. Investigations drew a blank, and the police mounted a search in the forest around the Davis' house. Tracker dogs were brought in but rain obliterated any scent there may have been.

On 18 August, Rosalind's father, a wealthy mining executive, arrived from Johannesburg to assist with the search for his daughter. He interviewed the three people who had allegedly seen a girl at the George post office and was convinced that she was Rosalind.

He conducted a thorough search of Knysna alone, questioned as many of his daughter's friends and acquaintances as possible, and reportedly considered the idea that she had entered a convent. For all his efforts, however, he unearthed no new clues as to her whereabouts.

The myth that Rosalind was a member of a strange cult or hippy commune began to grow when it was reported that 'A number of Rosalind's friends arrived in Knysna to help the police with their search,' among whom were a 'folk singer and two Rondebosch men … who arrived in a beach buggy wearing ponchos and playing drums and pipes …'.

Not surprisingly, Rosalind's apparently unconventional lifestyle became the focus of media attention and it was this, as much as her disappearance, that elevated her to celebrity status. In a much later report, she was described as a,

… tall, willowy extrovert who embraced the 'new society' of the '60s – the spirit of love and peace and miniskirts and Eastern mysticism; a girl who had shrugged off the security and comfort offered by her wealthy parents without a backward glance, choosing an alternative lifestyle and mixed with an off-beat crowd known as the 'cosmic butterflies'; someone who had cultivated the friendship of student drop-outs and those interested in the occult and was reported to have joined the butterflies in bizarre rituals which were conducted in Knysna forest.

On 26 August, fourteen days after Rosalind had gone missing, the police called off their search for her although the case remained open. They had followed up on all their leads but had no clues whatsoever as to her whereabouts. Rosalind's parents, however, never gave up hope of finding her.

Just over a month later, Rosalind's mother arrived in George on a personal investigation. 'Until she is found dead

we will not give up hope,' she said. 'The search must continue,' she added and speculated that her daughter may have been suffering from amnesia and did not know that people were looking for her.

There was no reason why she should have deliberately hidden herself. Although Mrs Ballingall made an appeal to her daughter to, 'come home, or to at least let us know where you are,' she denied that Rosalind had ever been involved in any sort of hippy cult.

The suggestion that Rosalind mixed with hippies arose from the time she settled in Cape Town to study at the University of Cape Town …

Rosalind Ballingall was last seen leaving the Davis' House on 12 August 1969.

'She found a house – admittedly not in the best part of town – for herself and a few fellow students. They painted it out and were as pleased as punch with it. I suppose a few hippy types did turn up there, but Rosalind being a honeypot and terribly kind, would not have turned them away.'

During April 1970, another search of the Knysna forest was initiated after reports of a hippy commune living there.

Mrs Ballingall rejected the idea that her daughter was involved, because it was 'not in her nature'. No trace of Rosalind was found, although a few weeks later there were reports that she had been seen in Cape Town. An article in the *Argus* referred to three witnesses, two of whom reputedly knew Rosalind well, who claimed to have seen the 'six feet tall, 21-year-old red-haired girl'.

One of the witnesses, Eddie Fourie, was emphatic that he had seen Rosalind in St George's Street.

'How could I have made a mistake?' he asked, 'I have known her for two years. I used to share a house with her and her brother, Andrew.

'I was surprised to see her. I walked round the corner into St George's Street and bumped into her. She was with a young man with long hair. I stopped and asked her how she was. She looked well and acted quite naturally.'

Another witness, William Phillmore, said he saw Rosalind Ballingall in Loop Street and recognized her from the picture in the *Argus*.

'The girl was dressed in hippy-type clothes and looked very pale – as though she had been ill or had not been outside for a long time.'

Although Mrs Ballingall had no knowledge of Rosalind and her brother, Andrew, having shared a house with Fourie, the police subsequently issued a statement calling on Rosalind to come out into the open and end a fruitless and time-consuming search.

PSYCHIC ALTERNATIVES

Ten months after Rosalind's disappearance the Ballingalls decided to consult the famous Dutch psychic, Gerard Croiset, known as the 'The Miracle Man of Utrecht'. Mrs Ballingall mentioned that neither she nor her family had ever had anything to do with clairvoyants before, but that they had received numerous letters from such people, many of them stating that Rosalind was still alive but afraid to return home. She placed a desperate plea for her daughter to return home in the *Sunday Times* ...

Come to England with me, Rosalind, next week. Phone collect or contact Basil. There is nothing to fear. We all love you very much. Mother.

But Rosalind did not come forward.

Croiset, a magnetic healer, apparently gifted with astonishing clairvoyant powers, had a record of helping police solve various crimes and over 400 missing persons' cases throughout the world – with an astonishing success rate. He normally made his predictions using only a photograph of the missing person and a map of the area where he or she was last seen. He was tested by scientists on many occasions and had always emerged with his reputation intact.

Unfortunately, the report he gave Mrs Ballingall was not good news.

He believed that Rosalind had met with a fatal accident and, according to a report in the *Sunday Times* of 25 October 1970, he is alleged to have said to her, 'Your daughter drowned in a river in the forest, probably on the very day she disappeared.'

THE CRUEL LIES OF EDWIN JOHN SIEBERT

The search for Rosalind Ballingall was complicated by the involvement of Edwin John Siebert, a hard-labour prisoner doing time at Johannesburg's Fort Prison.

In April 1970, nine months after Rosalind's disappearance, Siebert approached the police and made two declarations to the *Sunday Times*, claiming that he had been involved in her death. Although Siebert had been free at the time of Rosalind's disappearance, given his considerable criminal record, the police treated his claims with a degree of circumspection. But he could not be ruled out and his story had to be given due consideration.

In the statement Siebert made to the police, he claimed that he had knowledge of Rosalind's whereabouts. Later, he spoke to the grieving parents and made a number of vague statements until he extracted agreements from them to pay for the information. But whenever an agreement was reached, he found reason not to go through with his side of the deal.

Mr and Mrs Ballingall.

On 3 May 1970, Siebert sent a statement to the *Sunday Times* which began, 'Sometime beginning January 1970 ...' – but Rosalind had gone missing in August 1969 – in which he spoke of frequent trips to Knysna where he met a Mr X who promised to sell him drugs. After one of the deals had been struck, Mr X took him to nearby bushes where a woman – Rosalind – handed over the goods. At their last meeting, Mr X confided in him that they could make a lot of money by taking the woman to Johannesburg because she was a 'missing person' whose parents were rich and prepared to pay a lot of money for her safe return. Mr X claimed that Siebert's share of the reward money would be about R5 000.

According to Siebert, however, the woman overheard their conversation and this led to a violent argument between the two. Mr X swore at her and hit her, but 'she lifted her head to avoid the blow,' and Mr X 'landed the blow on her thraught (throat). She fell back and did not move but once or twice'.

Siebert and Mr X then had to dispose of the body, and they took a travelling rug from Siebert's car, wrapped the

body in it and carried it back to the car. They drove around Knysna until they found 'a likely place near the water where the ground was soft'.

After burying the body, Siebert took Mr X to the Royal Hotel where he bought him 'about ten canes and when he was nicely drunk I left'.

The distraught Ballingalls had spoken to Siebert before this account had been published, but remained cautiously optimistic that Siebert was lying. After listening to Siebert's sordid tale Mr Ballingall had asked him how tall the woman was and Siebert, who was himself about 1,6 m had indicated that she reached up to the bridge of his nose. Rosalind, however, was over 1,8 m tall.

On 17 June, Siebert again contacted the Ballingalls ...

I have been informed that the police has [sic] notified the Sunday Times *that I have retracted my statement and I have no idea why the police issued such a statement unless it be to prevent the* Times *from printing my full confession and adding to your already heavy burden of uncertainty I have tried to alleviate by telling you the truth.*
I am prepared to supply the name of the man involved with me at the time of your daughter's demise on condition that I will be granted the indemnity afforded to State witnesses.
You will remember my having mentioned to you that X is in prison.
I shall reveal his identity upon the conditions set by me.
I regret having to add to your grief, nevertheless the truth will eventually assist in the healing of your wounds.

Following this letter, the police began a series of intensive negotiations with Siebert. Mr Ballingall eventually offered a substantial reward if Siebert could locate the body of his missing daughter within seven days. Siebert agreed to this, and sent a letter to the *Sunday Times* shortly

afterwards announcing that he would be going to Knysna, in the company of a policeman, to unearth Rosalind's body. On the day of the trip, however, he backed out – his 'reason' being that Ballingall had not signed the agreement in his presence, and that there were no witnesses to his signature. He argued that he suspected he was being misled by the police, and was also suspicious of the document as it had not been folded, suggesting that it had been forged.

Stanley Hurst, a reporter for the *Sunday Times*, offered to ensure that each and every condition laid down by Siebert was met. A new round of negotiations began, during which Siebert laid down four conditions:

1. That the same amount of money as negotiated previously be paid if he showed the Ballingalls their missing daughter's grave;
2. That on his visit to Knysna he be placed under the custody of two warders, in addition to the two detectives who would accompany him;
3. That Hurst and a *Sunday Times* photographer be allowed to accompany the expedition as independent witnesses; and, finally,
4. One copy of his agreement with the Ballingalls be lodged in the office safe of the prison commandant and another entrusted for safe keeping to the Sunday Times.

With all of the conditions agreed to, the following Tuesday was set as the day on which the expedition to Knysna would take place.

At 9 a.m. on Tuesday morning, Siebert was brought to the commandant's office at Fort Prison where he was met by Colonel JJ Ferreira, Major van der Merwe and Stanley Hurst. Siebert was handed Ballingall's reward offer, which had been witnessed by Hurst and an attorney, and a covering letter from the attorney explaining that he had retained a second copy of the letter.

Siebert, who stared at the documents for a few moments, became increasingly angry and said, 'I am not going. Not with the Brixton police.'

Major van der Merwe pointed out to Siebert that as he had never had anything to do with the Brixton police in the past, there was no reason why he should object to them now.

'But I know about you,' Siebert retorted, 'you're all a bunch of sadists.'

Van der Merwe reminded him that he was going to be accompanied by two pressmen and that there was no chance of him being manhandled or mistreated in any way. But Siebert remained adamant about the issue, and said that he had just written to the *Sunday Times* and had recently posted the letter at the prison post office. While the letter was being fetched he outlined its contents.

'I am finished with Ballingall and the press,' he said. 'Ballingall can bottle his reward because he is more talk than anything else. As soon as one calls his bluff then he backs out and hides behind Brixton. Now he can have what's left of his daughter free of charge. Her passport he can also have and frame it to be hanged in his office to remind him of his big talk. Yes, he can have her bones to polish for his showcase ...'

Siebert was returned to his cell, and when Mr Ballingall was informed of his outburst, he heaved a sigh of relief.

'This shows at last that Siebert is lying. You see I have Rosalind's passport in the house. She did not take it with her.'

In January 1971, Siebert was declared a habitual criminal after being convicted of the theft of R19 104 from his former employers. An article under the heading 'Court rejects submission on missing girl' which appeared in the *Cape Times* on 21 July 1971 ended the Siebert affair.

The admission of habitual criminal Edwin James Siebert that the body of Rosalind Ballingall had been transported in his car was unfounded the Supreme Court heard here yesterday.

Siebert claimed in papers before the court that Miss Ballingall was murdered on June 27 1970 and transported from the crime scene in his car. Miss Ballingall, daughter of a wealthy Johannesburg mining executive, disappeared in the Cape nearly two years ago. The present action was brought by the New Zealand Insurance Company that claimed that two cars and a diamond ring at present with the police in Cape Town are their properties.

THE STORIES CONTINUE ...

Ever since Rosalind Ballingall walked out of the Davis' home and vanished without a trace in August 1969, her name is mentioned whenever someone goes missing or something unexplained occurs in the Knysna area. Not surprisingly, this has led to a number of unsubstantiated rumours ...

In 1972, for example, it was suggested that Rosalind had been murdered and that her body had been dumped in a large pit in the Knysna forest near to the Davis' house. This rumour, however, was proved to be entirely without foundation. On 16 October 1972, the *Cape Times* carried the following report:

Ballingall rumour rejected
The police have dug out a pit in the Knysna forest following rumours that the pit might hold the key to the mysterious disappearance of Rosalind Ballingall who has been missing since 1969. Police acted last week after rumours that she might have fallen or been thrown into it. They said: 'There is absolutely no truth in the rumour. We did dig up the pit but did not find the slightest trace of the missing girl or anyone else for that matter'. No signs of quicklime (which could consume human flesh and bone) was found.

Six years later, a skeleton, the skull of which had a broken jaw, was unearthed on a Sedgefield building site by building contractor, François Coetzee.

Did Rosalind Ballingall lose her way in the Knysna undergrowth? Stories and rumours continue to surround her disappearance.

There was some speculation that the skeleton could be the missing remains of Rosalind Ballingall. However, it turned out to be a find of historical, rather than criminological, importance.

At the subsequent site excavation, it was noted that the skull was filled with sand which indicated that it was at least 30 years old and may even have been centuries old.

After taking measurements, it was suggested that the skeleton was probably of Strandloper origin.

Rosalind Ballingall's mysterious disappearance was recalled as recently as

December 1992 when the following account appeared in the *Argus*:

In a strange twist, the mysterious disappearance of UCT student Miss Rosalind Ballingall in Knysna twenty three years ago, police yesterday denied that they were in possession of a statement implicating a homosexual in connection with her death. An Afrikaans newspaper yesterday claimed that it was in possession of a 'statement from the homosexual lover of the alleged murderer' who is said to have killed Miss Ballingall, 20, in a fit of jealous rage at a hippy commune near Knysna in 1969. It said the man had cut up the corpse and dumped the pieces around the Knysna forest. The report said the man allegedly murdered Miss Ballingall because she had become 'too intimate with his lover' who was now confessing the crime in order to ease his conscience. The report claimed the homosexual killer was 'repatriated' to Britain after serving a prison sentence for fraud. Police spokesman Attie Laubscher yesterday said that the report was 'false' and the police were not in possession of any statement implicating a person in connection with Miss Ballingall's death.'

To this day, the mystery surrounding Rosalind Ballingall's disappearance remains unresolved. No evidence of foul play has ever been found.

Perhaps new evidence will emerge in the future which will shed light on this intriguing mystery, but until that happens, we can only speculate ...

Mr and Mrs Ballingall died in the mid 1980s. Rosalind Ballingall was declared officially dead in 1986.

THE COLDSTREAM STONE
Forgery or phenomenon?

In 1911 a remarkable painted stone, which became known as the Coldstream Stone, was found at an ancient human burial site in a rock shelter near the mouth of the Lottering River, in what is now the Tsitsikamma National Park. The stone lay more than a metre beneath the soil, yet the painting was in almost pristine condition. And what makes the finding of this stone all the more amazing is that other burial stones found in its immediate vicinity were nowhere near as well preserved. The mystery of the Coldstream Stone is not its setting, nor the painted subject matter depicted on its surface – it is its superb state of preservation.

How could a primitive rock painting lie, undisturbed, in damp soil for hundreds of years, perhaps thousands, yet remain virtually untouched?

Is the Coldstream Stone a forgery or a bizarre natural phenomenon?

... The simple answer is that no-one really knows.

DISCOVERING THE STONE

In 1908, there was a buzz of excitement within the archaeological community when it was established that painted burial stones discovered in the Knysna region could be reliably linked to the somewhat mysterious Strandlopers, a nomadic people who lived along the south-eastern coast of South Africa. Prior to this date, only one other burial stone associated with the Strandlopers had ever been found and that was in a Knysna cavern in 1872.

Possibly as early as 1908, but certainly by 1909, excavations by CJ Whitcher at a shelter on his property near the small

village of Coldstream, revealed more painted stones but all were monochrome. In February 1911, L Peringuey, then director of the South African Museum, instructed the museum's taxidermist, James Drury, to excavate the shelter where the painted stones had been found by Whitcher.

In his notes, James Drury commented that, prior to his arrival, Whitcher had dug out part of the cave to a depth of ten feet. Drury continued digging the same trench for a further two feet and found the remains of a skeleton. The skeleton, however, was so badly decomposed in the damp soil, that he decided to begin working at another place in the cave where he hoped that any finds

The Coldstream Stone (lower row, centre) found at an ancient human burial site. What makes this stone so unusual is the almost pristine condition of the painting on its surface. Other burial stones found at the site were not as well preserved.

would be in a better state of preservation. Moving to the 'back centre' of the cave, he began excavating a second trench. Having dug to a depth of roughly four feet Drury came across another skeleton, which was also in a 'very rotten' state, but he had not come across any burial stones. Shortly afterwards, Drury encountered another skeleton, this time of a baby, and then a fourth skeleton lying a little deeper, underneath a stone, although the stone did not have any paintings. Continuing to dig, Drury unearthed a full skeleton of an adult on the same layer and, lying at its shoulder was a large flat stone with 'the finest painting I have so far seen anywhere ...'.

He had unearthed what became known as the Coldstream Stone.

James Drury at the excavation site where the Coldstream Stone was discovered.

The stone and its skeleton was displayed at the South African Museum in Cape Town for a number of years. When the display containing the Coldstream Stone was changed in the mid-1950s, it was placed in the museum's strongroom for safekeeping and virtually forgotten about until 1980, when it was returned to the museum's archaeology department artifact collection. Since then it has attracted a great deal of academic interest. The intriguing question for a number of investigators, including Peringuey, Drury, M Burkitt (author of *South Africa's Past in Paint and Stone*), ML Wilson and WJJ van Rijssen, is how such a fragile painting survived so well in the dampness of a coastal rock shelter. No-one has been able to explain the stone's superb state of preservation.

FRAUD, FORGERY, MIRACLE ?

Because the painting on the stone is so well preserved, many people have questioned its authenticity.

In 1989, ML Wilson and WJJ van Rijssen of the archaeology department of the South African Museum and DA Gerneke of the electron microscope unit at the University of Cape Town, conducted tests to determine the authenticity of the Coldstream Stone.

An analysis of the paint used on the stone was compared with that from other stones of similar origin, and the results of the tests strongly suggested that the paint was genuine in every way. Similarly, the style of painting found on the stone was, in the opinion of experts such as Burkitt in the late 1920s, and more recently, Rudner and Rudner in 1976 and L Abel in 1985, similar to that of mural rock paintings and other rock art in the area.

If, indeed, the painting is a forgery it is either an extremely skilful one or it has been touched-up or repainted by an unknown artist. Of course, even if the painting is 'artificial', why anyone would want to perpetrate such an elaborate fraud it remains uncertain.

There is the possibility, of course, that the painting was 'improved', in 1911, by an anonymous research assistant in a genuine attempt to preserve it, and that the researcher, whoever he or she was, simply forgot to report the fact because it was not thought to be important enough or necessary to record their restoration. But if this is the case, then why were the other stones not treated in the same way? A more standard practice in preserving this type of artifact would have been to paint it with clear varnish.

There is nothing to suggest that the Coldstream Stone is anything but genuine. Perhaps the answer to this intriguing riddle was buried along with the stone itself? Until new evidence is uncovered, the Coldstream Stone is destined to remain a mystery.

MODJADJI, THE RAIN QUEEN
'She' who must be obeyed

Modjadji V.

In a valley of the Molototsi River live the Lobedu, led by Modjadji, the most famous rain-maker of the African continent, and even the most savage and warlike peoples regarded her with awe.

But who was the original Modjadji and why does her descendant, also called Modjadji, still hold them in thrall?

According to ancient tradition, the rain queen is ensured of immortality through a ritual of reincarnation. This event followed in the wake of a great initiation ceremony for boys which occurred every fifty years. At this time the old queen would drink of the poisoned cup, then rise young again from the old queen's wrinkled body. The queen is primarily a rainmaker, not a ruler, and is regarded as a changer of seasons whose power derives from her ability to control Nature's cycles. Several steps can be taken to procure rain, depending on what is thought to be the cause of the drought; sometimes it may be the queen herself, and then she must be pacified with gifts.

Ceremonies take place at the royal kraal.

ter, Dzugudini, gave birth to a son, Makaphimo, but refused to divulge the identity of the child's father – alleged to be her own brother – despite Mulozwi's angry insistence. In the face of her father's mounting suspicion, Dzugudini was eventually forced to flee the kingdom. She took with her rain charms and sacred beads, and the knowledge of how to use them. Accompanied by a few followers, Dzugudini headed south.

The group settled in a remote valley of the Molototsi River, east of Duiwelskloof, in what is now the north-eastern Transvaal, and by virtue of Dzugudini's incestuous relationship with her brother, came to be regarded as a new people – the Lobedu.

Around 1800, long after Dzugudini and Makaphimo had passed away, a period of civil strife struck the Lobedu and eventually a woman, Modjadji I, ascended the throne. She was to be the first of a long line of all-powerful, legendary rain queens.

Modjadji I brought a long-overdue period of peace and prosperity to the tribe. In time, she became known as the 'ruler of the day' and was reputedly a four-breasted rainmaker who never revealed herself to the outside world and lived in a sacred grove of cycads on the edge of a precipice, high on a cloud-enveloped hilltop. She was also said to be white and, even nowadays, young women of the tribe with pale skin are thought to be of royal blood.

From the seclusion of this remote camp, perched like an eagle's eyrie on the edge of a forest, Modjadji I won fame and reverence as the greatest of all known rainmakers.

RAIN MAGIC

The strength and size of the Lobedu were insignificant when compared to the Zulu, Xhosa, Venda and Pedi – yet Modjadji's rain magic was believed to be so powerful that she received offerings and requests from the mightiest of lead-

The queen's moods and feelings are said to have a direct bearing on the weather and, not surprisingly, to earn her displeasure is equal to courting disaster.

FLIGHT FROM DANGER

During the 16th century, the sons of Mwene-Mutapa, the paramount chief of the Karanga of Zimbabwe, began quarrelling among themselves about how to divide their ageing father's realm. Eventually, each son established his own separate kingdom and declared himself an independent *mambo* or chief – fragmenting the once-mighty empire of the Mwene-Mutapa/Karanga in the process. One of the sons later took the name Mulozwi or Murozwi, and assumed control of a mountainous region of Zimbabwe. Shortly after this schism occurred, Mulozwi's unmarried daugh-

The home of the modern-day rain queen, Modjadji V, situated in the north-eastern Transvaal. It is said that the rain queen's descendents successively inherit her rain-making formula and reputation. It was the legend of Modjadji that inspired Rider Haggard to write She.

ers, including Shaka. Indeed, to the Zulu she was the greatest magician in the north and possessed the ability to transform the clouds into rain.

The Rain Queen's power was inviolable and even during the period of *Mfecane*, when a wave of death and destruction swept through the land, her kingdom remained a sanctuary – unharmed and invincible.

Modjadji I, who was to remain on the throne for over half a century, was held in awe by her followers and, in time, it came to be believed that she was immortal. She was aloof and inaccessible – even to members of her own tribe – and the fact that the she lived in seclusion in a remote region no doubt fuelled the imagination of her subjects.

Around 1850, Modjadji I died and the power and authority of her office as rainmaker was passed in secret to her daughter, Modjadji II. (Modjadji II, who was to reign for 44 years, was also reputedly the result of the incestuous union of Modjadji I and her own father.) Modjadji II handed the mantle of rainmaker to Modjadji III; and she in turn to Modjadji IV, who entrusted the rain magic to the present-day queen, Modjadji V.

There is no doubt that the world has changed greatly since Modjadji I ascended the throne *circa* 1800, but even today the traditions and mystique of the rain queen persist. Significantly, the ritual of the stolen magic has never been revealed to the outside world.

REALM OF THE RAIN QUEEN

In the Duiwelskloof area, a steep winding road leads to the capital of the rain queen, which is perched on a hillside below a forest of trees known as Modjadji cycads. The capital itself, a collection of circular thatched huts, is surrounded by a palisade of wooden staves which are decorated with strange, carved shapes and faces, frightening spear-like shapes, tufts of unrecognizable hair and strange skulls. Within this stronghold there is a large open courtyard, at the centre of which is a magical staff embedded in the earth, and the place where gatherings are held. The queen's quarters are secluded and she can be seen only by favoured visitors.

The queen will not act until those who seek her aid beg her to and then she may show her displeasure by refusing to co-operate until her demands are satisfied. For example, one year when the rains failed to arrive until December, it was thought that she was venting her anger about her daughter's liaison with a commoner.

Of necessity, therefore, the people are forced to temper their requests for rain with caution and, often, a degree of circumspection. Sometimes they will inform the queen of their wishes in an informal way, perhaps by speaking loudly when near her kraal or 'accidentally' mentioning during a conversation with her, that they hoped the season would be a good one. On other occasions, when the person feels a more formal approach is necessary, a ritualistic offering of gifts is made. Those people with requests sometimes dance at her kraal for long periods during summer, when they should be ploughing, in the hope that this will move her to take pity on them. If it is thought that the queen is displeased with someone in particular then the married women from all the villages in the vicinity may assemble at her stronghold every morning to dance and sing, declaring, 'We are being killed on account of a bogeyman in skins' meaning, in other words, that they are being punished for an offence committed by someone else.

THE SECRET CEREMONIES

The queen does not work alone but is assisted by one or more of the many rain-doctors within the tribe.

These rain-doctors are themselves influential figures and can act independently on occasion. A rain-doctor, for example, may be approached to bring rain to a certain district, but the power he possesses is totally dependent upon the queen – if she wishes to withhold rain, for any reason, it will not fall. The queen's power, however, is also thought to be dependent, at least in part, on the acquiescence of her ancestors and, just as the queen can stay the hands of her subordinates if she so wishes, so also can the ancestors stay hers.

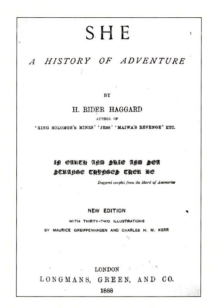
The actual rain-making ceremony remains a closely guarded secret, known only to the rain queen herself.

It has been rumoured that the rituals and practices of rain magic are only passed on to a chosen successor – a girl who has been prepared since childhood – when the rain queen is on her death bed.

The queen's rain medicines are said to be stored in rough earthen pots kept in specific areas of the village where only a few have access. These vessels are considered to be extremely valuable and are only shown to a person after many years of friendship.

Some of the power of the queen's rain magic is said to derive from a human skull. Animal horns are also used in the ceremonies, but the chief ingredient of the rain pots is said to be the skins of the deceased chiefs and important councillors. (It is believed that when an important chief dies, his body is left in the hut for some days and then treated in a certain way that remains a closely guarded secret so that the skin comes away easily.) Other ingredients used in the rituals are thought to be the fat of the scaly anteater, which is considered a royal animal, parts of kudu, sea water because it foams and froths, the feathers of the lightning bird, black and white sea shells and various roots and barks. On occasions, a black sheep is also killed, which is said to add strength to the queen's magic.

Now, of course, the world has changed for Modjadji and, for some at least, the 'old ways' are no longer as important as they were. Even so, the power and influence of Modjadji appears undiminished. In fact, it is said that in times of drought even the European population of the Duiwelskloof region join her in her rain-making prayers.

Perhaps one day, the secrets of the rain queen will be revealed to all. But for now they remain closely guarded.

And the Queen herself? She continues to perform her miracles, as remote and awe-inspiring as ever.

THE COELACANTH
Creature from the Lost World

Top: Professor JLB Smith with the second coelacanth at Mayotte, 1952.

Above: Marjorie Courtenay-Latimer, curator of the East Londen Museum in 1938.

With the publication in 1912 of his book *The Lost World*, Sir Arthur Conan Doyle, the celebrated writer and creator of Sherlock Holmes, turned his attention to science fiction.

In *The Lost World* three intrepid adventurers - Professors Challenger and Summerlee and a reporter, Malone – ventured deep into the unexplored jungles of South America and discovered a strange and frightening land on the summit of an isolated plateau.

In this remote setting, time has stood still and prehistoric creatures, long thought to be extinct, still survive.

The book not only caught the interest of an avid reading public, it also gained the attention of Hollywood directors and a number of films based upon the book were made.

Closer to home, in 1956, a South African ichthyologist, Professor JLB Smith from Rhodes University, Grahamstown, wrote *Old Fourlegs – the story of the coelacanth*. The book became something of an international best seller and a classic of science non-fiction. The book was translated into eight languages, yet the story Smith told concerned one fish – one of more than 26 000 species.

Why did *Old Fourlegs* capture the public's imagination? Like *The Lost World*, Smith's book concerned a living creature from prehistoric times. And the coelacanth is indeed a living fossil.

GOING BACK IN TIME

The coelacanth has a lineage that dates some 400 million years – almost 150 million years before the first dinosaurs roamed the Earth. It is part of a group of fish called *Crossopterygii* that is well known in fossil records and one of 121 extinct species that have been found in the dried-out beds of shallow seas and lakes that existed millions of years ago.

Some scientists have suggested that the coelacanth with its lobed fins, which resemble 'legs', is a distant ancestor of all land vertebrates and is a kind of 'missing link' between aquatic and land animals. Others claim that lungfish, which are fleshy-finned bony fish and, in addition to gills, have 'lungs' with which they can breathe air during drought periods, are closer in ancestry to four-legged land animals. However, one problem for scientists attempting to accurately place the coelacanth on the evolutionary ladder, is that the fish possesses none of the anatomical features which one would expect from a species thought to link aquatic and terrestrial animals. It is important to remember, however, that the coelacanth is not a primitive creature, but a highly sophisticated and well-adapted fish which makes extremely efficient use of its environment, and has evolved much slower than other fish species.

Scientists agree that the coelacanth has a central role to play in the evolutionary debate, although its exact importance is still a matter of conjecture.

Fossil coelacanths have been discovered in many parts of the world, including the Karoo, which once contained an inland lake, Somkele in northern Natal and the Graaff-Reinet district, but the coelacanth fossil record ended abruptly at the end of the Cretaceous period approximately 70 million years ago. It was thought that the coelacanth became extinct at about this time and no-one considered the possibility that it could survive in deep waters. For the last 70 million years the coelacanth has lived on unnoticed - until December 1938 ...

THE FIRST COELACANTH

Captain Hendrik Goosen, master of the fishing boat *Nerine*, and a good friend of Miss Marjorie Courtenay-Latimer, curator of the East London Museum, always kept an eye out for unusual fish, knowing they might be of interest to her and potential additions to the museum's extensive collection.

On 15 December 1938, after three days of stormy and unpleasant weather, Goosen sailed out of East London harbour and headed south-east, past Bird Island with the intention of trawling for sole. After twenty-four hours of poor catches Goosen headed back towards Bird Island Passage and cast his trawl net close inshore where the sea was calmer.

When he hauled in the net he was surprised to find it full of fish normally found in deeper waters.

After spending some time in Bird Island Passage, Goosen headed towards the Chalumna River area for one last haul. The fish netted at this location once again comprised mainly deep water species, although they had been taken close to the shore. As the *Nerine*'s crew sorted the catch, dumping the 'rubbish' over the side, Goosen noticed a metallic-blue coloured fish, the likes of which he had never

seen before. When he had a closer look the fish lifted its lip and snapped its mouth shut. Knowing instinctively that Miss Courtenay-Latimer would be interested in the specimen, he ordered the crew to keep it separate from the rest of the catch.

On his return to shore a day later, Goosen asked Pim Jackson, a clerk, to telephone Miss Courtenay-Latimer and tell her that he had caught an unusual fish which she might like to see. Fortunately, Miss Courtenay-Latimer was working at the museum when the call came in, but she was in two minds whether or not to go to the harbour – it was Christmas time, she had work to finish and was not particularly inspired at the thought of viewing yet another collection of unusual fish. At first she decided to ignore the call and then changed her mind because she wanted to wish the crew of the *Nerine* a merry Christmas. She took a taxi to the wharf,

and began going through a pile of sharks Goosen had dumped on the wharfside, Then she saw 'that fish'.

As soon as Miss Courtenay-Latimer saw the fish she knew that she was on to something special – although she didn't know exactly what it was. The fish was 1,4 metres long and weighed just over 57 kilograms; her first impression was that it was some sort of lungfish, although, as she admitted later, 'I hadn't the remotest idea as to which order the fish could belong'.

She knew, instinctively, that the fish had to be preserved. She asked Enoch, the taxi driver who had brought her to the quayside, to help her carry it to his vehicle. He shook his head. 'No stinking fish in my taxi!' he said resolutely. 'Well you can go,' she retorted, 'the fish is not stinking and I'll call another taxi!' Faced with this, Enoch relented and allowed Miss Courtenay-Latimer to place the fish in the boot.

At the museum, Miss Courtenay-Latimer's first task was to identify the fish, but it defied classification. In fact, the more she examined it, the more mystified she became: the head plates, fin and tail belonged to no lungfish she had encountered before. She needed expert help and the one person she knew she could turn to was Professor JLB Smith from Rhodes University in Grahamstown. Smith, who was both a keen angler and had an encyclopaedic knowledge of the fish of southern Africa, was the honorary curator of fish at the East London Museum. But this meant that the fish had to be preserved until such a time as Professor Smith could look at it.

Although she didn't realize it at the time, Smith was on holiday in Knysna and couldn't be reached by telephone for advice. Miss Courtenay-Latimer then wrote a letter in which she described her find and drew a simple diagram of the fish. It took eleven days for the letter to reach Professor Smith, and during this time, the fish was deteriorating ...

Miss Courtenay-Latimer first tried to get the fish admitted to the mortuary at Frere Hospital in the city, but was sternly rebuked by the mortician for even considering such a thing.

'What will the people think?' he asked.

'I don't think they'll be worried,' she replied, 'they're all asleep.'

She then tried local taxidermist, Mr R Canter, who often worked for the museum. Not surprisingly, he was not too keen to be disturbed at Christmas time by a woman who seemed unnaturally preoccupied with preserving a fish that looked to him like a rockcod. But in the face of insistence, he obtained formalin from a nearby chemist, wrapped the fish in strips of sheeting impregnated with the chemical and then cloaked it in wads of newspaper for extra protection.

Twelve anxious days followed during which Miss Courtenay-Latimer eagerly waited for a reply – but it never came. By 27 December the fish was exuding an oil which counteracted the effect of the formalin and it was beginning to decompose. In consultation with the taxidermist she realized that the only way to preserve the fish was to skin it and prepare a mount which would incorporate the skull. Although this would mean losing the internal organs, which were very important, at least the rest of the fish would be saved. Once the decision to preserve the fish was made, Mr Canter began his work.

When Professor Smith received Miss Courtenay-Latimer's letter he knew instinctively that the fish was one of significance. In a letter, he advised her to

treat the fish with the utmost care because he suspected it to be of great scientific value.

Professor JLB Smith first saw the fish for himself on 16 February 1939, some seven weeks after it had been caught.

'That first sight,' he said, 'hit me like a white hot blast and made me feel shaky and queer. Yes, there was not a shadow

Professor JLB Smith with one of the coelacanths caught in 1952.

of doubt, scale by scale, bone by bone, fin by fin, it was a true coelacanth ...'

Four days later the sensational scientific find was made public in an exclusive interview published in the East London *Daily Dispatch*. It was announced that the coelacanth would be displayed at the museum for two days and the general public, infected by the furore of seeing such a 'sensational scientific discovery', flocked to the museum.

'I wouldn't let a soul nearer than six feet and I stood next to it all the time we were invaded,' Miss Courtenay-Latimer wrote to Professor Smith.

As it was Professor Smith's job to identify and categorize any new species of fish, he took the specimen to Grahamstown with him as soon as the exhibition closed and, despite its 'curious, powerful and penetrating odour', kept it at his home where he conducted a detailed examination.

When he described this remarkable fish in a scientific paper for the first time, he gave it its official name – *Latimeria chalumnae*. The name honoured the efforts Miss Courtenay-Latimer had gone to to preserve the fish and the Chalumna River close to where it was caught.

Given the unprecedented world-wide public and scientific interest in the coelacanth, the trustees of the East London Museum soon realized that the fish was an extremely valuable acquisition and at one stage considered selling it to the British Museum of Natural History to raise much-needed funds. On this issue, however, Miss Courtenay-Latimer was adamant – if the fish went, then so would she! Needless to say, both remained in East London.

In April 1939, the coelacanth was returned to the East London Museum by Professor Smith, where it went on permanent display and attracted thousands of visitors. Unfortunately, though, it had been insufficiently de-greased during its initial preservation and was once again showing signs of deterioration. Although temporary steps were taken to protect the specimen, such as spraying it with alcohol, it had to be re-mounted. It was initially suggested that it be sent to expert taxidermists at the British Museum but Miss Courtenay-Latimer was determined that it should not leave the country. It was eventually sent to James Drury, a highly respected taxidermist who worked at the South African Museum in Cape Town.

On 19 August 1939, Miss Courtenay-Latimer and the coelacanth travelled to Cape Town.

On seeing the coelacanth, Drury assured her that he had 'every hope of being able to return her charge in a safe and sound condition'.

Over the next four months Drury painstakingly treated and remounted the head and skin of the fish, attaching them to a plaster-cast of its body. On completion of the remounting process, Drury took two plaster moulds of the entire fish. These casts were painted metallic blue, which was believed to be the colour of the living fish, while the actual specimen on which the models were based was left unrestored and unpainted. Drury kept one plaster cast for Cape Town Museum as payment for his work and returned the other to Miss Courtenay-Latimer along with her restored fish.

The rejuvenated coelacanth reached East London on 8 December 1939, just in time for the summer season and an ecstatic Miss Courtenay-Latimer reported to Professor Smith that 'Latimeria has arrived back from Cape Town looking really wonderful. Drury has done marvels ... one could hardly recognize the tattered specimen I took to him in August.'

OLD FOURLEGS

The word coelacanth means 'hollow spine' (Greek koilos, hollow; akantha, spine) and this name is given to these fish because the spines of the first dorsal fin are hollow. Adult coelacanths are very large blue fish with armour-like scales and small teeth. They do not have an ordinary backbone similar to other fish, but have a hollow tube comprising thick cartilage filled with fluid.

The name 'old fourlegs' originated from Professor Smith's remark that the fish had four lobe fins – two towards the front of its body and

two further back – which appeared leg-like. These lobe fins are similar to those of the first amphibians which crawled on to land and are thought to have evolved from fossil fish similar to the coelacanth.

The coelacanth, contrary to popular belief, does not use its fins to walk on the bottom of the sea bed. Studies by the French scientists, J Millot and J Anthony in the Comoro Islands have shown that they are nocturnal, carnivorous drift-hunters which paddle around slowly and majestically, occasionally rising and falling with the currents, and use their paired fins to control movement. They also perform beautiful 'headstands' but no-one knows why.

A £100 reward was offered to anyone who caught a coelacanth and made it available for scientific research. Similar rewards were offered by several countries.

Coelacanths are essentially nocturnal, deep water fish that apparently return repeatedly to the same caves during daylight hours, possibly in order to escape predators. The females produce up to 26 very large, live young.

THE COELACANTH SAGA

In the early 1940s, the Sea Fisheries Research Institute vessel *African I* repeatedly trawled off the continental shelf along the coast near East London, but no coelacanths were ever caught. And in 1950 a research vessel from the National Institute of Oceanography in England searched for coelacanths in the same region – without success.

It took fourteen years before a second coelacanth was caught, this time off the Comoro Islands in the Indian Ocean, situated between northern Mozambique and the island of Madagascar. This coelacanth was caught in 1952 by a hand-line fisherman off Anjouan Island and the then South African Prime Minister, DF Malan, arranged for a South African Air Force Dakota to take Professor Smith to the Comoro Islands in order that he might obtain the specimen and continue his research.

After the first coelacanth had been caught in 1938, Professor Smith predicted that the fish would be found in moderately deep waters off the East African coast and distributed thousands of pamphlets in September 1939 offering a reward of £100 for the capture of a specimen. In 1953 this amount was doubled by the Scientific Research Institute of Madagascar, a French organization, and in 1955, the American government offered the princely sum of $5 000 for a coelacanth. Since 1953 at least 175 specimens have been caught.

Before the 'discovery' of the coelacanth in 1938 the fish was avoided by Comoran fishermen as it was known to have a strong oily taste and an unpleasant smell. However, since the early 1950s, the coelacanth has been actively sought. There has also been a growing black market for the fish, particularly in the Far East where there is the (mistaken) belief that, because the coelacanth has survived for millions of years, it contains a chemical which will prolong life, enhance sex drive and generally affect the quality of life.

In 1991 a female coelacanth weighing 98 kg was trawled off the coast of Mozambique. This catch was important, not only because it was the second fish caught off the African coast, but because it was carrying 26 baby coelacanths, almost ready to be born. She was caught off a sandy continental shelf of about 40 metres' depth, which was peculiar as coelacanths are known to prefer the habitat off the Comoros – steep rocky shores with caves and overhangs, and depths of up to 250 metres.

THE BEST FISH STORY FOR 50 MILLION YEARS …

In a 1956 article written by Nancy Spain in the London *Daily Express*, the coelacanth was described as 'the most important scientific discovery of the century'. In spite of this somewhat exaggerated claim, it nevertheless remains true that scientists can learn a great deal by studying the anatomy and habits of a living creature.

Whatever the reason, this living fossil has certainly captured the imagination of both the public and the scientific community alike.

Literally hundreds of popular articles, songs and poems about the fish have been published since 1939. Apart from Professor JLB Smith's book *Old Fourlegs,* there have been several other publications including *Search for a Living Fossil* by E Clymer (1963), *Old Man Coelacanth* by S Bell (1969), *Operation Coelacanthe* by J Anthony (1976), *The Coelacanth* by R Brakenbury (1979) and, most recently, *Gombessa* by Y Suyehiro (1988), all of which have served to popularize the reputation of this amazing fish.

THE FINAL MYSTERY OF THE COELACANTH

Despite having survived for millions of years, the coelacanth is now thought to be in danger of extinction.

One negative effect of the increase in public and scientific interest in the fish since its rediscovery, is that there has been a drive by scientists from a number of countries to capture specimens for further study.

In 1954, a furious debate erupted in scientific circles concerning just how many coelacanths should be caught, and in 1963, on the 25th anniversary of the first coelacanth find, Professor JLB Smith delivered a rousing speech entitled *The Atom bomb and the coelacanth*, in which he lamented the fate of the fish and suggested that an international body be proclaimed to protect the species from extinction.

Apart from the efforts of Professor Smith and several other scientists, attempts to protect the coelacanth have, in the main, been poorly co-ordinated and under-funded.

It was not until July 1987 that the formation of the Coelacanth Conservation Council (CCC) was announced at a conference in Grahamstown.

The present status of the coelacanth is uncertain. It is currently listed as one of the 'vulnerable' species on the International Red List. (It is not listed as an 'endangered' species because insufficient data on the fish is available.) It is also listed in Schedule 1 of the Convention on International Trade in

Endangered Species (CITES), which means it is considered 'severely threatened by trade' and may not be traded for financial gain.

Whether or not the coelacanth will be able to survive the assault being made on it by man is yet to be decided. At present, however, the fate of 'old fourlegs' appears to hang precariously in the balance.

GHOSTS AND SPIRITS
Do they really exist?

From left to right: Lizl Strauss, Zelda Cloete, Lizette van Wyk, Maretha Burger and Martha Esterhuizen, the five girls affected by the Rietfontein hauntings.

... People won't believe in anything they can't explain ... Ghosts, for instance, may be like a footprint which some event has left imprinted in time ... But refusing to believe can be just as dogmatic as believing.

(Dr K Pedler; *The Guardian*, 18 June 1980)

THE HAUNTED HIGH SCHOOL OF RIETFONTEIN

The small town of Rietfontein is close to the Namibian border, on the edge of the Kalahari desert, and it is here that a series of mystifying events occurred at the local secondary school during 1992.

The incidents affected five teenage girls – Lizl Strauss (18), Maretha Burger (18), Lizette van Wyk (15), Martha Esterhuizen (16) and Zelda Cloete (16) – all of whom boarded at the school hostel. They reported being attacked and lacerated by unseen hands; the cuts or scratches, of about eight to ten centimetres in length, appeared under their clothes without damaging the garments. Normally, there were four or five cuts or scratches in a row and, according to the girls, they appeared randomly and spontaneously. The attacks often occurred for weeks at a time. Then, just as suddenly as they had begun, the attacks would cease. On some occasions, instead of being lacerated, the girls would have their clothing slashed, their hair hacked, or pins driven into their arms and legs.

Apart from the fact that the girls were all boarders at the same school hostel, the only other connection between them was that they all lived in, or had ties of some nature to, the town of Welkom.

Neil Oppelt, the headmaster of Rietfontein Secondary School since 1986, explained to reporters that the girls were all average pupils who had no problems at school and were not harassed or ostracized by their friends.

'The attacks are random,' he said. 'There is no pattern. In the past we've found the attacks usually stop when they leave school. The girls are definitely not doing it themselves. They are well-adjusted and attractive girls who have no reason to draw attention to themselves. They are also from poor families and I genuinely can't believe they would cut up the little clothing they do have.'

Neil Oppelt also revealed that these were not the only attacks of this kind that had taken place at the school. Similar incidents had occurred as far back as the early 1980s, but they had been kept secret to avoid 'sensational' media attention. Oppelt, who is convinced that a paranormal force was at work, said that the school had held prayer meetings but these had failed to help. He maintained the problem was a spiritual one and was considering having the school exorcised by a priest.

'There is something evil here. I have seen scratches grow and bleed on Lizl's arm. We have prayed. That's all we can really do.'

Lizl Strauss, a matric student and one of the victims, claimed to have suffered attacks for four years. They had started in Standard 7 when she woke up one morning to find her legs burning and blood running down her calves. Since then she had been constantly plagued by mysterious 'attacks'. The week the Rietfontein story hit national headlines, for example, her hair was mysteriously hacked off. Two weeks prior to this she had suffered a fit. The hostel attendant and three other men had been unable to hold her down because she was thrashing about so violently. Lizl had no explanation for these strange phenomena.

'I do not believe in spirits,' she said. 'I just want it to stop. I am a child of God. I can only trust in God. My parents consulted a witch doctor two years ago, but I know of no-one in my family who has dabbled in satanism.

'I have a strange premonition before these things happen. I just feel something is going to happen. Last week, I was on my way to church. When I walked downstairs my dress suddenly felt uncomfortable and I looked down to see the whole front was cut up.'

Above: Johanna Cloete with an example of slashed clothing.
Below: An x-ray of an arm with evidence of needles in the flesh.

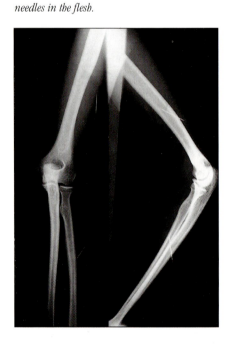

In another incident Lizl's hair had ignited spontaneously while she was at her parents' farm in Welkom. Afterwards she had fainted and remembered nothing more. Her eight-year-old brother,

however, who witnessed the incident, said that she had run out of the toilet with her hair burning, collapsed to the ground and then the flames had 'just disappeared'.

'Her hair was burnt. It was stinking. We battled to bring her round after that,' Lizl's mother said. 'I've seen white lines appear on her skin. Then the skin just opens up. Sometimes they're just surface cuts which become inflamed but others are deep and then the blood runs out. I never used to think supernatural things happened, but now I think there is no other explanation.'

One of the other victims, Zelda Cloete, started experiencing problems at primary school in Welkom during 1989 ...

'I woke up one Thursday to find scratches on my thighs. I went to school and felt my breasts burning ... there were more scratches.'

At Rietfontein the attacks manifested themselves once more. One afternoon she was sitting in her hostel room when she realized something was hurting her leg. When she looked down she saw the eye of a needle sticking out of her thigh. On another occasion she had arrived home one day to find all the clothes in her cupboard slashed.

Reverend Andrew Julies visited the school and led the children in a church service. He was reported to have ruled out mass hysteria as an explanation for the attacks.

'Satan has come to Rietfontein,' he said. 'We can only fight this with prayer and faith ...', an assessment supported by Lieutenant-Colonel Kobus Jonker, head of the occult and related crimes unit based in Pretoria.

'It sounds like a fairy-tale, but I have spoken to the girls, I have spoken to their parents and I have spoken to two policemen and one of their wives who have seen these incidents taking place before their eyes. Some people just don't want to believe it can happen.'

To this day, the events at Rietfontein remain unexplained.

The Uniondale ghost lady.

UNIONDALE'S 'LADY IN WHITE'

In the Eastern Cape, on the road from Oudtshoorn to Port Elizabeth, lies the farming town of Uniondale, and it is here, or so the story goes, that the ghost of a young girl killed in a motorcycle accident during the Easter weekend of 1968, occasionally appears. There are reports of motorists who claim to have seen a forlorn-looking young woman standing at the side of the road and even stranger tales of those who have ventured to give this mysterious 'lady in white' a lift, to find her having disappeared into thin air. The last reported sighting occurred in 1987.

In 1980, Ken Dodds mentioned to an *Argus* reporter that he'd felt the presence of another person on the back of his motorcycle, shortly after he had seen a young woman standing at the side of the road. He had felt the pressure of arms around his waist, panicked and accelerated, and was then struck repeatedly on his helmet. When he stopped to investigate the cause of the blows, there was no-one behind him, but his spare helmet had been placed neatly on the seat behind him.

The last sighting of the ghost occurred one night during May 1987. A young woman was seen near the Langkloof Pass road around 9.30 p.m. by the Van Jaarsveld family while they were driving from Oudtshoorn to Port Elizabeth. The three people in the car, Willem van Jaarsveld, his wife Rita, and their four-teen-year-old daughter, Marietha, all saw the same sight – a woman in white standing at the side of the road with one leg slightly raised as if about to climb on to an invisible motorcycle.

Rita van Jaarsveld was about to remark on the fact that the girl was miles from anywhere, when her husband said, 'There she is!', and at that moment their daughter, who had been asleep in the back of the car, sat bolt upright and complained about the cold. They all felt 'an eerie presence' in the car and when Rita van Jaarsveld glanced at her hus-

band, she noticed that he was in a cold sweat and his hair was rising. Twenty kilometres later, the 'presence' left the car, leaving behind a smell of apples. Later Rita van Jaarsveld, who stressed that both she and her husband were down-to-earth people, said that she had been too scared to speak to the ghost. Later, she wished that she had and even expressed a measure of sympathy for the ghost, whom she believed to be troubled. With hindsight, she realized that the ghost was in no way dangerous.

'At the time I never thought of speaking, but I know how I would feel if my dead son could not find peace. I just wish there was something that could be done for her.'

THE TOKOLOSHE

In southern African folklore there exists a small but malicious 'creature' known as the tokoloshe. The tokoloshe, which is normally described as small, hairy and beast-like, appears to take pleasure in causing damage and distress. Rather like the poltergeist, it reveals its presence with wanton acts of destruction, but if some newspaper accounts can be believed, it can be 'called up' to persecute or punish a particular individual or household.

The tokoloshe legend is a familiar one, and it is traditionally associated with the black community; but there is a measure of ignorance, and scepticism, regarding its existence within other sectors of society. In an article published in the *Sunday Times* on 27 January 1987, however, there was a detailed account of a harrowing ordeal suffered by the Ramlall family of Northdale, at the hands of a 'fierce, hairy, paraffin-spitting tokoloshe'. According to the article, the Ramlall family had moved into their modest house in October 1986 and their problems began almost immediately.

'I was out of the house visiting neighbours when someone broke in and ransacked our cupboards. Then the first fire started,' explained Mrs Ramlall.

This was just the beginning. In the days and weeks that followed, curtains, bedclothes and mattresses burst into flames, and a series of unpleasant 'accidents' made life a misery for the family. At first the Ramlalls assumed they were merely the unfortunate victims of local vandals and contacted the police. An investigation followed, but reached no conclusion. Eventually, the police decided the matter was not of a criminal nature and, therefore, outside their jurisdiction. According to a police spokesman the investigating officers were satisfied that it was not a 'person' causing the damage ...

Following this, the Ramlalls made no less than twelve unsuccessful attempts to exorcise the evil presence possessing their home, including engaging the services of a Hindu priest and a Muslim faith healer.

But the damage continued. Eventually, a sangoma was called in and, according to Mrs Ramlall, after a lengthy ritual and a difficult struggle, a 'fierce little tokoloshe with a face like a monkey and body covered in coarse hair' was captured underneath a cupboard in her son's bedroom.

The sangoma 'put the creature into a bottle and we went with him to the Bulwer River where he performed another ceremony before throwing the tokoloshe in ...'

From that day on, the Ramlalls were never bothered again.

GHOSTS PAST AND PRESENT

What are ghosts and poltergeists? A poltergeist is recognized as a household spirit renowned for throwing things, making noises and generally causing a disturbance. The word itself is of German origin (*poltern*, to be noisy; *geist*, ghost) – and, going back in time, there are literally thousands of anecdotal accounts of their activities. The first well-documented case history of poltergeist activity, however, occurred in England in 1661 and was known as the 'Drummer of Tedworth' affair.

The home of a local magistrate was beset by bangs and crashes every night after he had imprisoned a local pedlar

Artist's impression of a Tokoloshe, a malevolent, mythical creature, often invisible to humans.

and confiscated his stock-in-trade, a drum. Once the pedlar was sent abroad to a penal colony the hauntings stopped, but later began again on his return.

In fact, during the sixteenth and seventeenth centuries, the existence of

witches and spirits was common knowledge. King James I of England, wrote a book about demonology, witch trials were common and there were even officers of the court known as 'witchfinders' who roamed the countryside seeking out the agents of evil.

During the late nineteenth century there was a definite move away from the concept that poltergeists and the like were human souls or spirits of some sort. Thomson Jay Hudson, author of *The Law of Psychic Phenomenon*, advanced the theory that all 'spirits' were simply products of the subjective mind. He further concluded that those who denied spiritualism were not sceptics – they were merely ignorant. He maintained, in other words, that ghosts were a product of the mind and not an independent entity and added that, as a Christian, he believed in the survival of the soul after death but that this had nothing to do with spiritualism, which was an entirely separate phenomenon. Although Hudson was not able to explain how the subjective mind could move individual objects, play musical instruments, cause fires to occur and the like, he had no doubt that such things were possible.

During the 1930s Hungarian psychoanalyst, Nandor Fodor, extended Hudson's analysis. He agreed that poltergeists were not spirits and argued that they were in fact the manifestation of repressed sexual energies. Forty years later, the British investigator of psychic phenomena, Guy Playfair, would reject this assessment. Playfair challenged Fodor's theory and suggested that poltergeists were spirits 'playing' with the energy exuded from those in a condition of tension, such as teenagers at puberty.

It is certainly true that one can dismiss many 'hauntings' as fake: they can be ascribed to human trickery, to a psychological imbalance on the part of the observer, or even strange, but quite natural, shadows, shapes and noises.

Nevertheless, there remains a number of 'ghostly' contacts which even the most sceptical among us would find hard to explain. The Psychic Club in Cape Town has investigated a host of inexplicable phenomena over a period of nearly fifty years. In a 1988 interview with the *Argus*, Max Frank, then president of the club, remarked:

Most people are ignorant or hostile towards the subject. They show their prejudice without knowing much about psychic phenomenon. In my respectful opinion this all stems from a fear of the unknown ... so why don't people read up on the subject and find out about it?
There's nothing wrong with exploring the subject as long as you do not harm anyone in the process. I want to make it quite clear that we seek only truth ... this is a club of interested people – it's not a church and does not hold religious services ...

Max Frank has personally investigated psychic phenomena for over thirty years and he is now convinced that the subject warrants serious scientific research. It is for this reason that he has suggested that universities establish a chair for scientific research.

Different accounts of poltergeist activity have had the tendency to bear remarkable resemblance to each other. Apart from the noise and general disturbance, factors which are frequently reported, a common feature is showers of stones. Often these fall around people in a room and sometimes hit individuals, but rarely hurt them.

A particularly well-documented incident was reported in the *Sunday Times* on 20 July 1980 and concerned two young tennis players, Okkie Kellerman and André Wolfse, who were travelling from Cape Town to Pietermaritzburg. At one of the stations en route, they inadvertently offended a 'witch doctor' and the man cursed them. For the rest of the weekend, showers of stones rained down on them wherever they went.

They even had to vacate the room where they were staying after being pelted with stones *inside* the house. Neither Kellerman nor Wolfse had any explanation for the phenomenon and were uncertain whether the fact that they had been 'cursed' by the witch doctor was in any way connected to the showers of stones which fell on them.

Other poltergeist-type activity is a frequent phenomenon in South Africa. In August 1986, for example, some of the residents of Hout Bay in the Cape found themselves on the receiving end of some strange and alarming incidents which they attributed to poltergeists. Wet washing burst into flames while hanging on the line, clothes mysteriously burst into flames in the house and the report also maintained that some clothes burst into flames while they were being worn, although the wearers themselves were not harmed in any way. There were also incidents where curtains were torn apart by 'unseen hands'.

In the article *Feeling Haunted?* in the *Johannesburg Star* of 26 April 1987, Harriet Pienaar, a member of the South African Society for Psychical Research, described her contact with a poltergeist which was persecuting a Klipfontein family. Beds in the home would catch fire for no logical reason and children's school lunch boxes were interfered with, their contents being replaced with lumps of coal for no apparent reason.

Another alleged incident took place at the Light Horse Band clubhouse in Kelvin, Sandton, where several uniforms belonging to the band members were thrown about and paint was daubed on the floor and the cupboards of the clubhouse.

In November 1991 a report was published in the *Argus* concerning the picturesque town of George, in the southern Cape, where the Du Plessis family were planning to leave their home which they believed to be haunted.

George du Plessis said that he and his family had been living in the house for

only four days when strange things began to happen – cups fell off hooks, locked doors opened and closed of their own accord, tables were knocked over and a fish tank burst. His wife, Ina, repeatedly told him that she felt as if someone was touching her neck or shoulder and was having much trouble sleeping at night as a result. Their two-year-old daughter, Sara, also woke up in the middle of the night, screaming, and kept pointing to what she said was an 'old lady' looking at her. It was later established that previous tenants had also 'seen' an old woman ...

There was neither an explanation for these strange incidents, nor did there appear to be any cause-and-effect relationship between the alleged poltergeist and the persons or places affected by them. It seems that poltergeists, which remain invisible to the human eye, materialize out of the blue, strike at random and depart as mysteriously as they arrive.

DO GHOSTS REALLY EXIST?

Before you dismiss the incidents mentioned above, consider the conclusion reached in Arthur C Clarke's book, *World of Strange Powers*, in which he investigated several cases of unexplained phenomena of various kinds from around the world.

He created a 'scale of possibility' in which he attempted to assess the likelihood of such things as poltergeists, precognition, telepathy, apparitions and other similar phenomena. The scale of possibility runs from +5 (certainly true) to -4 (certainly untrue). Poltergeists, he maintains are +2 (possible) and apparitions +4 (highly probable).

In the final analysis, however, believing in ghosts has to be attributed to an act of faith because we certainly don't know all there is to know about the subject. So beware, a ghost may be waiting for you behind the bedroom door this evening ...

THE MYSTERIOUS RUINS OF ZIMBABWE
Capital of an Empire?

For hundreds of years the magnificent Zimbabwe ruins have been steeped in mystery, their origin uncertain. Who constructed this magnificent complex of wall and temple, the like of which is found nowhere else in the world? Was it the fabled land of Ophir, an outpost of ancient Phoenicia as some popular novelists would have us believe, or perhaps even a temple dedicated to King Solomon? Maybe it was a fortress belonging to the legendary Queen of Sheba? Or did its builders live closer to home? And was its purpose more functional, less glamorous?

Recent research has thrown much light on this intriguing mystery, deep in the heartland of southern Africa.

THE GREAT STONE BUILDING

About thirty kilometres from Masvingo (previously known as Fort Victoria) lies Great Zimbabwe, one of the most famous ruins in the world. The site takes its name from the Shona word *maDzimbabwe*, or *dzimbahwe* meaning 'great stone building' and comprises a vast complex of elaborate stone walls, built without foundation or mortar, extending over more than 24 hectares.

Great Zimbabwe, which is situated in the fertile and well-watered Mutirikwi Valley, dates back to the eighth century AD, although the site had been occupied for about 600 years before that.

Between 500 and 1500 AD, the area was dominated by the Karanga-Rozvi group of people.

The ruins themselves may be roughly divided into three parts: the Acropolis or Hill Ruin, the large Elliptical Building and the Valley of the Ruins.

The Acropolis is situated on the summit of a granite hill over one hundred metres high and was at one time believed to have been both a military stronghold and holy place. It comprises a number of dry-stone walls of varying thickness which are constructed entirely from granite fragments.

These walls, which are built on or around great natural boulders, have created several stone enclosures, of which at least one was used for smelting gold. The Hill Ruin also has a cave with unique acoustic properties and it is thought that Mwari, the Karanga-Rozvi god, would, through the priests, speak to his people from this cave, his voice booming out over the valley.

The Elliptical Building (originally called 'The Temple' by European antiquarians) is estimated to have been constructed using almost a million bricks and contains large (10 m high) and small (2 m high) conical towers. It is believed that the Elliptical Building was used as living quarters by the resident king, his wife and servants. The enclosure wall of this section of the ruin is decorated in places with chevron patterns of black and white granite fragments. This pattern is thought to have indicated the presence of the king and signified his role as the great rainmaker.

The Valley of the Ruins extends between the Acropolis and the Elliptical Building. It is an area on which lie the

The legendary Zimbabwe Ruins, situated some thirty kilometres from Masvingo.

Above: The view of the Elliptical Building from the Acropolis.

Below: One of the conical towers which lie within the walls of the king's residence.

THE LEGENDS

It has been suggested that Great Zimbabwe was the fabled land of Ophir (*see* 1 Kings 9:26-8), an unidentified territory famed for its fine gold. It was also, allegedly, the site of King Solomon's gold mines, the Queen of Sheba's fortress, and even a mysterious outpost of the sea-faring Phoenicians – but all of these claims are contrary to the archaeological evidence available.

It is possible that at least one of these popular misconceptions was encouraged by Rider Haggard's novel, *King Solomon's Mines*, published in 1885. In his book, set in the 19th century, three European heroes, Sir Henry Curtis, Captain John Good RN and the narrator, Allan Quartermain, accompanied by their native servant, Umbopa, set off to find Curtis' missing brother, George, who vanished while searching for the treasure of King Solomon's mines. Heading inland from Durban, the intrepid explorers venture into the hinterland of Africa and confront the mythical lost people of the Kukuanas. They come across magnificent ruins abandoned by 'The Ancients' of generations before. On observing three colossal statues that guard the mines – called the Silent Ones by the Kukuanas – Quartermain suggests that, 'Perhaps these colossi were designed by some Phoenician official who managed the mines', and in this way Haggard may well have perpetuated the myth that the Phoenicians had established a powerful empire in southern Africa.

King Solomon, however, lived well over three thousand years ago, but historical research conducted on the site indicates that the Karanga-Rozvi people who established Great Zimbabwe, only entered the territory from the north around 500 AD, although there is archaeological evidence to indicate that the area has been inhabited by various races from earliest times.

The iron and gold mining industry and the practice of wall-building came much

ruins of numerous smaller structures, possibly dwellings, and continues for over a kilometre down the valley.

The foundations of small stone buildings can also be found in the Acropolis and the Elliptical Building. There is also the remains of an extensive drainage system throughout the ruins.

Great Zimbabwe was probably abandoned towards the end of the 15th century and it was not until 1868 that the ruins were 'discovered' by Adam Renders. Just over 20 years later, in 1889, a hunter, Willie Posselt, found the first Zimbabwe bird in the eastern enclosure of the Acropolis. Since Posselt couldn't carry it away as it stood, he hacked it from its pedestal and offered to sell it to President Paul Kruger. It was eventually bought, however, by Cecil Rhodes, then prime minister of the Cape, and it now stands in Groote Schuur library.

later, around the 9th or 10th centuries, and archaeological research indicates that Great Zimbabwe grew to become an important centre for trade and reached the height of its power around the mid- to late-14th century AD, and then fell slowly into decline until its virtual demise around 1500.

WHO BUILT GREAT ZIMBABWE?

There have been suggestions by novelists such as Rider Haggard (*King Solomon's Mines*) and even Wilbur Smith (*The Firebird*) that European nations – Phoenicia in particular – established outposts of their civilization in Africa thousands of years ago, long before the voyages of discovery. However, detailed research into the origins of Great Zimbabwe has proved that there is no historical evidence to suggest that this beautiful complex of ruins was built by anyone other than the Karanga-Rozvi people who have lived in and around the area for almost 1 500 years. Certainly the ruins are unique in their grandeur and size, and a number of granite-walled enclosures, seen nowhere else in the world, are found within a 160 kilometre radius.

GREAT ZIMBABWE

It would seem that between 500 and 1000 AD so many people came to live on the hilltop that it became overcrowded and more buildings were erected below the summit of the hill. It is thought that the priests and military lived in and around the Hill Ruin while the chief (or mambo) with the bulk of his family and people lived in the valley below.

Great Zimbabwe was not a military stronghold, however, and it is significant that the whole complex is laid out for domestic use.

Great Zimbabwe was not constructed with a view to defense as there is no evidence to suggest that there was an army in residence or a military barracks of any sort. It was, in other words, a centre for trade, not a fortress. Furthermore, the inhabitants could be numbered in hundreds and not thousands and it is likely, therefore, that most of the settlement

A section of the inner walling of the Acropolis which is sometimes referred to as the Hill Ruin.

was occupied by farmers, artisans and craftsmen living in traditional African huts. Traditional circular clay-walled huts were built against the protective stone walls that now look like a meaningless jumble and each complex of huts formed a family dwelling with huts for wives and children, for sleeping, cooking and entertaining guests. Furthermore, each of these domestic units was separated by a courtyard which offered a degree of seclusion and provided a working space

for skilled craftsmen who had established themselves within its boundaries.

CENTRE OF AN EMPIRE?

With very few written records to refer to, researchers have had to piece together the history of Great Zimbabwe using archaeological evidence gleaned at the site. The conclusion drawn by modern researchers such as archaeologist, Roger Summers, former curator and keeper of antiquities at Bulawayo Museum and author of *Ancient Ruins and Vanished Civilizations of Southern Africa*, believes that Great Zimbabwe was the centre of a great inland empire ruled by the Karanga people, who smelted and worked with gold, copper and iron which they traded on the shores of the Indian Ocean, and that it stood at the centre of a regional trading network.

Roger Summers was involved in a dig in 1958 which identified five distinct periods of occupation. The first, which began around 100 BC ended during the 4th century, when the second began. The third – which is when the stone walls were probably built – began around 1000 AD, and the fourth and richest period commenced during the late 14th century and continued into the 15th century. However, all the pottery, earthenware and coloured glass found at the site has been dated to around the 14th century, yet there is little or no Chinese porcelain. Since this was a major import to the east coast by the mid-15th century, it is argued that Great Zimbabwe ceased its trading contacts (and fell into decline) around this time. There is no evidence to suggest economic or building activities after 1500 AD.

UNANSWERED QUESTIONS

Although we know a great deal about Great Zimbabwe, a number of questions remain unanswered which explains why mysteries surrounding the ruins persist. No-one knows, for example, how the state which was centred at Great Zimbabwe originated, where its power came from, or how the society was structured. The evidence suggests that Great Zimbabwe was rather like a palace or capital which housed a ruling class, but the relationship between the rulers and the ruled remains unclear.

Also, it is fair to assume that religion played its part in maintaining the social order, but just how important or even what form that religion took is uncertain. Indeed there is every possibility that the rulers used the Mwari cult as a unifying force, through which they encouraged political support for themselves, but no-one knows how.

And, of course, there are the greatest mysteries of all: why did Great Zimbabwe fall into decline? And why was the site abandoned?

THE DECLINE AND FALL

According to Shona history (which is supported by near-contemporary Portuguese accounts), the first Munhu-Mutapa (Mwene-Mutapa) left his home in the south (Great Zimbabwe?) and moved north to settle in the Zambezi valley 'because of a shortage of salt', in the middle of the 15th century. This may mean that there were difficulties, either agricultural or economic at the capital, which may have proved insurmountable. Of course, this migration may also have occurred as a result of inter-family feuding within the ruling dynasty or because of arguments over succession. Whatever the real reason, it would appear that some time during the 15th century the Mwene-Mutapa took what was perhaps a dissident faction with him when he moved north. This event seems to have

heralded (or been a consequence of?) the decline of Great Zimbabwe as a trading power.

From this point onwards, the fortunes of Great Zimbabwe fell into rapid decline and the settlement was eventually abandoned, although the Rozvi people continued to work in the area.

Around 1835, Zwangendaba, leader of a Ndwandwe group fleeing from Shaka and the *Mfecane* (the 'crushing'), entered Zimbabwe, sacked the walled settlements of the Rozvi people and ravaged the territory in spectacular fashion before moving on to Tanzania. Three

years later the Ndebele followers of the Mzilikazi entered the territory from the west, continued the process of subjugation begun by the Zwangendaba and eventually settled in what is now central Zimbabwe. The African kingdom of the Rozvi, which had survived for over a thousand years, had been finally and irrevocably destroyed.

It is unlikely that we will ever know the entire truth about Great Zimbabwe, but the valley and the walls, stones and the terraces, remain – always silent, brooding reminders of a once-grand empire now vanished.

THE ZIMBABWE BIRD

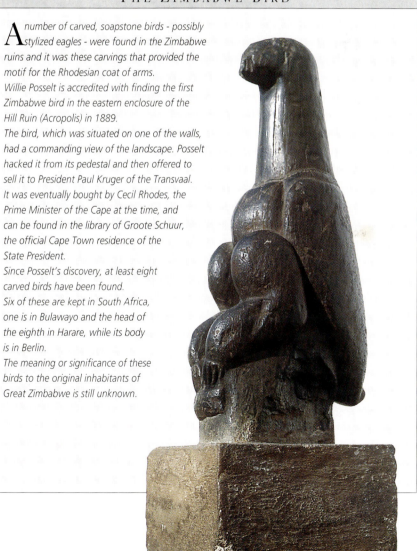

A number of carved, soapstone birds - possibly stylized eagles - were found in the Zimbabwe ruins and it was these carvings that provided the motif for the Rhodesian coat of arms.

Willie Posselt is accredited with finding the first Zimbabwe bird in the eastern enclosure of the Hill Ruin (Acropolis) in 1889.

The bird, which was situated on one of the walls, had a commanding view of the landscape. Posselt hacked it from its pedestal and then offered to sell it to President Paul Kruger of the Transvaal. It was eventually bought by Cecil Rhodes, the Prime Minister of the Cape at the time, and can be found in the library of Groote Schuur, the official Cape Town residence of the State President.

Since Posselt's discovery, at least eight carved birds have been found.

Six of these are kept in South Africa, one is in Bulawayo and the head of the eighth in Harare, while its body is in Berlin.

The meaning or significance of these birds to the original inhabitants of Great Zimbabwe is still unknown.

THE MISSING LINK
The southern African connection

Approximately 140 years ago, Charles Darwin unleashed upon the world a theory that was to rock Victorian society and shake the very foundations of the church. He maintained that human beings were not the descendents of Adam and Eve, but shared a common ancestor with an extinct ape and ultimately, 'some primordial cell'.

Critics of Darwin said that he proposed that Man was a descendant of an existing species of ape; but what Darwin actually meant was that Man and ape, though related, had evolved along different evolutionary branches.

Since the publication of Darwin's book *The Origin of Species,* there has been controversy within anthropological circles as to at what stage in the evolution of Man he developed characteristics which differentiated him from other primates with whom he shared a common ancestry. This ancient man-ape was popularly called the 'Missing Link'. But was there ever a missing link? And, if so, did this creature evolve in southern Africa as many modern scientists now maintain?

In 1831 a young naturalist, Charles Robert Darwin, joined the survey ship *Beagle* for a voyage of discovery, one which was to last five years. Darwin was 22 when he set out, but he returned to Britain a deeply thoughtful young academic. His observations, especially on the Galapagos Islands, which lie 800 kilometres off the coast of South America, suggested to him that the process of evolution was underpinned by natural selection. This important and formative period in Darwin's intellectual life was the basis for his wide-ranging theories on evolution.

Although Darwin purposely excluded discussion of 'man's place in nature' from his book, for fear of the furore it would cause within the staid Victorian religious establishment as it undermined the biblical writings of Genesis, he clearly understood the implications of his theories. Man did not emerge on Earth whole and complete, but evolved from a lower order of primate and was a possible descendant of tree-dwelling monkeys. It wasn't until 1871 that Darwin spelt out his conclusions concerning Man's role in the grand scheme of evolution in *The Descent of Man* in which he argues that 'Man in his arrogance thinks himself a great work worthy [of] the interposition of a deity. More humble and I think truer to consider him created from animals.'

Not unexpectedly, the book caused a tremendous stir and debates regarding Darwin's claim that Man was descended from a lower order of animal ranged the length and breadth of Britain. Scientists and laymen alike embarked on a search to determine the origins of Man.

One of the main problems of investigating the history of Man is that it all happened so long ago, and there is very little evidence of Man's ancient ancestors on which to base conclusions. Very few of the living sites occupied by our ancestors some two or more million years ago have been preserved, and, at those sites which have been identified, only a few stone implements and fragments of fossilized bone remain.

Despite these difficulties, tremendous progress has been made over the past 130 years. But the story is far from complete and, for this reason, the mystery of the missing link continues.

FROM MONKEY TO MAN

No-one is sure when the evolutionary course of ape and Man diverged. The first man-like creature is thought to have emerged during the Oligocene epoch, about 36 million years ago. By 14 million years ago, a variety of apes had evolved, including *Ramapithecus*, which is considered to be the first link in the chain leading to modern man.

ANCESTORS OF MODERN MAN

Australopithecus Between five and one-and-a-half million years ago, this man-like ape lived in eastern and southern Africa. He probably used tools, possibly walked upright, had human-like teeth but possessed a brain which was no larger than that of a modern ape.

Homo habilis About two million years ago, *Homo habilis* (*homo*, man; *habilis*, handy or capable) had evolved and for a time, apparently co-existed with *Australopithecus*.

Homo habilis, (also sometimes referred to as '1470 Man' taken from the museum number of a skull found in Kenya in 1972), was a new genus or 'class' of man-like creature and lived in east and central Africa. He had a much larger brain than his predecessor and archaeological excavations have shown that he actually made tools. For this reason, some anthropologists consider *Homo habilis* to be the first true human being.

There is little evidence of *Homo habilis* in southern Africa itself, apart from a few indeterminate fossil bones found in a Krugersdorp cave and a more recent find at Gladys Vale which may or may not be *Homo habilis*.

Homo erectus Following *Australopithecus* and *Homo habilis*, the next genus to emerge on the evolutionary path to *Homo sapiens* was *Homo*

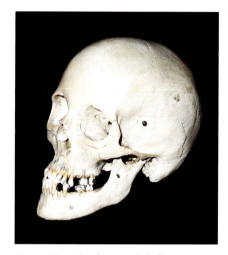

Homo sapiens (modern man) skull

erectus (*erectus*; upright), so called because he stood upright. He could move without the shambling gait of a monkey, hunted large animals, and archaeological investigations at the living sites of *Homo erectus* suggest he was the first to use fire for cooking and keeping himself warm. Charred embers were found with Peking Man's remains in a cave near the Chinese capital in 1929.

The term *Homo erectus*, however, may well be a misnomer since fossilized footprints were found in 1976 in Olduvai Gorge in Tanzania. These have been dated to *Australopithecus* times, three and a half million years ago.

Homo erectus was first 'discovered' in 1927 by Davidson Black of the Peking Union Medical College. For this reason, *Homo erectus* is sometimes referred to as 'Peking Man'. It is interesting to note that Eugene Dubois, a Dutch anatomist, found the skull and thigh bone of a man-like creature in Java in 1891, which later proved to belong to *Homo erectus*. It was not until 1940, however, that the significance of Dubois' 'Java Man', and the fact that his findings constituted evidence of a new chapter in Man's evolution, was fully appreciated.

The evolutionary path of the ancestors of modern man.
From left to right: Australopithecus, Homo habilis *(the first, true human being),* Homo erectus and Homo sapiens *(modern man).*

WAS THERE AN AFRICAN EVE ?

Is all of mankind descended from a single, female African ancestor? For almost a decade, this debate has raged in both academic circles and the popular press.

It all started in 1987 when Alan Wilson, Rebecca Cann and Mark Stoneking came to an amazing conclusion at Berkeley, California, after studying mitochondrial DNA in a number of living populations. They concluded that we are all descended from a common, female African ancestor who lived some 200 000 years ago. They named her 'Mitochondrial Eve'. Thus originated the 'Eve out of Africa' theory.

Many people were misled by this theory and believed that the Wilson group had stated that all mankind was descended from a single, female ancestor. In fact, the group had stressed repeatedly that the unknown 'Eve' was a type of ancestor and had a number of companions, of both sexes.

On the basis of the Wilson group findings, some molecular evolutionists claimed that anatomically modern man had burst out of Africa less than a quarter of a million years ago, spread over the entire world and eliminated the earlier man.

Significantly, even before these findings were made public, some anthropologists were convinced that there had been two human migrations out of Africa: the earliest more than a million years ago, and then a more recent one by truly modern humans about 100 000 years ago. These 'children of Eve', as the second group of migrants were called, replaced all populations from the previous migration. The Wilson group's hypothesis seemed to strengthen the 'children of Eve' theory, despite the fact that it appeared to contradict the available fossil evidence.

Many anthropologists, however, remained convinced that the more traditional theory of evolution, namely that there had been no second migration and that modern homo sapiens evolved from ancient ancestral populations well over a million years ago, still held true.

In 1992, Dr Phillip Tobias, professor of Anatomy and Human Biology at the University of the Witwatersrand, enrolled the assistance of Dr Christopher Wills, a molecular evolutionist at the University of California to examine this dichotomy.

After an exhaustive DNA study, Dr Wills concluded that the length of time since the so-called Mitochondrial Eve had existed was, more precisely, 750 000 to 1,1 million years ago, and not 200 000 years as some scientists had suggested. Dr Wills' investigation supported the fossil evidence and refuted the 'Eve out of Africa' theory.

'The "Eve out of Africa" theory was a flash in the pan,' Dr Tobias maintains. 'It was an exciting idea. It would have been very nice for us who live and work in Africa, but one must not allow oneself to get chauvinistic about these things.'

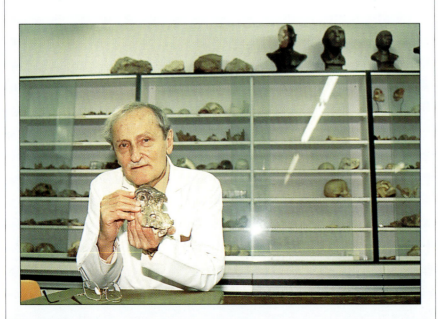

The terms '1470 Man' and 'Peking Man' are used in reference to particular anthropological specimen remains, as is 'Java Man'. 'Peking Man' has now been renamed 'Beijing Man' after the new capital city of China.

Homo sapiens, the specific name for modern man, is thought to have made his appearance on the world's stage 35 000 years ago. Modern man is more correctly classified as *Homo sapiens sapiens*, a subspecies of *Homo sapiens*. Ancient remains of *Homo sapiens* have been found in Hungary, England, Germany and France. *Homo sapiens* remains have also been unearthed along the banks of the Omo River in southern Ethiopia, in Kenya and Borneo and most anthropologists are now of the opinion that the genus most probably evolved outside Europe.

IS SOUTH AFRICA THE HOME OF THE 'MISSING LINK'?

The answer to this question depends upon how the term 'Missing Link' is defined. All the evidence indicates that Man's evolutionary ancestors evolved in central and east Africa. Only *Homo sapiens* may have emerged elsewhere. If one defines the missing link as that creature which most closely resembles modern man physically, then *Homo erectus* is the most likely candidate for this title. Remains of these hominids have been found in Europe, Asia and Africa.

If, on the other hand, one defines the missing link as that man-like creature which was the first to actually construct tools as opposed to simply making use of stones or other objects lying about, then *Homo habilis* fits the description – and is most closely associated with the continent of Africa.

A third contender for the title is our own *Australopithecus*. Man's distant ancestor, *Australopithecus*, was named by Professor Raymond Dart, professor of Anatomy at the University of the Witwatersrand, after he found a skull at

I n 1924, Raymond Dart, classified the first fossil remains of a man-like, higher primate, discovered near Taung in the north-eastern Cape, by naming it Australopithecus africanus (the southern ape of Africa). The Taung skull, as the fossil came to be known, was unearthed during excavations by the Northern Lime Company. It consisted of the greater part of a child's skull and contained a face, mandible (jawbone) and skull base with a brain cast, plus all twenty of the milk teeth and the first permanent teeth (the upper and lower first permanent molars). Since the cranial and dental characteristics of the specimen were not ape-like in any way, Dart believed this to be the fossil of an intermediate between ape and man. He published his findings in Nature in February 1925. However, as this was the first fossil of its kind that had been discovered, other scientists were sceptical.

In 1936, Dr Robert Broom, one of the few people who agreed with Dart's claims of the possible relationship between the Taung skull and modern man, was shown fossil remains discovered at Sterkfontein. These remains were also eventually classified as australopithicine. Over the next decade, more fossil australopithicines were identified in south and east Africa and Asia.

But Dart's claim was not truly vindicated until the 1950s and 1960s when the Leakey family, working in the Olduvai Gorge in Tanzania, found more fossils. They established that australopithecines were hominids, walked upright, made tools and lived as early as $5^1/_2$ million years ago. Today these hominids are classified as Homo sapiens australopithecus.
The skull is preserved in the Anatomy Department of the University of the Witswatersrand.

a cave near Taung, in 1924. Professor Dart concluded that the unearthed skull belonged to an early hominid which he named *Australopithecus africanus*, meaning the southern ape of Africa.

From the time of Dart's discovery, South Africa has produced more evidence of *Australopithecus* than any other country in the world, mainly from limestone deposits in Krugersdorp, Kromdraai, Sterkfontein and Swartkrans. Out of the hundreds of specimens found, however, not one complete skeleton can be constructed.

Then there is also the matter of Neanderthal man, a variant of *Homo sapiens*, dominating Europe and Asia between 100 000 and 40 000 years ago, before and during the last Ice Age.

He appears to have been an evolutionary dead-end – despite having a larger brain than modern man.

There is some controversy as to the taxonomic identity (classification) of skulls with heavy brow ridges and 'Neanderthal features' discovered at Broken Hill (now Kawbe) in Zambia and Saldanha, near Cape Town.

At one time, the so-called Neanderthal man was considered to be a distinct species of Man but modern taxonomists tend to attribute the whole group to a subspecies of *Homo sapiens* – *Homo sapiens neanderthalensis*.

Neanderthals were cave dwellers who had the use of fire and manufactured stone tools which would have permitted them to prepare skins for clothing and weapons to hunt with.

Excavations conducted at sites in Europe, the Middle East and then Russia show that Neanderthals buried their dead and on occasion provided the departed with goods arranged around the body.

Skulls of the cave bear were often found at their living sites and it is speculated that this extinct animal may well have had some sort of religious significance in their lives.

The reason that all trace of Neanderthal man suddenly vanished from fossil records, still remains a matter of some debate.

It has been suggested that extinction followed catastrophic disease, a failure to adapt to climatic changes, annihilation by more 'advanced' *Homo sapiens*, and even absorption by *Homo sapiens* – but to date no-one is sure.

THE MYSTERY CONTINUES

Despite almost 150 years of intensive investigation, there still remain missing chapters in the story of Man's evolution. The available evidence suggests that many millions of years ago the ancient simian ancestor of modern man – the so-called 'Missing Link' – began to change and evolve in Africa.

But why this change occurred or how long it took to reveal itself, remains somewhat uncertain.

Perhaps in the years to come, more light will be shed on this intriguing mystery and we will learn, once and for all, that our part of the planet provided the nursery for all human life on Earth.

THE STRANDLOPERS
The people who never were

Dotted along the length of southern Africa's coastline, both in the open and in caves, are ancient refuse heaps of compacted sea-shells. These 'middens' as they are more often referred to, have been found to contain the remains of birds and animals, human artifacts and, not infrequently, human skeletons and are the legacy of a nomadic people usually referred to as the Khoisan. (The Khoikhoi is the name the Nama, who were nomadic herders, used to refer to themselves and San was the name the Nama gave to people without domestic livestock, who lived by hunting and gathering. Khoisan is simply a combination of these names and refers to both groups as a whole.) Until the latter half of the twentieth century, however, they have been attributed to a somewhat mysterious group of people called the 'Strandlopers'. But for a long time no-one was quite sure who the Strandlopers were, how they evolved or why they had become extinct. In the face of so much uncertainty, the myth was created that the Strandlopers were a race of people separate, both culturally and physiologically, from all others in southern Africa. But were they?

The irony of the Strandloper issue is that there is no physical evidence to suggest that they were in any way different from the Khoisan. Even the name we know them by is one given to them by Leendert Janssen, a survivor of the *Haerlem*, which was wrecked in Table Bay in 1647 and, as a consequence, is likely to have been misleading.

Archaeological evidence indicates that at least 100 000 years ago, much of the

A painting of Strandlopers by John Thomas Baines.

coastal region of the Cape was occupied by late stone-age people who lived in caves and simple shelters – the hunter-gatherers and ancestors of the San or Bushmen.

About two thousand years ago, the Khoikhoi, a new people, entered the Cape coastal area and, not unexpectedly,

their arrival created competition for land, marine and food sources. This influx proved to be to the detriment of the San who were pushed away from the coast by the force of numbers of immigrating Khoikhoi pastoralists and black farmers, ancestors of the Nguni, who were also moving into the area, and into regions not occupied by the Khoikhoi.

The major Khoikhoi tribe in the Cape was the Cochoqua, who were referred to as 'Saldanha-men' by the Dutch. They lived near the coast, wintered in and around St Helena and migrated to Tygerberg in the spring. During mid-summer, if the rains were good, they moved across to Stellenbosch and then back along the banks of the Berg River to their winter quarters.

In the 1600s, Van Riebeeck witnessed this migration of the Cochoqua, whom he called 'Quena', and, as part of a military assessment, calculated that the number of men capable of carrying arms was around one thousand. He also noted that they were accompanied by thousands of sheep and cattle. If this estimate is correct, it would suggest that the entire tribe comprised five to six thousand people.

The Goringhaicona, who were also known as Watermen, Fishermen and Strandlopers were effectively led by a man known variously as 'Hadah', 'Harry' or 'Herry', but whose real name was Autshumao.

In 1630 or 1631, Herry was taken by the British to the East Indies and brought back to the Cape the following year. It seems that he learned to speak English during this journey and later, along with his 'niece' Krotoa (Eva) acted as an interpreter for the British when bartering for livestock from the Khoikhoi.

It is also possible that he learned to speak some Dutch. As a recognised interpreter, intermediary and postman, Herry had considerable influence with the colonists and the Strandlopers in Table Bay who were able to receive the rewards for his loyal services.

Herry died in 1663, by which time the fortunes of the Goringhaicona were already in a state of decline.

It would appear that the first specific reference to the 'Watermen' is to be found entered in the log of William Bayley, captain of the merchant ship *Mary*, in May 1639 ...

Satterday the 11th this morning about 1 aclock wee gott one Anchorr aborde and houe apeeke to the other ... About 9: or 10: Aclock this morning we sent our shallopp to Penguin (Dassen) Iland to carry Thomas with whom we lefte our lettres with the Rest of his family of watermen therre to resyde the whole number Consisting of 20 persons menn, weomen and Children, in the afternoon we sent our Joliwatt ashoare for water whoe retourned this Euen with 1 1/2 tonns as also our shallopp retourned from Pinguin Ile with divers fouls as Cormorants young geese 2 seales and but one Penguin leaving there 20 Persons affoernamd.

WERE THE KHOIKHOI AND THE STRANDLOPERS ONE AND THE SAME?

A smaller tribe of the Khoikhoi, known as the Goringhaiqua – *Capemans* or *Kaapmans* by the Dutch – numbered about one thousand people and lived on the Cape Peninsula, dividing its time between two main camps, one on the shore in Table Bay and the other along the False Bay coast near Muizenberg. It would seem that the Strandlopers, who probably numbered between twenty and eighty people, were in some way subservient to the Goringhaiqua since they were known to them as Goringhaicona, meaning 'children of the Goringhaiqua'.

In accounts written by some of the early European visitors to these shores, including Francois Valentyn who mentioned them in official records in 1681, the Strandlopers, who were sometimes called 'Watermen' or 'Fishermen', were a people who eked out a subsistence living by gathering shellfish from rocks and eating birds, seals and whales – reputedly a particular favourite according to European observers – which washed-up along the shore. It seems that the Strandlopers did not keep animals of their own, though the leader of the Goringhaicona, Autshumao or Herry, who had visited England in 1630/31, acted as an interpreter/ intermediary for the Dutch when they bartered for livestock with the Khoikhoi.

It may be suggested that the life style of the Strandlopers was adapted by, among others, Herry and his niece Krotoa (Eva) out of a desire to be the first to make contact with the European settlers and to derive the benefits from this contact.

In the same year, another sailor, Johan Albrecht von Mandelslo, stopped at Table Bay in the *Swan* and also made reference to the Strandlopers whom, he claimed, 'live very miserably by the waterside, but without ships or boats. They live on herbs, roots and fishes, and especially on the dead whales which are cast ashore by storms, which must serve as their best food. They are called Watermen, because they live by the shore.' [1]

In a later log entry, Mandelslo maintained that on one occasion he had transported fifteen 'Watermen' – four men, eight women and three children – to Penguin Island after they had begged him to do so. He claimed that this group hoped to live on the island by feasting on dead whales, seals, fish and penguins, and expected to be free from the persecution of the Khoikhoi in the area.

WHY WERE THE STRANDLOPERS THOUGHT TO BE A SEPARATE 'RACE'?

The confusion regarding the classification of Strandlopers began at the turn of the twentieth century. In 1907, Dr FW Shrubsall undertook a comparative analysis of 23 skulls taken from the South African Museum and elsewhere, including one reputedly of a Strandloper which had been obtained in 1872. Those from coastal contexts he classified as 'Strandloper', while those from the interior, or for which no locality was recorded, were classified as 'Bush'. He concluded that the Strandloper crania, 'appear in all respects to form a purer group than the Bushmen, and to be distinct from the Hottentots'. In other words, the Strandloper 'race' was quite different to all the others in the area.

Despite the fact that Shrubsall's theory was later proved to be incorrect, it managed to gain a measure of public acceptance and this led to the popular misconception that the Strandlopers were in some way unique.

In the book *Earthworks*, Lyall Watson suggests that the Strandloopers [sic] were part of a now-extinct people known as Boskopoids. (The term 'Boskopoid' is derived from the town of Boskop near Potchefstroom in the Transvaal where, in 1913, parts of a skull and fragments of limb bone were unearthed and attributed to the 'Boskop Man' – a more intelligent member of the Neanderthal race, but one which was destined to become a dead-end branch of the evolutionary tree.)

However, the Boskop Man theory has also been discredited, as the cranium on which it was based has since been proved to be part of a large but very Bushman-like skull and quite within normal parameters.

Southern Africa has been called the richest storehouse of prehistoric art in the world and the discovery of new sites is an all-but everyday occurrence, particularly when compared to Europe where the discovery of a new painted site is cause for much excitement. On the eastern slopes of the Drakensberg alone, there are over 29 000 recorded sites and no-one knows for certain just how many art sites, paintings and engravings there are in this part of the world.

Most European rock art is found underground, and so-called narrative scenes, such as those found at Lascaux in south-western France and Altimira in Spain, are extremely rare and, consequently, much publicized. In southern Africa, however, most of the abundant rock art is open to the elements or found under rocky overhangs. Narrative compositions are also far more common and people are clearly depicted dancing, fighting, hunting and performing ritual activities.

The subject matter of southern African rock art is varied, which suggests that the artists painted for a number of reasons. Some paintings may well have been created to accompany initiation ceremonies, illustrate folk tales, record contemporary life and denote ownership.

Establishing the age of paintings has proved somewhat difficult, since the paints do not contain sufficient carbon for radiocarbon-dating. The oldest paintings, however, are thought to be in the region of 10 000 years old and the most recent, 200 years old. Experts in the field are reasonably certain that most of the art was painted by the Bushmen.

With the arrival of European settlers and colonization during the 17th century, the traditional way of life of the Bushmen was severely disrupted. The colonists, who found it impossible to negotiate with the Bushmen as they had no chiefs, and agreements made by one camp were not binding to any others, eventually conducted an all-but systematic campaign of extermination.

WHAT HAPPENED TO THE STRANDLOPERS?

By the early 1700s the Strandlopers had virtually disappeared. In an official record made by Francois Valentyn in 1714 it was noted that the *Kaapmans* had all but died out following an outbreak of smallpox. Given that the Strandloper community was small to start with, and that it appeared to have fairly close ties with the European settlers, it is likely that those Strandlopers who did survive the sickness would have been assimilated into the settler community.

After 1714 there is little or no mention of the Strandlopers. Given the fact that they were a small group, possible outcasts of the Goringhaiqua, and therefore, a 'temporary' tribe, any further references to them were more likely to have been San seen along the coast.

REINCARNATION
Is there life after life?

*R*eincarnation refers to the belief that after bodily death, the soul or personality survives (often for an indeterminate intermediate stage) and then enters a new body and is reborn. It is often associated with two of the great religions of the East – Hinduism and Buddhism – but the notion is common among several religions as well as African and native American peoples.

Considerable research has been conducted by a number of scientists around the world but it has not been possible to prove conclusively that reincarnation has ever occurred.

UVASHNEE RATTAN

Possibly the most well-documented case of reincarnation in South Africa involves a young Indian girl, Uvashnee Rattan who, one Sunday in September 1974, quite spontaneously began to reveal details of a previous life.

Jugdees Rattan left his home in Lotusville, just outside Verulam, to deliver a load of sand to a house in the nearby suburb of New Glasgow. He took with him his three children, including his four-year-old daughter, Uvashnee. When he returned home, a very excited Uvashnee went running up to her mother.

'Mommy, Mommy,' she said, 'my name is Sudima, and I was staying at Kemla's house. Kemla's house is in New Glasgow. It is down a steep hill. The house is bluey in colour and inside there are planks ...'

Mr and Mrs Rattan were surprised by Uvashnee's outburst. Mrs Rattan understood Uvashnee's reference to planks to be a simple wooden floor, but when Uvashnee went on to describe her

'other' family, the Rattans became alarmed. Uvashnee was talking about things of which neither she nor they had any knowledge. How was this possible?

Their daughter then went on to describe how her 'other' family ate only potato curry and roti, but no meat, and that in front of her 'other' house there had been a pond and next to that, a river where they used to wash their clothes. Mrs Rattan knew instinctively that her daughter was speaking of a previous life of some kind. No other explanation made any sense.

'Who did all these things, Uvashnee?' she asked.

'Kemla's mother.'

'Are you trying to say that you were someone else? An old lady?'

'No, no! Kemla's mother is an old lady. I was the young daughter.'

'What young daughter? How old were you when you lived at Kemla's house?'

'I was the same as Asha.'

(Asha is the Rattan's eldest daughter who was eight years old at the time.)

'But what happened to you? If you were staying at Kemla's house, why aren't you staying there now?'

'Because I got sick and died. I had a bad stomach pain and died. They thought I was dead but I wasn't. I was only sleeping.'

It was later established that Sudima, the girl Uvashnee claimed to have been, had died of dysentery. This was a common sickness in the area, particularly among people who obtained their drinking water in the way Uvashnee had described. Uvashnee frequently talked about her previous life and, as word of the story spread, a number of people came to interview her and her family.

In the days that followed Uvashnee's initial revelation she told her family a great many other details of her previous existence. She spoke of how Kemla's mother used to wear a long skirt full of gathers underneath a short sari and how the house where she used to live was on the side of a hill so steep that, 'the vehicles can't come up to the house because they would get stuck'.

After listening to Uvashnee, Mrs Rattan became so intrigued that she decided to investigate the matter for herself and to go to the house where her husband had delivered the sand. When she called at the house, the door was answered by an elderly woman.

'I told her of my daughter's insistence that she had lived there with a man named Kemla. The old lady said that Kemla was her grandson but that she herself had not been there the previous Sunday, although her daughter – Kemla's mother – had been at home and the child may have seen her there. The old woman, who had herself only moved into the house two weeks before, did not know of anyone named Sudima.'

Mrs Rattan suspected that Uvashnee had seen the woman's daughter and that, for some reason, this had caused her to recall her previous life.

For some time, nothing was heard from the 'other family', then they invited the Rattans to their home so that they could hear the story for themselves. On the day of the visit there were a number of other guests at the house. Many questions were asked, and answered quite fully and without hesitation. Then something happened ...

'Uvashnee was sitting on my wife's lap at the time,' Jugdees Rattan explained. 'I pointed to a tray of sweetmeats near to her and said, "Give your mother some sweetmeats, Uvashnee". I expected that she would simply take some then turn around and give them to my wife, but instead she got off her lap, collected some sweetmeats from the tray and took them to an elderly lady, Mrs Baghwandeen, who was sitting on the far side of the room. This woman

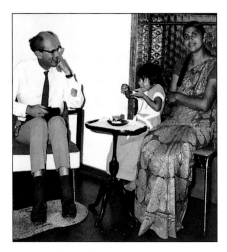

Above: Professor John Poynton, Uvashnee Rattan and her biological mother.
Below: Uvashnee Rattan and Mrs Baghwandeen, her mother in her previous life.

began to cry. She took the sweetmeats from Uvashnee, pulled her on to her lap and kissed her. She said she was crying for her daughter, Anishta, who had died of dysentery twenty years before, at the age of nine. Anishta had only been sick for a day and there had been nothing anyone could do for her. She then explained that although her daughter's name was Anishta, she also had another name bestowed on her by a priest at birth, according to Indian custom: Anishta's priest's name was Sudima.' [1]

At another meeting of the two families, Uvashnee saw a photograph of Mrs Baghwandeen's late husband. She called him 'my other daddy who was dead' and asked to keep his picture. At another visit, Uvashnee asked for her toys.

'What toys?' Mrs Baghwandeen asked.

'The ones on the wardrobe.'

Mrs Baghwandeen was very upset – Uvashnee's remark had reminded her that she once kept her daughter's toys on top of the wardrobe, but had given them away shortly after she had died.

Mrs Baghwandeen died in 1975, after a period of ill-health. Surprisingly, a few days before her death, Uvashnee had said, 'You know, I feel very sorry for the other mommy. She will die very soon.'

'Despite being a Hindu I am not a religious person,' Mrs Rattan explained, 'so at first I was sceptical when Uvashnee began talking the way she did. In fact, it wasn't until I saw her pick out a photograph of Sudima at the house of her "other family" that I became convinced she was actually telling the truth and that she was really reincarnated.'

There are numerous incidents in this account that appear to defy explanation. Perhaps the story was an elaborate fraud or a series of coincidences? Perhaps even a figment of a fertile imagination? But the possibility cannot be excluded that a case of reincarnation actually occurred.

Professor David Scott-Macnab carefully investigated the incident for the Natal branch of the South African Society of Psychical Research, and concluded that it appeared to be a classic case of recall. He added further that the *prima facie* evidence was 'strongly suggestive of a genuine case of reincarnation'.

On one occasion, Uvashnee had accompanied him to the site where her 'other parents'' home once stood. Viewing a pile of rubble – all that remained of the house – she had been clearly confused yet talked in detail about the house, the pool outside and the stream which ran nearby.

She also pointed to a spot where there used to be a swing. All of these points were later confirmed by the Baghwandeen family.

Both Professor Scott-Macnab and his colleague, Professor John Poynton, Chairman of the Natal branch of the Psychical Society, were convinced that the child's memories were genuine.

'Uvashnee has information which could not have come to her through her normal senses.

It is a classical case, an extremely clear-cut case of recall of an apparent previous existence.'

Uvashnee Rattan now lives in New Delhi, India, with her sister Asha.

FACT OR FICTION?

Dr Ian Stevenson has been investigating the phenomenon for over 30 years and published the paper, *The Evidence for Survival from Claimed Memories of Former Incarnations,* in which he studied 44 cases of supposed reincarnation, where the accuracy of the subject's previous life could be verified.

In addition to the more conventional cases of reincarnation, Stevenson also has on file a number of cases where the 'new' reincarnated body was several years old when the previous body died. This confusing situation suggests that the spirit or life-force of the reincarnated person entered its host after the host body had been living for some time. His investigations indicate that these anomalies are not a result of date mix-

ups and suggests that there may have to be a radical re-think of traditional reincarnation theory. Stevenson is now convinced that the most productive route for research in this subject involves investigating in detail the past-life experiences of young children.

Not only is there less likelihood that a child has accumulated a vast store of knowledge on which the 'past life' can be based, it is also easier to determine if a child has been coached in any way. Wherever possible, Stevenson first checks the authenticity of the past life and attempts to determine if the child has the same memories as the deceased by speaking to friends and relatives.

Professor Scott-Macnab, who investigated the case of Uvashnee Rattan.

Over the years, he has been able to establish that, in most cases of this nature, the child normally volunteers information from a past life without any warning or prompting (although subsequent investigation often indicates that the initial outburst is triggered by an event or location in 'this' life which is in some way related or similar to one from the 'previous' life).

The optimum age for past memories to reveal themselves is apparently between two and five years.

These memories begin to fade by the time the child turns five or six and are usually gone by the age of eight unless they are constantly reinforced.

Often the child uses language or particular language skills beyond his years and, in the more significant cases, not only does the child have visual and verbal memories but he or she will act in a strange or unexpected way, which is called atypical behaviour.

Also of significance is that about ten per cent of Stevenson's cases appear to involve birthmarks which are in some way related to the previous life.

Despite extensive research, Stevenson does not claim to have irrefutable proof that reincarnation occurs, although he argues vigorously that his research strongly suggests that this is the case. He argues further that it is overly simplistic merely to dismiss the subject of reincarnation as unproven and, therefore, non-existent.

REAL PROOF?

How does one prove the reality of reincarnation? The fact is, it's probably impossible to do so and some people dismiss all mention of the subject for this very reason.

Nevertheless, on-going research is continually generating interesting information on this intriguing subject and nowadays, few people would deny that our range of mental powers, our ability to put 'mind over matter', is clearly much greater than we give ourselves credit for. Perhaps reincarnation is a manifestation of an unrecognized mental power?

The Uvashnee Rattan story is not the only well-documented case of a reincarnation-type experience which has occurred in South Africa, but it does tend to raise just as many questions as it does answers. There is, of course, a distinct possibility that reincarnation has never occurred and it remains to be seen whether this is the best explanation for the apparently strange phenomena referred to in this chapter. Clearly, more research is needed, but it may well be that one day we will all discover the truth of the matter for ourselves.

MYSTERY FLIGHT N12062
Possible hijack?

On Sunday, 16 June 1991, Evan Boddy and his pilot, Elliot Hutchinson, took off from Reciffe Airport in Brazil for Abidjan on the Ivory Coast. They flew in a twin-engined Aero Commander 685 which Boddy had purchased to bring to South Africa in order to set up an air charter business.

The Aero Commander was equipped with an open five-man raft with a radar reflector, torch, dye, water and other emergency supplies. Although the aircraft was not equipped for a water landing, it was considered exceptionally buoyant and capable of staying afloat for several days.

Boddy and Hutchinson never arrived in Abidjan, and it was assumed that the aircraft had gone down somewhere in the Atlantic Ocean. But is this what really happened, or could some other fate have befallen the two men?

THE FLIGHT PLAN

The flight plan submitted to Reciffe Air Traffic Control indicated the shortest possible flight path across the Atlantic Ocean, then a route along the west African coast and finally inland to Pretoria. Flying time for the transatlantic leg was estimated to be just over thirteen hours.

The two men originally intended taking off while it was still dark, but were requested by the Brazilian authorities to delay their departure until after dawn. The aircraft apparently took off at 5.13 a.m. in near-perfect flying conditions – calm, cloudless weather with

Above: The missing plane.
Below: Evan Boddy.

excellent visibility – and 28 minutes after take-off the pilot made a routine flight call on Reciffe's radio frequency to inform air traffic control that they were changing to another frequency used by aircraft flying outside controlled air space.

Evan Boddy, Elliot Hutchinson and the aircraft have never been seen or heard from since.

BRAZIL AND THE IVORY COAST

When the aircraft failed to arrive at Abidjan, authorities at the Ivory Coast made no attempt to conduct a search for the missing men, despite numerous requests by the South African Department of Foreign Affairs and repeated appeals by distraught friends and relatives. On the other side of the Atlantic Ocean, the Brazilian government effectively disclaimed their responsibility in the affair, contending that it was up to the government of the country of destination, in this case the Ivory Coast, to initiate a search.

According to international law, legal responsibility for a search lies with the port of destination. Legally, therefore, the Brazilian authorities were justified in disclaiming responsibility. Unfortunately, however, the Ivory Coast had neither the equipment nor facilities to conduct an extensive search.

Nine days after the men went missing,

Robin Binckes, a friend of the two men complained, 'The South African consul in Abidjan is doing his utmost to get a response from the Ivory Coast government. He is trying to get an audience with the country's president. The family is distraught at the lack of action. If these two men are still alive in a dinghy in the ocean, a matter of hours if not minutes could count.'[1] At this point no-one had any idea of where or why the aircraft may have gone down.

A REASON FOR OPTIMISM

In the face of official indifference from the Brazilian and Ivory Coast authorities, a number of friends of the two missing men put pressure on the South African government to become more directly involved in the search, even though the search area was beyond South Africa's area of responsibility. The Department of Civil Aviation, acting through the Department of Foreign Affairs, applied for permission to launch its own search and rescue effort.

There was reason for optimism as a French satellite had recorded two automatic mayday signals which appeared to have been transmitted from points on or near to the original flight path. The first signal was received on 21 June, five days after the aircraft had gone missing, and the second, three days later. It was not possible, however, to establish the source or identity of the two signals.

This information came to light as a result of efforts made by Trevor Trautman, who first contacted the American Department of Aviation to ask if any US satellites had received an emergency signal from an ELT (emergency location transmitter). The aircraft had two of these transmitters, one of which was fitted in the tail and the other in an emergency rubber dinghy. Trautman then approached the French aviation authorities for their help. 'It was only on the off chance that we tried the French, and they confirmed receiving the sig-

nals,' Binckes explained. 'We are hoping the signals are coming from a drifting dinghy. An encouraging sign is that they came a few days apart.'

From the information received from the French, it was thought that the two men could be floating at four kilometres per hour in the Benguela Current, about 500 nautical miles from the west coast of Africa. On receiving the information regarding emergency transmissions, Trautman calculated several possible positions and gave sets of co-ordinates to the South African and French satellite

I did not know where he was for six days the first time and ten days the second time. On both occasions he had been unable to get fuel and I only found out where he was when he managed to get messages to me from other pilots. There are no telephones or communication channels on these isolated islands.

There are so many tiny islands dotted around and they could be stranded on any one of them. So I am still very confident and full of hope that they are alright.[2]

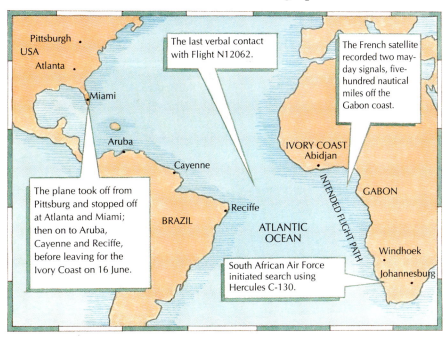

The proposed flight plan of Boddy and Hutchinson

monitoring teams in the hope that further emergency transmissions would be received. A second signal, received on 24 June from an area close to the missing aircraft's flight path, suggested that it may be located in the Atlantic Ocean about 500 nautical miles west of Libreville, the capital of Gabon.

Mandy Hutchinson thought that her husband may have landed at an airport in West Africa due to engine trouble. Confusion arose when a newspaper report quoted her as saying that this was not the first time her husband had gone missing ...

THE SEARCH

On 26 June, the Maritime Rescue Co-ordination Centre (MRCC), Silvermine, Cape Town, received the co-ordinates of the emergency transmissions which had been picked up by French satellite over the Atlantic Ocean, and on 27 June, the South African government announced that it was sending a plane to the area north of Ascension Island to mount its own search.

The first signal, picked up on 21 June , was 3 degrees 22,5 minutes south by 34 degrees 8 minutes west – a point just north of Ascension Island. The second signal, received three days later, was 2 degrees 1 minute north by 16 degrees 0 minutes west, or approximately 250 kilometres from the Brazilian coast. If both signals had come from the missing aircraft, they indicated that it was actually moving *westwards*.

A South African Air Force Hercules C-130 left Waterkloof Air Force Base, Pretoria, for Ascension Island and operated from an American air base there. (This was the first contact between the two air forces for two decades.) Over the next three days the South African team searched the area and spent over 36 hours in the air. Each run up and down the search area covered a three mile-wide strip. No debris or clues to the fate of the missing aircraft were found.

On 1 July the search was officially called off. A day later, in response to repeated appeals and bad press coverage throughout the world, the Brazilian authorities conducted their own one-day search off the South American coast, combing an area off the island of Fernandez de Royale.

DID FLIGHT N12062 GO DOWN IN THE OCEAN?

It has been assumed by all the countries involved in the search that flight N12062 went down somewhere between Reciffe and the Ivory Coast, although there is no concrete evidence to support this assumption. Trish Gordon, Boddy's fiancé, has continued to investigate the matter in the hope that she can shed some light on the fate of the two missing men.

If Boddy and Hutchinson had completed their scheduled journey they would have arrived off the Ivory Coast around 21h00 local time, in other words, after dark. The first country they would have come near to in Africa was Liberia and Robertsfield,

the international airport in Monrovia, the first alternative landing point listed on their flight plan. In fact, Elliot Hutchinson asked his wife to enquire about the political situation in that country. She told him that as the country was in a virtual state of civil war it would be extremely dangerous to try to land there. After the two men went missing, concerned friends and relatives contacted the staff of the American embassy in Monrovia who advised them that 'This country

A Hercules C-130 was sent by the South African Airforce to the search area.

is not functioning'. There is the possibility that the two men, running short of fuel, endeavoured to put down at Monrovia. They may have crash-landed as the airport would have been in darkness due to the fighting, been shot down on their approach, or attempted to land at the coast, away from the danger, and crashed into the jungle. There is even the possibility that they made a successful landing at the airport but were killed by rebel forces who were in control of the airport at that time. Certainly, the atrocities reported during the war suggest that if the two men had landed they would not have stood much chance of survival, and eye-witness reports claim that Robertsfield Airport is littered with unidentified burnt-out aircraft.

HIJACK IN BRAZIL

Trish Gordon also speculates that the two men were not on the aircraft when it left Brazil, that the aircraft they were scheduled to fly to South Africa was hijacked before they left South America.

She bases this theory on the discrepancy between a conversation she had with Boddy prior to departure and the flight plan submitted.

On 15 June 1991, Evan phoned me from Reciffe to advise me that the plane was in order and that they would be flying out that evening to Abidjan, Ivory Coast. The reason they intended leaving in the evening was to ensure that they arrived at the African continent in daylight. They were aware that after dark, airport runway lights would not be on and the tower would be closed. Elliot had flown this particular route twice before, so he was very conscious of the need to arrive before nightfall. A flight plan was filed for 10 p.m. local time. A report from one of Lloyd's Insurance agents advises the plane took off and came back. Another flight plan was filed for 5 a.m. and this is when the plane took off. According to another report from another Lloyd's agent, the original flight plan was filed for departure at 10 p.m. and then another was submitted for 5 a.m. At 5 a.m. the plane left Reciffe. The last radio contact was made 28 minutes after departure. There is no guarantee that Elliot and Evan were in that plane. They were aware it was approximately 10 hours before they would be near the African coast and it is very strange they should leave in the early morning knowing the possible consequences if they arrived after dark in Africa.

So what happened to flight N12062?

THE QUAGGA
Extinct or not?

Until roughly two hundred years ago, vast herds of quagga roamed South Africa. Now, this oddly striped member of the horse family is extinct. What happened? And perhaps equally mystifying, will we ever see their like again as geneticists are talking of re-introducing this extinct animal to the wild? And is such a prospect even conceivable?

The quagga (*Equus quagga quagga*), which is now known to be the southernmost subspecies of the plains or common zebra (*Equus quagga*), formerly known as *Equus burchellii*, gained its name from the Khoisan, who referred to it as the 'kwa-ha' because of its distinctive bark. But whereas most of the plains zebras are characterized by black striping on a white to brownish base colour, the quagga was reddish-brown in colour and possessed stripes on the head, neck and fore-quarters only, becoming progressively indistinct towards the back.

The numbers of this once-abundant animal began to decline drastically following the arrival of European settlers in this 'hunters' paradise' during the latter half of the seventeenth century.

In addition, the farmers hunted them for their flesh, made grain bags of their skins, and erected fences to restrict their range. In South Africa it is thought that the last of these animals was shot in 1878, some eight years before a law was passed to protect the species! The last known quagga in existence – a mare – died in her stall on 12 August 1883 at Amsterdam Zoo.

The quagga, on show in Munich, Germany, which was restored by Reinhold Rau.

A CAUSE FOR CONFUSION

The numbers and distribution of the quagga remain uncertain despite the fact that it was frequently mentioned by travellers to southern Africa during the seventeenth, eighteenth and nineteenth centuries. Unfortunately, however, chroniclers of the time frequently confused the quagga with some of its closest relatives and, on occasion, mistook the quagga for the female mountain zebra. Further complications arise from the fact that some descriptions given by early writers are clearly open to debate and must, therefore, be treated with a degree of circumspection. For example, many of the early records are not sufficiently definitive to separate the true quagga from other zebra and, in many cases, it is impossible to determine exactly which animal the writer is referring to. Some write of horses where they appear to be referring to zebras, others of asses, and where 'mules' would seem to suggest quaggas in one account, 'horses' would be appropriate in another. Some authors have credited long ears to the mountain zebra; others, to what seems to be the quagga. Today we associate long ears with donkeys and mountain zebra (*Equus zebra*), whereas some of the early travellers associated them with asses and wild horses.

Colouration has been equally misrepresented. There have been references to blue, yellow, green, black-and-white, white, chestnut, pure sky-blue, brownish, red, chestnut-brown, pale red and isabella quaggas. These varying descriptions may be accounted for by such things as the time of day at which the sighting was made and that individual animals were sometimes significantly different in appearance. But the fact remains that reports are unclear and there is a conspicuous absence of consistent terminology. It would appear that many writers were themselves uncertain of what they had seen! It is no surprise, then, that modern-day researchers have had great difficulty deciphering their comments with any degree of certainty.

In spite of these drawbacks, however, it is fairly certain that the quagga was encountered in vast herds on the great Karoo plains of South Africa between the Cape Province in the south and the Vaal River in the north; from Bushmanland in the west, to the Orange Free State in the east. But there is no record in the accounts of explorers and adventurers of the 18th and 19th centuries to suggest that the animal was found further north than Vanrhynsdorp on the western coastal belt. It is also questionable whether the quagga was ever present in Namaqualand – although it seems to have existed in fairly large numbers in and around what is now Piketberg. The quagga was also fairly common in the Paarl and Malmesbury regions (though not on the Cape Peninsula) and occurred throughout the Eastern Cape, certainly as far as Uitenhage and inland to Cradock.

TRAVELLERS' TALES

The first mention of wild equines in the southern Cape in Jan van Riebeeck's journals, occurred in 1657 – five years after he had established a settlement at the Cape. The account refers to a report written by Abraham Gabbema, who led the first expedition from the Cape that year. In his account, Gabbema reports seeing the footprints and dung of 'horses' approximately fifty miles north of Cape Town, [1] but whether these were left by zebras or quaggas, is impossible to tell.

Two years later, a man by the name of Dapper visited the Sonqua people living in the Hottentots-Holland mountains, and drew a distinction between wild

One of the last known quaggas at London Zoo.

'horses', which he described as having 'buttocks extra-ordinarily dappled, and over the rest of the body they are striped yellow, black, red and pure sky-blue' and 'mules', which he said, '... are also striped white and chestnut-brown, but not dappled, and are uncommonly beautiful'. [2]

This appears to be the first time a distinction was made between wild horses (zebras) and mules (quagga?), but it was certainly not the last. In many cases travellers' observations tended to increase rather than decrease the confusion surrounding the various species. Typical of travelogue entries at the time, was the one made by Anders Sparrman while travelling from Warm Bath to Zwellerndam and Riet Valley between 26 August and 3 September, 1775 ...

It was here that I saw for the first time in my life one of those animals called the quagga by the Hottentots and colonists. It is a species of wild horse, very like the zebra; the difference consisting in this, that the quagga has shorter ears, and that it has no stripes on its forelegs, loins, or any of its hind parts.

This partial resemblance has been the occasion of Mr Edward's delineating the quagga with the title female zebra. But in fact both the quaggas and zebras are species totally different the one from the other, keeping in very different tracts of country, and those frequently very distant from each other. The females of each species are marked like their respective males, excepting that the colour is somewhat more lively and definite in these latter.

That the zebras discover some trifling variations from each other with respect to their streaks, particularly down the legs, may be perceived by comparing the different skins of this animal; which, as I have remarked above, are sold by the furriers under the denomination of seahorse skins. I have never had an opportunity of comparing together the skins of quaggas, but have very little doubt that there is likewise some trifling difference between them.

A full grown foetus of a quagga, which I brought with me from the Cape, and kept stuffed with straw in the cabinet of natural history belonging to the Royal Academy of Sciences, seems to have livelier colours than

I have observed in the adult animal. The length of this foetus, from the ears to the tail is thirty-one inches, and its height about the loins twenty-two inches. The quagga I saw here, having been caught when it was very young, was become so tame, that it came to be caressed. It was said never to be frightened by the hyena, but, on the contrary, that it would pursue this fierce animal, whenever this latter made its appearance in those parts; so that it was a most certain guard for the horse, with which it was turned out to grass at night. ₃

In 1796, just over 20 years later, explorer-adventurer Francois le Vaillant, while in the region around the Fish River, and clearly conscious of the confusion that surrounded the quagga, determined to set the record straight ...

It was only under the twenty-fifth that I found a kind of wild ass, of an isabella or pale yellow colour. This animal, is by the Greater Nimiqual called the white zebra: but it is certainly a wild ass; for instead of having a striped skin like the zebra, it is of one colour, which has a yellow tinge. No animal in all Africa, perhaps, is so suspicious, and so shy as this kind of ass. It appears everywhere in large herds; but I could never get near enough to fire at any of them. I have, however, in my possession a skin, which I purchased in a horde where it was employed to cover the hut of a savage. There are, therefore, three different species of the ass in the southern part of Africa: the zebra, the quagga, and the kind above mentioned, which is neither spotted nor striped. At the Cape the zebra is known under the name streep-ezel (the striped ass), and the quagga under that of

wilde-paerd (the wild horse). In the colonies the names and the animals are sometimes both confounded; which, in natural history, may occasion errors, as has really happened; for the quagga has often been considered as the female of the zebra. But the quagga and the zebra are undoubtedly two different species, which, though they live in the same district, have no more intercourse with each other than they have with the flocks of antelopes that inhabit those regions. Vosmaer, who never travelled in Africa, and who, consequently, could know the quagga only from the accounts of others, pretends that it is a mixed breed, produced between the zebra and wild horse. False ideas are, in my opinion, entertained in Europe respecting the numerous supposed mixed breeds of desert countries. It is believed that nothing there is more common; but this is certainly a very great error. Busson himself, convinced of their multiplication in Africa, and endeavouring to explain the causes, ascribes it to the heat of the climate; which rendering springs scarce, and giving occasion sometimes to animals of different species to assemble around water at the same time, favours such extraordinary copulations. By assertions like

these, we may distinguish theories formed in the closet. A naturalist who has travelled will be very cautious of hazarding them; and experience will teach him how much the savage differs from the domestic animal in its appetite for procreation.

The quagga is not in reality, and cannot be engendered between a wild horse and the zebra; for there are not wild horses indigenous in the southern part of Africa. The horses seen there at present have been carried hither from Europe; but these never stray from the colonies, and none ever advanced, before mine, to the twenty-fifth degree of latitude, where there are both quaggas and zebras. Besides, if that animal were a bastard breed of the zebra, the young ones, while suckled by the mothers, would be seen following them in the herds of zebras: but this has never been observed; and the herds of both species have as little intercourse as the different herds of antelopes.

I have often seen, in the plains, herds of zebras and herds of quaggas at the same time, but I always saw them separate. To all these proofs I shall add that, before European horses were introduced at the Cape, the quagga existed there, and was known to the natives. This animal is much smaller than the zebra; and its cry has a perfect resemblance to the barking of a dog. With regard to that of the zebra, it is exactly like the sound of a stone sliding on ice, after being thrown with great force.

Disappointed in my hopes of getting near enough to shoot some of these isabella-coloured wild asses, notwithstanding the fatigue and trouble to which I subjected myself, I made amends for the loss by attacking the birds without number presented by this country ... ₄

In the early 1800s, T Phillips also described an encounter with quaggas ...

Our day was fast waning, and we were very desirous of reaching Graham's Town in good time; the road was stony, and the country not so picturesque. Some Hottentots passed us with a young quagga, which they had just succeeded in catching for a gentleman in the neighbourhood. The Hottentots gallop after a herd, separate the young one, which they drive into the bush, then dismount, and take hold of it around the neck, till the herd have disappeared; they then mount their horses, and the little animal follows without being fastened or led: they have not the strength to be made serviceable. The quagga is a species of zebra; striped like it on the neck, but it also resembles the ass; we passed some herds of them, fifty or sixty together.

In the face of so many varying descriptions, it is hardly surprising that zoologists were unable to agree as to whether the quagga was a species or a subspecies. At first it was given the scientific name *Equus quagga*, and the plains zebra, *Equus burchellii*, but because the plains zebra is a widely distributed species and shows a great deal of geographical and individual variation, the two forms were often confused. The situation was further complicated by the fact that although the quagga became extinct, the two names were retained by some scientists.

In fact, the quagga, which it was later established was a subspecies of the plains zebra, was named first, its name taking precedence. All plains zebra, become *Equus quagga* and not *Equus burchellii*. However, to differentiate between the subspecies a third name is added and the quagga more properly becomes *Equus quagga quagga* and the plains zebra of the northern parts

become *Equus quagga antiquorum*, *Equus quagga selousi*, and so on. The original Burchell's zebra, which should be known as *Equus quagga burchellii*, has been extinct since 1910.

THE OLDER THE BETTER

Cape Town taxidermist, Reinhold Rau, while remounting a quagga foal for the South African Museum in 1969, discovered fragments of fleshy tissue and blood vessels adhering to the skin. Although the animal had died more than a century before, the age of the specimen was a definite advantage as tanning

Reinhold Rau, who collected the quagga tissue samples in which DNA proteins had survived.

methods used on skins at that time – unlike modern treatments – did not destroy or chemically alter the molecular structure of the biological tissue.

Rau, who was aware of the advances made in the field of DNA research and dreamt that it may one day be possible to re-breed the quagga, carefully removed and kept the fragments of tissue in the hope that they would be of interest to molecular biologists. At that time he could not find a scientist willing

to work on the project. In 1979, while Rau was on holiday in West Germany, he was asked by the curators of the Naturhistorisches Museum at Mainz if he would be prepared to attempt the restoration and remounting of two quaggas and a Burchell's zebra. Shortly afterwards, Rau was granted leave by the South African Museum and returned to Germany to undertake the task.

He completed the work in July 1981 and returned to Cape Town, bringing with him the remains of a quagga foetus which had been badly burnt during an air-raid in the Second World War. A number of carefully labelled tissue fragments which he removed from the quagga skins during the remounting process are kept at the Naturhistorisches Museum at Mainz. The quagga foetus was subsequently restored by Rau, exhibited for a short period at the South African Museum, then flown back for display in Mainz.

During this period, Reinhold Rau was approached by Dr Oliver Ryder of the Research Department of the Zoological Society of San Diego, California, USA, with regard to obtaining blood and tissue samples of living zebras for cytological tests. When Rau mentioned that he had carefully preserved samples of quagga tissue, Ryder immediately offered to analyze the material. With the co-operation of the South African Museum and the Naturhistorisches Museum in Mainz, tissue samples from three quaggas and one true Burchell's zebra were sent to Dr Ryder in California.

It was subsequently proved that some of the original DNA proteins had indeed survived in the samples.

Preliminary studies by Dr Ryder indicated that proteins could be obtained from the tissue samples. An attempt was then made to extract the genetic coding substance DNA from the cells of the 140-year-old Mainz material.

A small piece of dried muscle and connective tissue was treated with detergents and enzymes to release DNA and, following this, Dr Ryder successfully extracted the almost unbelievably minute quantity of one one-hundred-millionth of a gram of DNA. At this stage, however, it was uncertain whether the DNA had come from fungal or bacterial contamination of the quagga skin. The DNA was tested against that from Hartmann's mountain zebra and found to be similar. On 4 May 1983, Dr Ryder wrote to Rau, 'So now we have pieces of the genes of the extinct quagga!'

After this material was cloned to obtain workable quantities of genetic material, comparisons were made between the quagga genes and those of other zebra species. It was proved that the quagga was one of the subspecies of the plains zebra and not a separate species altogether. This revelation later proved highly significant, as it meant that the gene pool of the quagga still existed.

RESURRECTING THE QUAGGA

The only remains of the once-abundant quagga are 23 skins (mounted in more-or-less-life-like postures), seven skeletons, some skulls and foot bones – all of which are housed in museums around the world, but mainly in Europe – and the accounts and illustrations of early travellers to the region.

For many years a debate raged in academic and non-academic circles on the advisability of attempting to 're-breed' the quagga through a selective breeding programme. Although individual specimens of the plains zebra exhibited quagga-like features, such as a lack of striping on the legs and their brownish colour (particularly in Zululand and the Etosha game reserve in Namibia), many scientists were against the idea in principle because they believed the quagga was a separate species of zebra and could not, as a result, be 're-created'. It was argued that any animal produced by a selective breeding process would merely look like the quagga but bear no true genetic relationship to the extinct animal.

Three groups of molecular biologists however, working independently in the United States and using different microbiological methods, have proved conclusively that the quagga and plains zebra belong to the same species and that the quagga was merely a sub-species. This is of paramount importance as it means that the original gene-pool necessary to re-breed the quagga – which was only identifiable because of its distinctive coat pattern – still exists in the plains zebra population but is merely dispersed and diluted. Given that there is no evidence to suggest that the quagga displayed any habitat adaptations or other characteristics distinguishing it from the plains zebra, it is considered possible to select those genes through a controlled breeding programme and reconstitute the quagga. Any animal created in this way would be, in every sense, a 'true' quagga.

THE QUAGGA PROJECT

During March 1986, a committee of leading scientists from the South African Museum, the Universities of Cape Town and Stellenbosch and the Department of Nature Conservation, was formed to

Reina, a first-generation lesser-striped zebra, at the Vrolijkheid Nature Conservation Station.

supervise and control a programme designed to re-breed the quagga. One year later, nine carefully chosen zebras were captured at Etosha and transported to the Vrolijkheid Nature Conservation Station near Robertson. In November 1988, four more zebras – this time from Zululand in Natal – were introduced to the breeding stock. The first foal was born in December of the same year.

At the Vrolijkheid Nature Conservation Station a series of enclosures separate the animals into selected breeding groups. Details of each animal in the programme, matings, births and other relevant information are carefully recorded, making it possible to trace the genetic history of each animal and find the most suitable pairings. There are plans to perform embryo transplantations into surrogates (donkey, horse, zebra) and artificial insemination.

A similar breeding programme conducted in Europe over recent years led to the re-introduction of the Mongolian wild horse (Przewalski's horse). Let us hope that a similar story of success can be achieved in this country.

THE PORTHOLE MURDER
Death on the high seas

On the night of 17 October 1947, a young up-and-coming actress, Gay Gibson, was pushed through the porthole of her cabin by James Camb, a steward on the ship on which she was sailing from Cape Town to Southampton. Camb, who admitted having sex with Gay Gibson but denied killing her, was charged with murder.

Was justice done? Or was James Camb, who admitted disposing of her body, guilty only of stupidity and *not* murder?

At 9.57 a.m. today Mr HH Knight, Chief Steward, reported to the Master that a first class lady passenger from Cabin 126 named Miss Eileen Gibson could not be found. She had failed to appear in the Dining Saloon for breakfast. The Master proceeded immediately to check that an efficient search had been conducted. This enquiry was held in the presence of the Chief Officer and the Purser and the Chief Steward. At 10.20 a.m. being satisfied that Miss Gibson was not on board the Master gave orders for the ship's course to be reversed. ₁

At 4 o'clock on the afternoon of 10 October 1947, the *Durban Castle* left Cape Town harbour en route to Southampton. One of the 57 first class passengers on board was the budding young theatre star, Eileen Isabella Ronnie Gibson, better known to her audiences as Gay Gibson. The promenade-deck (first class passenger leisure area) steward on the same voyage was a popular, good-looking young man named James Camb. Allegedly, Camb had an eye for beautiful women and

Above: The Durban Castle.

Right: Gay Gibson, who was pushed through the porthole of her cabin by James Camb.

Eileen Gibson, he would later suggest, was not averse to his advances. One week into the voyage, she invited him to her cabin just before midnight and, according to Camb, during a bout of enthusiastic love-making, she suffered heart failure. In a futile attempt to protect his job, he pushed her body through the cabin's porthole and then denied all knowledge of the affair. Unfortunately for him, however, another member of the crew knew exactly where he had been that night.

Eileen Gibson was never seen again and Camb was subsequently charged with her murder. The prosecution alleged that she had been raped and murdered – but there was always the possibility she had indeed died of 'heart failure' as Camb maintained. Would a modern jury trying the case have come to the same conclusion as the one in 1948, namely that man was naturally the predator and woman the prey? Given this perception, is it so surprising that the jury found that James Camb had forced himself upon an innocent and susceptible young woman and then killed her to protect himself?

Times have changed, and there is a distinct possibility that a present day jury would come to a completely different conclusion when presented with the facts of this case.

The *Durban Castle* arrived at Cowes Road off the Isle of Wight on the night of Friday 24 October. Camb had been under suspicion of murder by the police, who knew from one of the other crew members of his visit to Miss Gibson's cabin on the night she disappeared. When Camb was first questioned, after the ship docked, he lied about his relationship with her. A day later he was

James Camb, who was found guilty of the unlawful disposal of Gay Gibson's body. But did he murder her?

charged with the murder of Gay Gibson and made a full confession. But, he added, her death was entirely accidental – he hadn't murdered her.

Following a brief investigation, Camb's murder trial began on 18 March 1948. The accused, who admitted that he had pushed Eileen Gibson's body through the porthole, claimed that she had died 'naturally' during sexual intercourse. Certainly, there seemed to be no overt sign of a struggle, either in the cabin or on Camb himself. He had scratches over the back of his right shoulder, which could possibly have been inflicted by Miss Gibson during their love-making, scratches on his collar-bone that he claimed were caused by towelling himself too vigorously, and scratches above his right wrist which one of the pathologists, Dr Denis Hocking, described as 'of intriguing interest'.

These wrist scratches, the prosecution would argue, were caused by Eileen Gibson as she attempted to pull away his arms as he strangled her. The defence maintained they were caused by the deceased's death spasm. Both explanations were reasonable. The defence also attempted to prove that Eileen Gibson was little short of promiscuous, but this suggestion was strenuously denied by her mother, who maintained that her daughter was both chaste and innocent – a paragon of virtue.

Given the absence of a body and the limited forensic evidence available, the pathologists of the case disagreed over whether Eileen Gibson had died of heart failure or strangulation, although they did agree that she was most probably dead when James Camb pushed her through the porthole.

According to Camb's testimony, Eileen Gibson had invited him to her cabin after he had made a half-joking remark about bringing her a drink, and when he went to visit her that night, she greeted him at the door wearing only a dressing gown and nothing underneath. Shortly after he arrived, they got into bed and started making love. Then 'suddenly she heaved under me as though she was taking a deep breath ... her body stiffened for a fraction of a second and then relaxed completely limp ... one eye just slightly open'.[2] Realizing that she was dead, he panicked and pushed her body through the porthole.

His crime, in other words, amounted to the unlawful disposal of a body, not murder, and was not a capital offence.

The judge, Sir Malcolm Hilbery, appeared to take a dim view of this explanation and seemed unable to appreciate that a single woman – particularly one travelling first class – could willingly invite a handsome steward into her cabin for the sole purpose of sex. Indeed, one can argue that his summing-up, before the jury retired to consider their verdict, all-but assured James

Camb's conviction. But the year was 1948 and sex was neither a subject openly discussed by polite society, nor something one lingered over in a public courtroom. In the minds of some people it was inconceivable that a respectable young lady – and who was to say Eileen Gibson was not respectable since a number of attempts to introduce evidence to the contrary were stifled – would even contemplate such a liaison as James Camb had suggested.

It took the jury less than an hour to return a verdict of guilty and James Camb was sentenced to death. However, he was later reprieved by a House of Commons vote which suspended the death penalty was and finally released in 1978, suffering from a heart condition. He died in Leeds in July 1979.

The bizarre nature of the 'porthole murder case' has always elicited a great deal of public interest. But was justice done? James Camb's description of events is certainly plausible and a number of rumours suggesting that Eileen Gibson had had sex with a number of men prior to meeting Camb, surfaced only after the trial. It is certainly not beyond the realms of possibility that the entire affair occurred entirely as James Camb had described – indeed, some would argue that some of the 'sensitive' aspects of the trial were suppressed or, at the very least, not fully explored. If James Camb took the stand today, perhaps the jury would return an entirely different verdict.

But we are still left with an intriguing and unexplained mystery. Was Gay Gibson brutally murdered and her body callously disposed of by her killer in an attempt to protect his identity, as the jury concluded, or was James Camb the innocent victim of a narrow-minded society focused on protecting the somewhat tarnished reputation of a promiscuous young woman?

Right: Gay Gibson's cabin and the porthole through which her body was pushed.

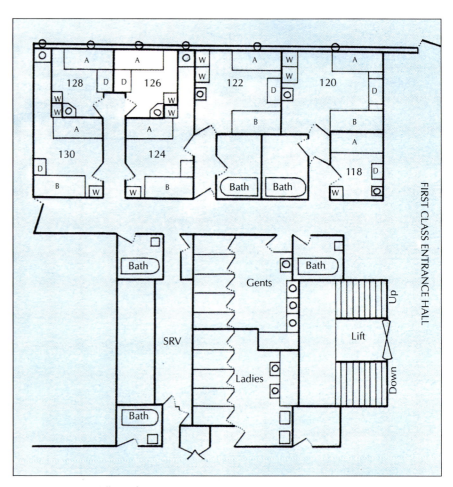

Above: A diagram of Cabin 126 and adjoining cabins.

98

WHALE AND DOLPHIN STRANDINGS
Why do they occur?

Almost since anyone can remember, whale and dolphin strandings have been known to occur throughout the world. Indeed, it is probably as a result of strandings that man first came to realize that these creatures could be used for food and oil. We know, for example, that whale oil was stored by the Khoisan and was greatly prized as a body oil and for other purposes.

Stranding is the most common and mysterious of cetacean behaviour and appears to affect all species, at any location, and at any stage of life; and they occur more frequently than most people suspect. Strandings, however, are not suicides and there is no reason to believe that mass stranding is nature's method of population control. Unfortunately, despite considerable scientific research, investigators are no closer to understanding or explaining this phenomenon, although there is no lack of theories.

Whales and dolphins are extremely advanced mammals. Though sea creatures, they are air-breathing, warm-blooded, give birth to live young (which the mother suckles) are able to communicate across vast ocean distances, live their lives entirely in water – sometimes at great depths, and have fascinated man for thousands of years. As far back as 335 BC, the renowned Greek philosopher, Aristotle, wrote authoritatively about the common dolphin in his book *Historia Animalium* ...[1]

What causes groundings and strandings? Despite several scientific investigations undertaken in recent years, no-one has been able to pin-point a conclusive answer.

All these creatures which have a blowhole breathe and inhale air; and the dolphin has been observed while asleep with a muzzle above the water, and it snores in its sleep. The dolphin and phocaena give milk and suckle their young. They also receive their young into themselves. The growth of the young dolphins is rapid, for they attain their full size in ten years. The female is pregnant for ten months. The dolphin produces her young in the summertime, and at no other season, they also seem to disappear for thirty days during the season of the dog-star. The young follow their dam for a long while and it is an animal which is attached to its offspring. It lives many years; for some have been known to live twenty five or thirty years; for fishermen have marked them by cutting their tails then giving them their liberty. In this way their age was known.

GROUNDING OR STRANDING?

There is a distinction between 'grounding' and 'stranding'. 'Grounding' occurs when a whale or dolphin intentionally or unintentionally becomes grounded, gets into difficulty and is unable to move

because the water is too shallow. What often happens is that the animal, while waiting to be refloated, turns broadside to the beach, is rolled over and disorientated by incoming waves. As long as the whale or dolphin is surrounded by water it is regarded as 'grounded'. Only after it has been left high and dry – usually as a result of the receding tide – is it termed 'stranded'.

Several research projects have shown that many of the whales and dolphins which beach themselves are either sick or injured and it has been proposed that some may have come inshore to shallower water, thereby decreasing the risk of drowning, to rest and recuperate. However, this does not explain mass strandings where sometimes hundreds of whales and dolphins are involved.

Although 'grounding' always precedes 'stranding' it does not always follow that a grounded animal becomes stranded. The incoming tide could enable the animal to refloat itself, but whale experts have no idea how frequently whales or dolphins ground themselves, accidentally or intentionally, and then get out to sea again.

HERD STRANDINGS

The term 'mass stranding' or, more correctly, 'herd stranding' is used to describe the situation where four or more animals become beached at the same time. Again, no-one fully understands why this happens. Most, if not all of the animals found, appear to have been in good health and, often, their stomachs are found to be empty.

Some say the answer to this mystery could be that a single or 'key' animal, swimming a short distance from the main herd, becomes preoccupied or distracted, inadvertently swims too close to shore, accidentally becomes grounded and, while lying on its side, draws in

other members of the herd with its distress calls. It is known that cetaceans 'speak' to each other using a sophisticated system of communication and that they are very 'social' animals, so it is not unreasonable to assume that they help each other in times of danger or difficulty. It may be that a domino effect follows, whereby one by one others are drawn inshore.

Several strandings of Risso's dolphins have been recorded. These dolphins were found at St Helena Bay, on the Cape's west coast.

There is some evidence from investigations conducted in New Zealand by, among others, the internationally recognized whale and dolphin expert, Frank Robson, to suggest that pelagic (deep water) species of whales and dolphins are more inclined to strand than others which habitually live closer to shore. There is speculation that they may be more prone to getting into difficulty and becoming disoriented when they come close to the land. The possibility also exists that some grounded animals have been led into danger by sick or senile herd leaders. Alternatively, whales, which clearly use sound for communication and possibly as a kind of sonar for navigation, may have become lost or disorientated as a result of unusual or unexpected 'echoes' given off by inshore obstacles. However, this does not explain why whales which have been refloated, often strand themselves on the same beach again and again.

FACTS AND FALLACIES

It has been suggested by some researchers that whales and dolphins which become grounded are attempting to follow ancient or traditional migratory routes which have been interfered with in some way by man. The noise and activity associated with coastal towns and cities, for example, may have led migrating herds to bypass the area, causing them to swim through 'uncharted', and possibly more hazardous waters. But the facts fail to support this hypothesis as a number of groundings have occurred beneath cliffs or in areas that have remained unchanged for many years.

There is little evidence to suggest that weather conditions play any part in groundings since they have been known to occur during both calm and stormy conditions. The one exception, however, would appear to be migrating bachelor herds which for some reason have difficulty compensating for drift. There is speculation that they may get into difficulties, particularly if there is a strong on-shore gale driving them landwards.

It may be possible to correlate strandings with the phases of the moon, severe weather, inclement tides, magnetic storms, gently-sloping sandy beaches (where echoes are not returned) and many other physical factors – but one should not forget that whales and dolphins are intelligent creatures which can become lost and confused, take wrong turns and make bad decisions.

Cetaceans appear to understand their predicament and often display more intelligence than they are credited for. Nan Rice of the Dolphin Action and Protection Group, for example, believes that cetaceans co-operate with their rescuers, 'seem to know what we want them to do – before we do anything' and 'sense somehow what our next move will be'. Robson also maintains that cetaceans have a unique aptitude to understand the state of mind of their rescuers and their intentions.

Despite extensive scientific study, a number of misconceptions persist. For example, a whale or dolphin which is righted after lying beached on its side often swims seawards hesitantly, circles to shore and may beach again. This can happen a number of times and observers often think the animal has a suicidal tendency. The fact is, however, that when cetaceans are forced to lie on their sides, their internal balance mechanism is disturbed, making it impossible to swim in a straight line. The experience of seasoned rescuers indicates that on occasions where a whale or dolphin regains its equilibrium, it swims out to sea, rejoins its herd, apparently unaffected by the ordeal.

WHAT CAUSES STRANDINGS?

It is important to remember that some of the whales and dolphins found along the coast have died at sea and been brought ashore with the tide. Sometimes young and sickly animals may have been abandoned by their mothers; others may have been injured, drowned in nets or affected by pollution – particularly oil pollution as all cetaceans have to come to the surface to breathe.

An investigation conducted on dolphins in 1972 by SH Ridgeway and MD Dailey [2] indicated that stranded animals had an extremely high incidence of brain lesions caused by a trematode worm. In a study by William Walker [3] of 43 cetaceans stranded in California in 1981, postmortems showed that most of the stranded animals were suffering from parasitic infections.

It was thought that the effects of these infestations on the inner ear and brain were the main cause for the strandings, as they were likely to have affected either the balance mechanism and/or the sonar ability of the animal.

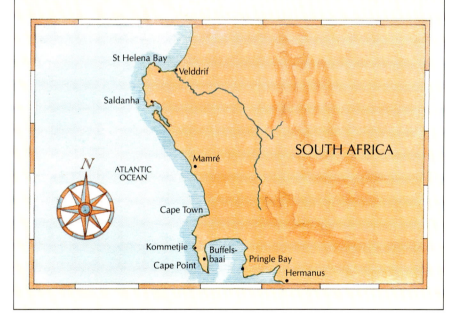

Dr M Klinowska of Cambridge University in England, has theorized that toothed whales navigate using geomagnetic topography; in other words, by making use of the earth's geomagnetic fields. Dr Klinowska believes that in certain areas these geomagnetic fields are distorted by rock deposits containing minerals with magnetic properties such as iron. Where this happens, geomagnetic 'anomalies' mislead the whales and subsequently create 'whale traps'. But there is insufficient evidence at present to confirm or disprove this theory.

Despite considerable investigation, we do not appear to be close to finding the reason why whales and dolphins strand, although there has been some progress made in attempting to understand this disturbing phenomenon. Possibly, there is no single or simple reason to explain this strange behaviour.

UFOs
Have we been visited from outer space?

It has been estimated that the number of stars in the cosmos is in the region of ten billion trillion. Given such compelling numbers, it is unlikely that 'Earthlings' are the only intelligent life form in existence. Indeed, perhaps the question one should ask is not 'Is there other intelligent life in the universe?' but rather, 'Have any of these intelligent life forms visited our planet?'

The earth is situated in an almost forgotten corner of the cosmos, vast enough to be almost beyond comprehension. Indeed, inter-galactic distances are so immense, it is impossible to talk of them using conventional terrestrial units of distance. Instead, scientists measure distance in light-years. A light-year is the distance a beam of light travelling at 186 miles per *second*, can cover in one year.

There are a number of South Africans who would argue that not only have intelligent alien life forms visited our planet, they have also visited our country. Marco Corrado, a spokesperson for the South African UFO Society, based in Pretoria, claimed in an article published in *Fair Lady* magazine in March 1993, that he was receiving an average of three calls a day reporting sightings. There are also oft-repeated allegations that governments across the world are continually squashing reports and research findings, presumably to avoid outbreaks of public panic.

Despite all this interest, however, the fact remains that there are very few well-documented UFO sightings and some of the accounts that do reach the newspaper headlines can sometimes appear to border on the ludicrous.

But perhaps we should not be too hasty in our judgments ...

Above: The comet of 1843, drawn by CP Smyth.

Below: A portrait of Akon, Elizabeth Klarer's lover from the planet Meton, painted according to her directions.

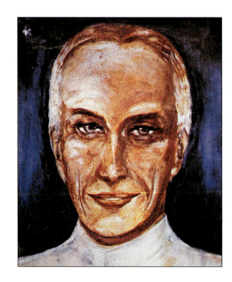

THE ELIZABETH KLARER STORY – CONTACT WITH ALIENS?

Without a doubt, South Africa's most celebrated UFOlogist is Elizabeth Klarer who, in 1956, claimed to have begun a life-long love affair with an astrophysicist by the name of Akon, from the planet Meton. She maintains that she visited Meton where she gave birth to a son, Ayling, and for the last twenty years has been waiting for Akon to return. Although doubted, ridiculed and scorned over the years, she has never changed her account.

Elizabeth Klarer, who was born in Natal and grew up on a farm in the Drakensberg mountains, recalls knowing that there were 'people in the sky' even at the age of three. Her first contact with alien intelligence, however, occurred when she was about seven years old ...

Just after sunset, she and her sister saw an enormous orange-red ball blazing its way across the sky. While the two girls were looking at it in wonder, a round metallic-like object appeared out of nowhere, circled the orange-red coloured ball three times and appeared to deflect it from its collision course with Earth.

Elizabeth's parents explained the phenomenon by suggesting that the metallic thing had been a meteor or meteorite.

'I never forgot it,' she says. 'It triggered off my interest in the sky ...' [1]

This first sighting of what Elizabeth believed was an alien spaceship had a profound effect on her. She began to go off alone whenever she could in the hope of seeing it again – her favourite spot being the summit of a hill which gave a commanding view of the area.

Elizabeth went on to study music in Florence, Italy, and later moved to England to further her studies at Trinity College in London. Driven by her fascination with the sky, however, she later changed courses and enrolled for a four-year diploma course in meteorology at Cambridge. Up to and during the Second World War, Elizabeth and her first husband, Captain Philips, a test pilot for De Havilland, lived in Hatfield, England, at De Havilland's experimental station, although they visited South Africa a number of times.

Elizabeth's second UFO experience occurred one evening in 1937 while she and her husband were flying from Durban to Johannesburg. They had just taken off when she looked to the east and saw what appeared to be a blue-white sphere heading directly for them. The sphere was an enormous circular spacecraft. Light was streaming from its many portholes and underneath, it was illuminated by a variety of flashing colours. As the spacecraft drew near, its colour darkened from blue-white to golden; it came very close, turned, and for a short while followed a parallel course, buffeting their small aircraft with the turbulence it created in the air. Then, without warning, the alien craft veered away, flying over them and disappeared as swiftly as it had appeared.

THE SPACECRAFT RETURNS

After the war, Elizabeth divorced Captain Philips, remarried and gave birth to a son. Although they lived in Johannesburg, Elizabeth returned to Natal regularly during the holidays. It was during the Christmas period in 1954 that she first saw the alien she would later refer to as Akon.

At about ten o'clock in the morning, the day after Boxing Day, Elizabeth heard some of the farm workers making a fuss and pointing to the sky. There was a brilliant flash of light in the clouds and an immense disc-like spacecraft, about

18 metres in diameter, descended from the sky and hovered about four metres from the ground near to where she was standing. There was a humming sound coming from the spacecraft and its tremendous displacement flattened the grass beneath it. At first the ship was too bright to look at but when her eyes

adjusted to the glare she was able to make out some of its features. It was smooth and shiny; its centre section was dome-shaped and around this was a flat rotating skirt. Along the side there were three portholes, and behind one of them was a humanoid figure staring at her. The figure, which was standing with his

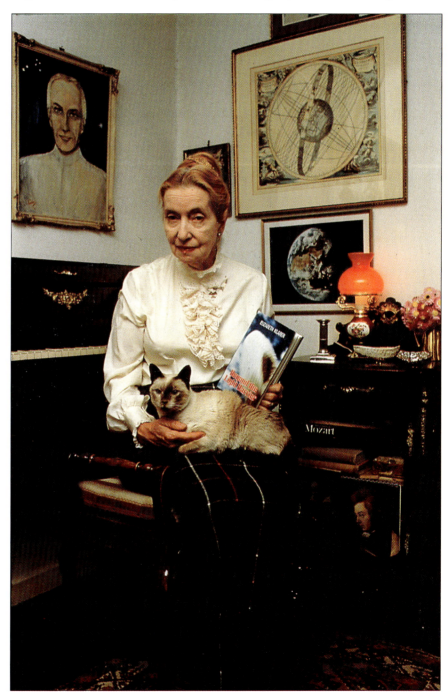

Elizabeth Klarer

arms folded across his chest, 'had a thin, ascetic face, with an aquiline nose and high cheekbones. He was a handsome man and there was a hypnotic attraction about his eyes ...' ₂ After a few moments, there was a tremendous increase in air pressure, the skirt of the ship started spinning and the spacecraft rose into the air and flew off at a tremendous speed.

CLOSE ENCOUNTERS

During the Easter holidays of 1956, which Elizabeth spent with her children in Natal, she had a compulsion to return to what she now called 'Flying Saucer Hill'. But as she drove to the farm she felt a strange, unexplained nervousness. There had been a spate of reported sightings of flying saucers in the newspapers and she was somehow certain that the figure she had seen before would return.

When she went to Flying Saucer Hill, the same spacecraft she had seen previously was resting in a dip on the hill's summit – only this time the figure was standing on the ground, next to the craft, near an open doorway. He was almost two metres tall and was wearing a cream coloured one-piece garment which had close-fitting cuffs at the ankles, wrists and neck. His hair was long and white at the temples.

'I ran straight into his arms and he said in perfect English, "You are not afraid this time". It was such a lovely voice, like a caress, soft, modulated, natural. I knew he had to be gentle and understanding.' ₃

He then led Elizabeth into the spacecraft and, once they were inside, a second figure, which appeared to be sitting at a control console, pressed a button and the doorway closed soundlessly behind them. The room was large with shiny curved walls. The red carpet-type material on the floor was soft and springy. Light seemed to come from the walls and ceiling, and the atmosphere contained a high percentage of oxygen. In the centre of the control room stood a large moon-shaped lens flanked by two benches. Elizabeth was guided to one of these seats and invited to sit down. She felt a slight vibration in the floor and realized that the spacecraft was moving, but when she went to look through one of the portholes she saw that it had closed and fused perfectly with the wall.

The tall figure, the one who had greeted her outside the spacecraft, said that his name was Akon, and explained to her that she was to sit at one of the benches and look out through the viewing lens. Elizabeth followed his instruc-

Some of the artifacts collected by Elizabeth Klarer during her visit to Meton.

tions and found herself awe-struck by the magnificent view she was afforded in every direction. Akon merely stood looking at her with a smile on his face.

The spacecraft climbed swiftly through the atmosphere and at a height of approximately 1 600 kilometres (according to Akon) a larger vessel came into view. Akon explained that it was a scientific survey ship known as the Mothership, and that he was an astrophysicist with the task of moving from one solar system to another to observe variable stars and determine whether they could be controlled. The spacecraft

drew alongside the mothership and the two were connected by an 'expanding funnel'. The mothership was filled with men and women dressed in clothing similar to that worn by Akon. On board, Elizabeth was shown a film of the visitors' home planet, Meton, which orbited the star, Proxima Centauri. The film also included shots of Durban's promenade and she was amazed because the conversations of the people in frame could be heard. She was given a tour of the vessel which included a visit to an enormous room with blue walls – a form of park with trees, plants and flowers.

The visitors' home planet, essentially an ocean world dotted with mountainous islands, was a virtual utopia bereft of civil strife. There were no continents, big cities or pollution, and the inhabitants lived in flat-roofed houses (to accommodate the small aircraft they used for personal travel) amongst the trees and spoke a language which sounded similar to Latin. The Metons also had the ability to communicate telepathically.

Elizabeth was offered food – salads, fruits, oatcakes and fruit juice – and discovered that the Metons were vegetarians and grew food on the ship using a system similar to hydroponics.

Akon's brother, who commanded the mothership, came to meet Elizabeth, and she learnt that the Metons could move easily between planets and regularly travelled from one solar system to another. They had not, however, mastered the problems of crossing the immense distances involved in inter-galactic travel.

When the time came for Elizabeth to return to Earth she felt extremely unhappy. She was very close to Akon, and all the more so when he revealed that he had been watching her since she was seven years old.

Elizabeth was returned to her farmhouse a few hours later. She went back to Johannesburg, excited and emotional following her experiences in Natal – she could not get Akon out of her mind. During the months that followed, she returned to Flying Saucer Hill on a number of occasions to meet him.

Eventually, Akon explained to her that the people of Meton needed new blood to revitalize the race, and that she had been chosen as a subject for one of their 'breeding experiments'. Shortly afterwards, Elizabeth, who was 47 at the time, became pregnant.

She stayed with her sister on the farm in the Drakensberg during much of her pregnancy, because Akon maintained that it was a healthy environment for his son to develop in. But when the time came for the child to be born, he said he would return to take her to Meton, because his son '... cannot be born on an alien planet where the time vibratory is too slow'. [4] (Elizabeth claims that Akon knew that she would give birth to a male child because he had chosen the time of mating when she was in the right condition to ensure this, although she could not elaborate on exactly how this could be deduced.)

When Elizabeth knew that the time had come for her to give birth, she went to Flying Saucer Hill and waited for Akon to arrive. Soon after she boarded, the spacecraft began to rise, slowly at first so that Elizabeth's body could adapt to the electrical gravity within the ship. Once outside the earth's atmosphere, she felt a tingling sensation as the ship 'passed from one dimension to another' [5] and, moments later she was looking down on Meton. When they landed, Akon's mother and Pleia, his brother's mate, were waiting to greet them. Pleia, a beautiful woman with golden eyes, high cheekbones and browny-gold hair, was wearing a kaftan-like garment of silk and

led them into a nearby house. They went down a spiral staircase, through the top floor where the storerooms were situated, past bedrooms on the middle floor, to a large living room on the lowest level. Pleia brought refreshments, including a type of herbal tea which was to regulate Elizabeth's heartbeat.

Akon then took Elizabeth to see some tame white horses grazing nearby, and they went riding together. She used the mane to stay on and was able to guide the animal through mind control. (Elizabeth is convinced that the people of Meton brought horses to Earth when they first colonized the planet and that Arabic horses are descendants of this breed.) Akon and Elizabeth were treated

by Pleia and his brother to a picnic in the shadow of a nearby mountain. Elizabeth was then informed by Pleia that it was time for her to give birth.

Elizabeth stayed on Meton for another four months until Ayling matured, but was eventually forced to return to Earth. Not only was her heart being weakened by the different vibratory pulse rate of Meton, but she also had a mission to tell other people of her experiences.

The people of Meton are apparently concerned by the rampant materialism seen on Earth and the apathy with which most Earthlings regard nature. They believe that man's indifference not only contributes to the destruction of the environment, but also retards spiritual development. Unless fundamental changes take place, they fear that planet Earth is heading for disaster.

The last time Elizabeth Klarer physically saw Akon was in 1963, although she claims to have had a number of telepathic contacts with him since then.

There have been numerous reported sightings of UFOs, and some people claim to have captured the event on film. Often the authenticity of such photographs can be neither proved nor disproved.

In an interview with *Fair Lady* magazine in 1978, she said that Akon was on a mission for his people and would return for her once the assignment was complete, probably sometime after 1982. At the time of writing, she is still waiting.

SIGHTINGS IN SOUTHERN AFRICA

UFOs in one form or another are sighted more frequently than most people imagine. Of course, many so-called UFO sightings can be explained as completely normal astronomical phenomena. However, there remains a number of incidents for which there is simply no scientific explanation available ...

In June 1972, Bennie Smit, a businessman from East London, was on holiday with his family at his farm, Braeside, in Fort Beaufort, when he was summoned to a nearby reservoir by one of his labourers, Boer de Klerk.

De Klerk was highly agitated – an hour earlier he had noticed smoke in the vicinity of some nearby rocks; then there had been an eruption of fire and a ball of flame had suddenly emerged.

Smit accompanied De Klerk to the reservoir and saw a 'fiery red ball hovering at tree-top level and the bush seemed to glow red. It was approximately 76 cm across, with flames shooting out. As I watched it, it turned from bright red to dark green and then to a yellowish white.' [6]

Alarmed by what he had seen, Smit returned to the farm to telephone the Fort Beaufort police and to collect his rifle. An hour and a half later, Warrant Officer PR Van Rensburg and Sergeant PC Kitching arrived at the scene. The object, which was constantly changing colour, moved in and out of the bushes and Smit and Sergeant Kitching began firing at it, hitting it at least once – without any visible effect. Eventually, the object made a loud whirring noise, cut a path through the foliage and vanished

into thick bush. Circular 'footprints' were found in the area where the object was last seen, but all the soil tests that were conducted to establish whether any alien substances were present, proved negative.

At first glimpse, this appears to be a photograph of a flying saucer. However, it is the result of photographic manipulation and is, in fact, an image of a hubcap superimposed on an image of Cape Town.

Further sightings of the flying object were made in the area and Smit confirmed that a photograph of a UFO which had been seen in Port Elizabeth a week later, closely resembled the craft which he and six other people had watched that morning.

DANIE VAN GRAAN: LOXTON – JULY 1975

Danie van Graan left his house and went to explore a local kraal following reports of UFOs in the vicinity. The kraal itself was hidden from the village by a three-metre high bank and it was not until he reached the top of this bank that he could see the aluminium roof of what he first took to be a caravan. The 'caravan' was about 200 metres away and it wasn't until he got much closer that he realized that it was in fact an oval-shaped machine of some sort with four people moving around inside.

He described the visitors as very small – about one and a half metres tall – pale and unhealthy looking. They wore cream-coloured coveralls, had fair hair, slanting eyes, high cheekbones and sharp chins. He managed to get within a few metres of the shape before they reacted to his presence. A beam of brilliant light shot out of the craft and temporarily disoriented him, forcing him to step back. The craft lifted off and disappeared into the sky at a tremendous speed.

Danie's account was partially supported by one of his neighbours who reported hearing what sounded like a helicopter at the time of the sighting. Danie, who at first thought he had come across 'Russians', could not explain what he had seen and consequently treated the whole subject with a degree of circumspection.

Although there *were* some unexplained markings and footprints on the ground at the site where the spacecraft had been seen, there was no conclusive physical proof that Loxton had been visited by aliens.

GROENDAL NATURE RESERVE: 2 OCTOBER 1978

On Sunday, 1 October 1978, four boys – Peter Simpson (16), Jannie Bezuidenhout (15), Hugo Ferreira (12) and Joe Perino (13) – embarked on a hike in the Groendal Reserve just outside Uitenhage in the Eastern Cape. After camping overnight, they set off early the following morning in the direction of the monument.where they had arranged to be picked up by Peter's mother at midday.

They reached the monument early and were sitting under a tree when they noticed a 'silver thing' in the trees less than a kilometre away. At first they thought it was a large stone, then noticed two men dressed in silver coveralls, going over a hill about 250 metres away. At first, the boys thought they were looking at ordinary men, even though they were wearing strange silver-foil uniforms that made them look like fire-fighters. Then the 'men' started to move uphill at a rapid rate ... without any noticeable walking movement; they appeared to glide over the ground, and did not bend forwards as one would expect a person climbing a hill to do.

The two 'men' were joined by a third with a small silver suitcase. But the man wasn't carrying the suitcase, nor did it seem to be strapped to his back or connected in any way to its owner. The three 'men' continued to walk away from the four boys, but at one stage one of them paused and looked at them.

'They moved only from the knees down,' Peter explained. 'It was almost like a fin ... then he turned to look at us. I could see then that the silver suit he wore came down over his forehead and then where his face was, that was just grey.'7

Then, the men 'disappeared', and the boys also noticed that the 'silver thing' had also gone. The incident was reported to Mr DP Zeelie, the official in charge of the Groendal Reserve. After questioning the boys for some time, Zeelie real-

Below: Peter Simpson (left) and Hugo Ferreira, two of the four boys who saw strange figures, dressed in silver, at the Groendal Nature Reserve in 1978.

ized that they had seen 'something strange'. He had also seen a 'saucer-shaped green light' in the reserve some months before – the same strange light that eighteen-year-old Johan Kleynhans had pursued through the reserve one night eleven months earlier.

In the face of considerable scepticism, the boys were reluctant to contact the police until they heard of the 'strange tracks' which some forestry workers discovered in the area the next day.

A report of the incident under the heading 'Space visitors in E Cape', appeared on the front page of the Port Elizabeth *Weekend Post* on 21 October 1978. The article began,

Reports of eerie sightings of what appeared to be a UFO and of strange beings that move by gliding over the ground and the finding of tracks in the remote Groendal Wilderness area

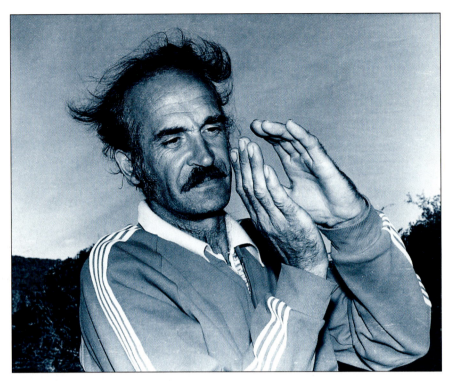

Mr Zeelie: 'A green light, shaped like this, moved across the sky and disappeared.'

near Uitenhage, have led to speculation that the region has been visited by cosmonauts from space. Investigation of the reports which at first appear to be fantastic, suggest that they cannot be casually dismissed. Extra credence is lent to the reports by the fact that they do not come from one person but from several different sources, including four schoolboys, a forest ranger and experienced bush-trackers.

The report went on to add,

> ... Mysterious tracks were found by responsible bush-trackers in the vicinity of the sighting. At least one other person has seen a 'green saucer-shaped' light over the same area, at least one other person has followed a 'strange light' in the area of the reserve. Independent reports of strange lights in the sky over Port Elizabeth were made to the Evening Post recently ....

The hill which the three 'men' had been climbing was densely covered with two-metre-high fynbos and was almost inaccessible to ordinary people. The spot where the 'silver thing' had rested was also investigated by a lecturer from the Geology Department at the University of Port Elizabeth and it was discovered that there were nine separate symmetrically-arranged impressions on the ground. Four of the impressions were oval in shape, and each had four small holes which could have been made by a tubular prong or tine. Despite a degree of initial scepticism, the researcher was later to admit that he had no explanation for the phenomenon. Furthermore, given the remoteness of the position in which the indentations were found, it was extremely unlikely that they could have been made by equipment transported through the dense bush.

LIGHTS IN THE NATAL SKY

Not all UFOs appear as shining disks, as indicated by the following account which appeared in the *Natal Mercury*.

> An unidentified object was seen in the sky off the Natal north coast early yesterday morning.
>
> A north-coast farmer woke at 2 a.m. yesterday and looked out of his window. He saw what looked like a pencil with a glowing end. He woke his wife and they both observed the object for 40 minutes as it moved across the sky in a west to east direction before apparently splitting and disappearing over the sea.
>
> The object started about halfway up the sky and disappeared about 20 degrees above sea level.
>
> The Natal Centre of the Astronomical Society of Southern Africa, to whom the event was reported, is anxious to know if there were any other observers.
>
> 'A comet was first observed in this area of the sky – about in line with the star Spica in the Constellation Corvus – last week by Jack Bennett of Pretoria, who has discovered several such bodies and given his name to them,' said Andrew Gray, Chairman of the Natal Centre yesterday. 'But it is unlikely that this is what was seen yesterday morning – it would still be too faint. If someone else observed this object, we can then work out by triangulation its position, and whether it was a small object close at hand or a large object far away,' said Mr Gray. 'If the position can be established, the US Information Office will be contacted to find out whether any of the 3 000 odd objects in space was in the vicinity at the time of the sighting,' Mr Gray added.
>
> When comet expert Mr Bennett was contacted, he agreed that it was highly unlikely that it was a comet.

JOHANNESBURG 1975

During Christmas 1975, Rhoda and a friend drove to a hilltop south of the city. Shortly after they arrived they both noticed a bright light hovering over the car. The light, which was too bright and too close to be a star, appeared to have no shape, but when the light dimmed it was possible to discern the outline of a craft of some sort. They also became aware of a barely audible hum or whine. After a short while the craft appeared to move away and Rhoda and her companion attempted to follow it in the car, but it shot off at a 30 to 40 degree angle at a tremendous speed.

The object, which Rhoda was able to draw, appeared to be dark-grey metal, was extremely large and shaped like a flattened cotton-reel, although 'probably more oval than round'.

The craft was turning all the time, not terribly fast at first but then it gathered momentum. I felt the object was ponderous, heavy. I also had the distinct impression of 'portholes' which were glowing red (like traffic-lights) ... At the end of the craft was a thin perpendicular ray of light ... yellowish-white in colour ... that remained at the rear of the craft even when it was moving. When the craft sped away it was like a ray of light, too fast to follow. The movement of the craft was like a flat spiral, each rotation taking in a little more space as it gathered speed. [8]

NOORDHOEK, CAPE TOWN

An hour or so before dawn on 14 May 1992, Nigel Espi woke up and looked out of his bedroom window to see what he first thought was a falling star. However, the 'star' slowed down, eventually stopped and then began moving towards him, though not in a straight line. He ran to fetch his mother, but by the time she arrived the object had retreated slightly. His mother thought the light was a star or a planet until she saw it move, then, thinking it might be an experimental plane of some sort, went to fetch her husband. Mr Espi, was unable to identify the object.

Nigel's sister and grandmother were also awakened. They all saw the object go behind a neighbour's house and then zig-zag far out over the sea, flashing many different coloured lights: red, yellow, blue and green. Nigel who later drew a sketch of the craft they had all seen, believed the object was circular in shape, was spinning and had a row of 'windows' around the middle. [9]

ARE WE BEING VISITED BY BEINGS FROM ANOTHER PLANET?

Of course, if intelligent beings from another solar system are visiting our planet then they possess a technical superiority which is possibly beyond our comprehension, so it would be reasonable to assume that they have the ability to keep their presence secret. It is also conceivable that such beings would wish to avoid influencing or affecting – perhaps catastrophically – our own social evolution. (Earth-bound researchers are only too aware of the dangers of disrupting the habitat of an animal species under investigation.

It would be fairly logical to assume that any off-world visitors would attempt to conceal their existence while studying us.

In response to an article about sightings of an UFO at a drive-in at Honeydew, Johannesburg in the *Sunday Times* on 9 July 1992, an anonymous spokesman from the Johannesburg planetarium voiced considerable scepticism about the whole idea of flying saucers and visitors from outer space.

'Have you ever heard of any of the professional astronomers seeing such things?' he asked.

'And believe me, we spend our time looking at the sky day and night. It is our life ...'

Nevertheless, there is a serious attempt being made by scientists across the world to establish whether other intelligent life exists in our part of the galaxy.

For a number of years radio astronomers have been engaged in a search for extraterrestrial life through the SETI programme (Search for Extraterrestrial Intelligence), and in October 1992, NASA announced that some of its equipment was to be used in the search.

Dr John Billingham, the head of the SETI progamme, explained that scientists had received radio waves matching the

Groendal Nature Reserve workers (from left to right) Alfred Pope, Cedric Kaptein and William Fire, who found strange oval-shaped footprints in the sand.

expected signature of a message from space about 60 times, but that the messages, if that is what they were, had not been confirmed as genuine contacts because they were fleeting and unverifiable.

He then went on to say that it was thought that when, or if, a genuine message was received, the Earth should reply with one voice rather than individual countries responding.

GEORGE REX OF KNYSNA
King's son or commoner?

George Rex, pioneer of Kynsna, was allegedly an illegitimate son of Prince George, who later became George III, King of England.

Rex came to South Africa in 1797 where he was appointed Marshal of the Vice Admiralty Court – he was also notary public to the Governor and Advocate for the Crown, probably two sinecure appointments, since he was not qualified to practise law at the Cape. According to local legend, he was later banished to the southern Cape coast where he established a large estate at Knysna. Certainly, George Rex existed, but whether or not he was the son of a king, remains a matter open to some speculation to some people ...

A BRIEF BIOGRAPHY

A considerable amount of research has been undertaken into the life of George Rex. What is known with some certainty, is that he was born in London in August 1765, that he was articled to Edward Cooper, a notary public in London in 1780, that he emigrated to the Cape in 1797 where he took up a lucrative government post, that he later moved to Knysna after having been granted a huge tract of land by the government in what was then a virtual wilderness and that he established a fine estate which he named Melkhout Kraal.

He subsequently became the richest landowner in the Knysna district and was frequently host to a number of important guests, including Lord Charles Somerset.

Rex had impeccable credentials and influence with the Government – but his royal ancestry has yet to be proven ...

Above: The church where Hannah Lightfoot and Prince George were said to have married.
Left: Artist's impression of Hannah Lightfoot.

THE 'FAIR QUAKER'

On 12 October 1730, Mary Lightfoot (*née* Wheeler), the wife of Mathew Lightfoot, a Wapping shoemaker and cordwainer, gave birth to a baby daughter, who they named Hannah. For the next five years the Lightfoots prospered, but in 1736 disaster befell the family with the death of Mathew Lightfoot. Confronted with destitution, Mary Lightfoot went to live with her uncle, Henry Wheeler.

Wheeler, who owned a linedraper's shop on the corner of Market Street and St James' Market, London, later adopted Hannah and brought her up as his own daughter. His premises were near to the old Opera House and the story goes that it was here that the young Prince George first cast his eyes upon the 'Fair Quaker', Hannah Lightfoot, on his way to the theatre. The heir apparent was very much attracted to the pretty young shopkeeper's daughter but had not bargained on the young woman's strict religious convictions. She refused to become his mistress and in the end he determined to marry her. Legend has it that he married her not once, but twice – the first in 1753 after her abduction from Isaak Axford, and the second in 1759 when the young Prince came of age. Indeed, two marriage certificates exist, although both have been proclaimed forgeries.

According to popular belief, the catalyst in this saga of love and intrigue was none other than Elizabeth Chudleigh (later Duchess of Kingston), one of the Ladies of the Royal Court. The Lady Elizabeth, who, it seemed, had established for herself a position of some influence with the ageing King George II and his wife the Dowager, Princess of Wales, had ambitions of securing the support of young Prince George to consolidate her position at court. To this end, some time in December 1753, she allegedly negotiated a sham marriage between the reluctant Hannah and an eager young grocer from Ludgate Hill named Isaak Axford. There are even some who suggest that Isaak Axford was merely a pawn in the entire affair and was bribed to marry Hannah simply to make the scheme work.

The Lady Elizabeth was aware that there was much anger within the royal household at the conduct of the young Prince and Mistress Lightfoot, so possibly reasoned that once Hannah was 'a respectable married woman' there was every reason to expect that outrage would be assuaged. And, of course, there was every likelihood that as the architect of this 'marriage' she would gain favour with the king.

Equally important, at least as far as Lady Elizabeth was concerned, was the fact that as the marriage was one in name only, and had been contrived to provide the Prince with the opportunity to pursue Hannah, she would earn his favour also. Pulling off such a coup would be a significant achievement.

Whatever the case, it is recorded that as Hannah left the church after her (first) wedding, a carriage awaited her and she was spirited away to the city – pursued for a time by an irate bridegroom – to a secret rendezvous with the young Prince.

Some accounts claim that Axford searched for his reluctant bride and at one stage petitioned the king for the 'return of his wife', albeit unsuccessfully.

After the marriage, the whereabouts of Hannah Lightfoot becomes a mystery. According to a report in the *Daily Dispatch* of 9 January 1931, she moved (or was moved) from one elegant London apartment house to another and that she gave birth to three children, George Rex being the eldest (although some claim the second eldest), John, and a daughter, Sarah. There are numerous accounts of Hannah being seen in and around London, in Devonshire and, in the company of two children, as far afield as Germany. (It is believed that John went to India where he later drowned, Sarah moved to Bath, where she died without marrying, and George stayed in London where he acquired legal training.)

The story goes that in 1760, when Prince George ascended to the throne, he was obliged to take a royal consort, Charlotte (later Queen Charlotte) and, consequently, severed his ties with Hannah Lightfoot.

His son, George Rex, who was considered something of an embarrassment to the Crown, was sent to the Cape of Good Hope in 1797, and was immediately appointed Marshal to the Vice-Admiralty Court.

What the pious Hannah thought of these manoeuvres – if they ever occurred – is never mentioned.

FACT OR FICTION?

The fact that Prince George and Hannah Lightfoot were lovers and that she bore him two sons and a daughter is not in dispute – according to *In the Land of Afternoon* by Lawrence Green.

There is even consensus that they married legally, but in secret. A marriage certificate and will allegedly made by Hannah Lightfoot was produced as evidence during a court case brought about in 1866 by Caroline Margaretha Ungerer, Rex's second wife, in which she attempted to establish her husband's ancestry. The will read: [1]

Schoonerzicht, the estate bought by George Rex on his arrival in the Cape.

Hampstead, July 7th, 1768
Provided I depart this life, I commend my two sons and my daughter to the kind protection of their Royal Father, His Majesty, George III, bequeathing whatever property I die possessed of to such dear offspring of my ill-fated marriage. In case of the death of each of my children, I give and bequeath to Olive Wilmot, the daughter of my best friend, Dr Wilmot, whatever property I am entitled to or am possessed of at the time of my death. Amen.

Witnesses
J Dunning   *Hannah Regina*
William Pitt

But if this document is authentic, why did Hannah Lightfoot sign her name as Hannah Regina? And was witness William Pitt, William Pitt the elder? If so, then in 1768 he was effectively completing his second term in office as prime minister of the coalition government of the time. If Hannah Lightfoot had these connections, surely more would have been heard of her?

There is also an account by one of Rex's sons ...

My father was the second son of George III and Hannah Lightfoot. He lived in South Africa on land provided by the government, with an annual grant from the government on condition that he did not return to England and that he did not marry. He did marry, but the grant continued.

Clearly, there is a selection of incidental material to support the claim that George Rex was a son of Prince George and Hannah Lightfoot, but emphatic proof is notoriously scarce. Despite this, Sanni Metelerkamp, a great-granddaughter of George Rex and the author of the book *George Rex of Knysna*, maintained that at least nine facts concerning Hannah Lightfoot could be proven true. [2]

1. Hannah was born in 1730, the daughter of Mathew and Mary Lightfoot.

2. Her father died when she was five years old and she was adopted by her uncle, Henry Wheeler, a draper.

3. She was married to one Isaak Axford at Keith's Chapel, Mayfair on 11 December 1753, their names being entered in the marriage register on that date.

4. She vanished mysteriously and there is no record of her after her marriage.

5. After a 15-month search, she was disowned by the Society of Friends in a Testimony of Denial for having been married 'by a priest to one not of our society'.

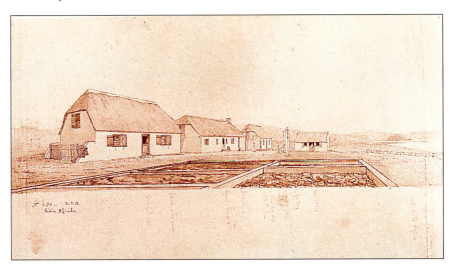

Melkhout Kraal, Rex's home in Knysna, drawn by WJ Burchell.

6. She was painted by Sir Joshua Reynolds. (Her portrait shows her dressed as a woman of fashion – rather than in the more sombre dress of a Quaker.)

7. She was bequeathed money 'for her own sole and separate disposal, and for her sole use and behoof' by Robert Pearne of Isleworth, in his will proved in April 1757.

8. From Mary Lightfoot's will, proved in 1760, Hannah was known to have been alive in 1758, three years after her disappearance, though Mrs Lightfoot had not seen her since that date.

9. More than one family claims descent from her union with George III.

However, not one of these 'facts' makes reference to a son named George Rex. Nor does everyone agree with this version of events. One of the most ardent critics of the saga was WJ Thoms, editor of the London magazine *Notes and Queries* who, in his book *Hannah Lightfoot*, ridiculed the affair:

Once upon a time there was a Fair Quaker, whose name was Hannah Lightfoot. No, Anne Elanor Lightfoot. No, Whitefoot. No, Wheeler. Well, never mind what her name was; her father was a shoemaker, who lived near Execution Dock, Wapping. No, he was a linedraper and lived at St James' Market. No, that was her uncle. But these are mere trifles. She no doubt had a name and lived somewhere.

Well, the Prince saw her as he went from Leicester House to St James'. No, that's wrong; it was as he went to the Opera. No, you are both wrong; it was as he went to the Parliament House!

Never mind where he saw her: he did see her, and fell in love with her, and, as neither his mother the Princess Dowager nor Lord Bute looked after him, and he was then sixteen years

old, he married her in 1754!
No, that's not right: it was 1759.
But it does not matter when he married; he did marry her at Keith's Chapel in May Fair.
No, it was at Peckenham.
No, it was at Kew.
No, that is all a mistake.
Her royal lover never married her. Isaak Axford married her and left her at the chapel door, and never saw her after that. Yes, he did; they lived together for three or four months, and then she was carried away secretly in a 'carriage and four', and he never saw her after that.
Wrong again.
It was the King from whom she was so strangely spirited away, and he was distracted; and sent Lord Chatham in disguise to hunt for her, yet he could never find her.
No, that's all wrong. It was Axford who could not find her, who petitioned the King to give him back his wife at St James' Park, as directed.

GEORGE REX AT THE CAPE

George Rex arrived in Cape Town during October 1797 and bought Schoonerzicht estate, which he subsequently shared with a widow, Johanna Rosina Ungerer, who bore him three sons and a daughter. There is no record, however, of their marriage.

Whatever the reason for Rex's departure from England, there seems to have been little or no attempt to hide his ancestry.

According to anecdotal evidence, it was common knowledge that he was the king's son, and that one of the conditions of his glorious exile from England was that he was expressly prohibited from marrying.

In 1801, for example, one Mr Twistle, an obscure government official at the Cape, complained in a letter to his sister that Rex had only received his position because of his influential connections ...

Sanni Metelerkamp.

This so-called Rex is fêted and the recipient of much honour on account of his being the son of the King by a Quaker. He has been sent here with every comfort. Those who have called themselves the servants of the Colony are now the servants of Rex. You ask the reason? Rex is not only the son but the legitimate heir of our King, for his mother the Quaker and King George, were joined in marriage before ever Queen Charlotte was thought of ... ₃

REX MOVES TO KNYSNA

In 1803, the Cape reverted to Dutch control, with the establishment of the Batavian Republic, and many British subjects employed in the government either lost or relinquished their posts. To make matters worse, Governor Janssens issued a proclamation commanding that all British-born or naturalized British subjects leave the country within two months – and there were strict penalties imposed upon those who had any contact with these 'undesirables'.

In light of this, Rex chose to sell his house at the Cape by public sale on 23 February 1804. Nine months later he moved his entire household to Melkhout Kraal in Knysna, a large farm which had earlier been granted to him by the British government and named by its previous Dutch owners.

Relocating was a considerable undertaking given the difficulties and dangers of the journey and the comparative isolation of his new home. Apart from his 'wife' and children and the household servants, Rex took with him over one hundred slaves (slavery was not abolished in the British Empire until 1834) and sixteen wagonloads of supplies, furniture and equipment.

According to Sanni Metelerkamp, the first Mrs Rex, Johanna Rosina Ungerer passed out of the picture four years later and was replaced by her daughter, Caroline Margaretha Ungerer, but no marriage certificate relating to either of these two women now exists. Caroline Margaretha bore her husband three sons and six daughters.

In those days Knysna was a veritable paradise, untouched by man, with a huge forest, abundant wildlife and a diverse range of flora. There is also the legend that Rex was authorized by George III to claim all the land he could see from a high point near the mouth of the Knysna River. But this can probably be discounted and was possibly based on the fact that his first property was a Crown grant of 4 000 acres of land between Knysna and Plettenberg Bay to which he gave the name Springfield.

Later, Rex purchased other desirable properties in the district, including several properties held by Dutch occupiers on loan from the government – one of them Melkhout Kraal – and ruled over an estate of over 20 000 acres.

THE MAN HIMSELF

Rex affectionately referred to Melkhout Kraal as the 'Old Place' and over the years the estate matured and grew. A farm was established, orchards and gardens planted and a blacksmith's shop built, but we know little of Rex himself.

Rex's children said that he was a loving father and a cultured man who employed tutors in mathematics, French, Latin, drawing, music and dancing for his children. Everyone always dressed for dinner and guests to Melkhout Kraal were received with splendid and lavish hospitality. Indeed, the estate was visited by all the prominent people of the time including the travellers, Burchell and Thompson, Dr James Barry - the woman physician who masqueraded as a man and worked in the Cape for a number of years - and, on a number of occasions, Lord Charles Somerset.

One visitor, William Harrison, an English traveller who visited Melkhout Kraal in 1831, later wrote an article which was published in *Notes and Queries* on 10 February 1861, in which he maintained that Rex was of 'the exact resemblance in feature of George III'.

Unfortunately, there are no portraits of Rex that we might judge this matter for ourselves.

It is also said that he refused to have his portrait painted, although there is a painting of his son Frederick which, some maintain, shows a remarkable likeness to George III.

DEATH OF A LEGEND

George Rex died on 3 April 1839 and, according to the provisions of his will, his estate was divided into sixteen equal parts – one part going to each of his thirteen children and three parts to Caroline Margaretha.

His tombstone is to be found less than a kilometre outside Kynsna on the Plettenberg Bay road.

The inscription reads:

In Memory of George Rex, Esquire, Proprietor and Founder of Knysna 1839

Sanni Metelerkamp possessed an obituary which was printed in an unknown newspaper shortly after his death ...

There died recently at the HUYSNA, South Africa, no less a personage than George Rex, the morganatic son of George III. In the early part of this century a sailing vessel left England under sealed orders. It made for the Cape, and the illustrious son of a morganatic union between George III and Hannah Lightfoot, the Quakeress, got a grant of land, as much as he wished for, in our then new South African possessions. He selected the HUYSNA, a beautiful, well-wooded and well-watered tract of land and was made Marshal of the Cape. A great many relics of George III are preserved as heirlooms in the family. George Rex was always very reticent as regards his descent. A few years ago a gentleman who did not know

of his descent was touring through Germany and at the castle of Nurnberg he saw a large painting of George III. 'How very like my old friend George Rex in South Africa!' he exclaimed to a friend who knew of the romantic life of George Rex. 4

Another obituary written along similar lines was as follows:

This month there died at Knysna, South Africa, a mysterious person known as George Rex, believed to be a morganatic son of the late King George the Third, and a lovely Quakeress, Hannah Lightfoot. He was sent out to South Africa in the early part of the century and received large grants of land in the beautiful wooded lake district of the Cape Colony; he was also given the post of Marshal to the Admiralty in Cape Town; a great many relics of our late monarch remain in the possession of the family, for George Rex had many children. He was buried on a portion of his estate which he had specially chosen for the purpose, on a day of wild wind and rain, and the whole population of Knysna paid tribute to the founder of their town, recalling his dignity; his regal bearing; his reputation as a family man and squire, and the manner in which he ruled over his vast estate. Of him it can be truly said – he left no enemy behind.

NO SMOKE WITHOUT FIRE?

It would seem that the available evidence suggests there is some fact behind the story that George Rex was the son of George III, but many people have vehemently argued otherwise. Fact and fiction have often been intertwined.

Certainly, several questions remain. If George Rex was the son of George III, why did he leave England so suddenly in 1797? No-one knows. If the reason for his departure was to bury the story in oblivion at the remote Cape, why did the British authorities wait over thirty years to act, particularly as his existence appears to have been an open secret at the Royal Court in London for a number of years?

There have been rumours that Rex, while an equerry for the King, formed an 'unsuitable' liaison with a Princess at Court. If Rex was the King's illegitimate son, his presence at Court under any circumstances had the potential to cause untold embarrassment to the Crown and possibly even a constitutional crisis as, in theory, he had a direct claim to the throne, but why he should ask, be encouraged or choose to leave England in 1797 remains a mystery.

According to Sanni Metelerkamp, Lord Chief Justice Wilde ordered that all documents relating to the alleged marriage between Prince George and Hannah Lightfoot be impounded in a strongroom at Somerset House in London, the principal Probate Registry in England. Many historians have attempted to examine the documents but have been denied access to them.

Unfortunately, George Rex himself seems to have made no attempt to shed any light on the situation, but whether this is significant, is impossible to say, as his diary was destroyed in one of a series of disastrous fires at the 'Old Place'.

There is the (unsubstantiated) story, however, that he purposefully destroyed many of his private papers. Why he should have thought this important also remains a mystery.

Further 'proof' of Rex's illustrious ancestry is said to be a number of relics, including a medallion with a bust of George III by Wedgewood, a rosewood chair which he brought from England, some wine glasses, some coins and a seal engraved with the words, 'Though lost to sight to memory dear', which was reputedly handed to Rex by George III when he left England.

THE CASE AGAINST REX

The first reference to the supposed connection between George Rex and King George III is said to have occurred in a letter written by a government official at the Cape, Mr Twistle, to his sister living in England.

The story goes that this letter was sent to the editor of the *Cape Post*, who decided not to publish it. However, a newspaper by the name of the *Cape*

GEORGE III (1738-1820)

George III came to the throne in 1760, seven years after he'd allegedly married the 'fair quaker', Hannah Lightfoot. His reign is regarded by many historians as covering one of the most brilliant periods in British history. However, George III himself was a controversial and often unpopular figure. He came to power during the Seven Years' War and established a peace which effectively isolated Britain from Europe for the next thirty years. During his reign, the American Colonies declared their independence, the Industrial Revolution transformed British society and the British population doubled.

He also instituted wide-ranging agricultural reforms and became known as 'Farmer George'. George III suffered from a disease of the nervous system, now known as porphyria, which was characterized by occasional bouts of delirium, paralysis and agonizing pain. Although we now know that porphyria is not a mental illness, George was declared insane in 1811, and his son by his wife, Charlotte Sophia of Mecklenburg-Strelitz, became Regent.

Post never existed, nor is there any mention of a Mr Twistle in the Cape Archives. In other words, the legend of George Rex is based on a letter of which there is no record, written by a man whom no one knew, to a newspaper that did not exist!

In a somewhat similar vein, local rumour also has it that on his deathbed, Rex requested that the Royal crest be obliterated from the family silver. Unfortunately, this, like most of the other stories, is not supported by any documentary evidence. Furthermore, no-one who visited Melkhout Kraal – and there were many visitors, a considerable number of whom recorded their observations – made reference to a royal crest. Surely the royal crest, if it existed, would have drawn comment from someone?

There is no evidence to connect the two men in any way, other than speculation and hearsay. Nor is there a shred of evidence to suggest a 'last interview' between George Rex and King George III just prior to Rex's departure for South Africa. Although there is a valuable Wedgewood portrait medallion of George III, which is now in the possession of a descendant of the family in Knysna, there is still no evidence to connect this item with the king. The Josiah Wedgewood factory in fact produced a number of medallions of famous people and owning one was not in itself particularly significant.

Although there are those who would argue otherwise, the claim that George Rex of Knysna was the son of George III is based entirely on hearsay, and *not* proven fact – disappointing as it may seem. But the legend of George Rex's illustrious ancestry will no doubt persist.

BUBBLES SCHROEDER
Death by accident?

Bubbles Schroeder. What happened to her on that fateful night in August 1949?

The murder of eighteen-year-old 'Bubbles' Schroeder on a balmy August night in 1949 remains a matter of public curiosity even today, and, because of the fact that no-one was ever convicted for the killing, rumours persist.

It was a perplexing crime that had all the ingredients of a best-selling novel – a young and beautiful victim, a cast of rich and prominent suspects and, not least of all, a mystifying murder without an explanation …

THE BODY IS DISCOVERED

Bubbles Schroeder's body was discovered by Samuel Ngibisa Mabela on the morning of Thursday, 18 August 1949, on the grounds of the Birdhaven plantation at Illovo. She had been missing for thirty hours. She was lying on her back on burnt-out grass about thirty metres from the road; her face was turned to the right, and her left leg was lying over her right. Her left arm was pressed against the side of her body, while her right was flung out at an angle of about 75 degrees.

She was hatless, shoeless and her coat was missing. The soles of her stockings were intact and no grass or other substances such as mud, gravel or dust were found on them, which indicated that she had not walked to the spot where she was found.

The stocking on Schroeder's right leg was snagged and her panties were torn on the right side from the leg upwards to the waistband, but her black petticoat and brassiere were intact.

In her mouth were some pieces of hard clay-like material, and although some of the bits lay deep in her throat, there were no particles in her lungs, which indicated that the clay had been forced into her mouth and throat after she had stopped breathing.

Although there was evidence of light scratches and abrasions on different parts of Bubbles Schroeder's body, scratch marks on her throat, and a particularly ugly strangulation mark on the front of her neck – all of which bore testament to a rather fierce struggle with her assailant – she had not been sexually assaulted.

THE POSTMORTEM

Dr Jack Friedman, then Johannesburg District Surgeon, conducted a postmortem soon after the body was discovered and estimated that Bubbles Schroeder had died around 2 a.m. on the morning of Tuesday, 16 August. Cause of death was recorded as asphyxia and inhibition as a result of the pressure on her throat and the impaction of a hard clay-like substance (similar to that in a heap of builder's lime found a few metres away from the scene) in her hypopharynx.

A significant fact that emerged during the postmortem was that Bubbles had suffered from a condition of the thymus gland which would have caused her to fall unconscious from only slight pressure round the neck. The bruising on her neck indicated that she had been strangled from behind, probably with a scarf or belt, and had scratched herself in an effort to tear the restriction from her throat. It was possible that Bubbles' assailant or assailants assumed she had suffered a heart-attack after falling unconscious and then carried the body into Birdhaven plantation and placed the clay in her mouth, inadvertently perhaps, causing her to suffocate.

Dr Friedman concluded that the position of the body indicated that the victim had been carried (possibly over someone's shoulder) into the plantation and that she probably died at the place where her body was discovered.

THE GOOD-TIME GIRL

Jacoba 'Bubbles' Schroeder was born in Lichtenburg on 8 June 1931 and was educated at Benoni and Vereeniging. At the age of thirteen she moved to Johannesburg with her mother. Four years later, in March 1948, she moved back to Vereeniging for a few months, then returned to the city and moved into an apartment with fifty-two year-old bookmaker Philip Stein, whom she had met at a dance in Orange Grove. Stein liked having a beautiful young woman around, but the situation did have its inherent drawbacks.

'She was a young woman, a little loose in her morals,' Stein said, 'but she was very sweet – except when she had been drinking. She used to become rather unmanageable.'

Bubbles Schroeder, the good-time girl.

Matters finally came to a head in June 1949 – Bubbles had come home drunk once too often and Stein asked her to leave. She moved to Dorchester Mansions in Rissik Street where she shared an apartment with a 'hostess' by the name of Mrs Griffin, and despite the fact that Bubbles didn't have a regular paying job, she never seemed to be short of money.

'Bubbles was a glamour girl,' according to Mrs Griffin. 'She'd spend her days at the beauty parlour and her nights at night clubs. And she could be charming, until she had a few drinks in her, of course. Then she became rather obstinate and difficult.'

THE FINAL HOURS …

On Thursday, 11 August, 21-year-old Morris Bilchik visited Dorchester Mansions. He made a date with Bubbles for the following Saturday night. After spending some time with each other, they went back to Bilchik's home and spent the night together.

The following Monday, Bilchik boasted of his conquest to his friend, David Polliack. The two men visited Bubbles at her apartment and proposed making up a foursome, the plan being that Bubbles would contact her friend, Penny, and they would all go out together that evening. Unfortunately, Penny couldn't be found at any of her old haunts so, in the end Bilchik, Polliack and Schroeder decided to go out without her.

That afternoon, Bubbles went to see Philip Stein at his apartment and eventually arrived at her own place around six o'clock. Bilchik and Polliack were waiting for her, so she dressed quickly, putting on a green dress and some make-up.

BIRDHAVEN PLANTATION

TO WANDERERS CLUBHOUSE

VENUS STREET TO TYRWHITT AVENUE

The body was found on Birdhaven plantation.

They set off together around half past seven, and headed for Polliack's house, Hlatikulu, in the affluent suburb of Illovo. (Polliack's mother was in Durban, so the three had the house to themselves.) Bubbles travelled with Polliack and Bilchik followed in his own car.

They reached the house at eight o'clock just as Polliack's cousin, Hyman Balfour Liebman (20), was leaving for Houghton to pick up his girlfriend. The two men invited Liebman to bring his girlfriend back to the house to join the party, but Liebman declined because they had already made arrangements to go to the cinema that evening.

After Liebman had driven off, Bubbles, Polliack and Bilchik went into the house. Polliack asked the cook, Irene, to prepare food for them and at about half past nine, they sat down to a meal of asparagus soup, followed by chops and chips;

for dessert they had a tin of peaches. Afterwards, they went into the living room where Bubbles drank a few glasses of brandy and snacked on peanuts.

At about 11.15 p.m. Bilchik left because it seemed obvious to him that Bubbles and Polliack wanted to be alone. After he had left, Bubbles and Polliack cleared up in the living room, and went upstairs to listen to records in his bedroom. Not long afterwards, Bilchik phoned. Jealousy, it seemed, had finally got the better of him. First he spoke to Bubbles, and then he apologized to Polliack for disturbing them; after about fifteen minutes he rang off.

Around midnight, Hyman Liebman returned from his cinema date. Polliack met him in the hallway and told him that Bubbles was in his room. The trouble was that she had had too much to drink and he wanted to get her home before she passed out. Liebman went upstairs to see for himself, and discovered that

Bubbles had been drinking but that she wasn't drunk. After another drink, Bubbles decided she wanted to go home and mentioned that her mother was staying with her and expected her home around one o'clock.

Eventually, at about half past one, the three of them went out into the driveway – Polliack wanted to take her home but she got into Liebman's car and wouldn't get out. Liebman offered to drive her home and, with Bubbles insisting that she wanted to drive, the two of them set out for Dorchester Mansions. About twenty minutes later Liebman was back at the house, alone.

'That girl's a lunatic,' he told his cousin. 'She wanted to drive and when I wouldn't let her she made me stop and got out. I told her to be sensible but she wouldn't listen.'

Polliack was angry and concerned.

'You mean you let her walk? Where did you let her out?'

'At the Dunkeld bus terminus.'

'And did she say anything?'

Liebman nodded. 'Yes. She said, "Which way to town?" I told her to follow the bus wires along Oxford Road. The last thing she said to me was, "You will be surprised to read about my corpse in the morning papers".'

Polliack was so concerned about Bubbles, he decided to get into his car to go and look for her. Liebman, on the other hand, had had too much of Bubbles already and went off to bed. After driving around for about an hour Polliack returned home alone and went to bed. He assumed that Bubbles had managed to get a lift with a passing motorist. Neither Polliack nor Liebman suspected anything was wrong until they received a phone call some hours later. That morning, Bilchik had been to Dorchester Mansions to see Bubbles and had learnt from her mother that she had not returned home the previous evening. Soon after hearing the news, Polliack went to see Mrs Schroeder himself. Polliack, Bilchik and Mrs Schroeder then went to the police station to report Bubbles missing. Polliack telephoned the general hospital to see if she had been admitted there, but she had not.

THE INVESTIGATION

When Bubbles Schroeder's body was discovered, the police opened a murder docket. But despite an extensive search of the area around Birdhaven plantation, little or no evidence came to light. There were no footprints to or from the spot where Bubbles' body had been found, no fragments of torn clothing that might have given a clue as to the identity of the killer or killers, nor any witness to the crime. On 13 October, almost two months after the murder, Liebman and Polliack were arrested and charged with the murder of 'Bubbles' Schroeder; their trial began a few days later at the Johannesburg Magistrates' Court. The evidence the police presented to the court was almost entirely circumstantial. The prosecution based its case upon the fact that Liebman and Polliack had been with Miss Schroeder late on the night of her death but there was no direct evidence to connect either of them to the murder itself. Both men were eventually acquitted.

WHO MURDERED BUBBLES SCHROEDER?

The police contended that Liebman had strangled her in his car using a scarf, after driving her to Birdhaven plantation and attempting to have sex with her. When she fell unconscious, as a result of the attempt to strangle her into submission, he had carried her body away from the road and left it in the plantation. But there was not a shred of evidence – apart from the fact that Liebman had given Bubbles a lift – to support this claim.

A second hypothesis was that Bubbles had been murdered by a passing black man, following a failed robbery attempt. This theory was supported by the fact that her mouth was stuffed with clay. (Among certain African peoples it is customary to place something in the mouth of a victim who has suffered a violent death, to prevent him or her from speaking ill of the killer in the afterworld.) But this theory has a number of obvious flaws – for example, if the motive for the crime was robbery, why had nothing apparently been stolen? Why was she killed? And why had her body been carried so far from the road? This seems inconsistent if the assault had been opportunistic, and the attacker would have been more likely to have fled the moment Bubbles 'died'.

A third, and possibly the most plausible answer, was that Schroeder tried to hitch a lift with a passing motorist. (If there had been two men in the car, the passenger would have moved into the back seat, and been in the perfect position to hook a scarf around Bubbles' neck.) She was assaulted, fell unconscious, was (accidentally?) asphyxiated and her body dumped, probably in panic. Clay was placed in her mouth to confuse the police investigation.

Despite speculation, the question remains – who killed Bubbles Schroeder? It now seems unlikely that the answer will ever be known.

Hyman Liebman and his parents after being acquitted in the Johannesburg Magistrates' Court.

LORD LUCAN
Where is he now?

On 7 November 1974, a member of the British aristocracy, Richard John Bingham, the seventh Earl of Lucan, allegedly murdered Sandra Rivett, his childrens' nanny at the Belgravia, London, home of his estranged wife, Veronica. After fleeing the scene, Lord Lucan vanished and, despite the fact that he later became, for a time, one of the most wanted men in the world, no definite trace of him has ever been found.

However ...

LONDON Detectives hunting Lord Lucan, wanted on a murder charge, watched passengers board a South African Airways flight to Johannesburg after an anonymous tip that a woman carrying money to the missing Earl would be aboard the aircraft. In recent weeks there have been rumours that Lord Lucan is in southern Africa and being supplied with money by friends in England.[1]

FROM BALACLAVA TO BELGRAVIA

The Charge of the Light Brigade at Balaclava in the Crimea on 25 October 1854, one of the major disasters in British military history, was led by the seventh Earl of Cardigan, on the orders of his brother-in-law, George Bingham, the third Earl of Lucan, the Major-General commanding the cavalry.

Above: Lord and Lady Lucan.
Did Lord Lucan, mistakenly murder the family nanny, Sandra Rivett, believing her to be his wife? Are the circumstances surrounding his disappearance in fact related to the murder?

Although the ambiguous command to advance into what the poet Tennyson would later describe as 'the valley of death', in his poem, *The Charge of the Light Brigade*, actually originated with the Commander-in-Chief, Lord Raglan,

it was Lord Lucan who subsequently carried the blame and disgrace for the catastrophe. Lord Raglan issued an order to his aide-de-camp, Nolan, that 'the cavalry should attack', which Nolan dutifully relayed to Lord Lucan who was in command of the Light Brigade.

Since the enemy was ranged on a number of sides, Lucan replied, 'Attack sir? Attack what? What guns sir?' Nolan then reputedly threw out his arm towards the north of the valley where the heaviest concentration of Russian guns lay and said,

'There, my Lord, is your enemy! There are the guns.'

Of the 673 soldiers who took part in the charge, there were 272 casualties.

Not, of course, that Lord Lucan was a stranger to controversy. Prior to this momentous event, he had singularly distinguished himself through the callous and brutal treatment he had meted out to his Irish tenants during the years of the Irish potato famine (1845–48).

Historians have noted that his inhuman evictions caused the starvation of countless numbers of people and it was for this reason that he became known as 'the exterminator'.

Richard John Bingham, the seventh Earl of Lucan, the man with whom this story is concerned, was one of the direct descendants of 'the exterminator'.

He was true to his family history, or so it seemed ...

THE PRIVATE LIFE OF LORD LUCAN

Richard John Bingham married Veronica Duncan on 28 November 1963. He was 28 at the time. Two months after the wedding, his father died suddenly and he became the seventh Earl of Lucan.

Before this date, Lucan had had something of a chequered life. He had been sent to the very best schools, had struggled through university, later completed his two years' national service in the

The Lucan's London residence at 46 Lower Belgrave Street, scene of the murder.

prestigious Coldstream Guards, then joined a merchant bank in the city of London. He was, however, a compulsive gambler and following a run of luck at the card tables – hence his nickname 'Lucky' – he chose to abandon his somewhat conventional career in banking to become a professional gambler.

After ten years of marriage, the relationship between Lord Lucan and his wife, Veronica, had deteriorated to the point of open hostility. Domestic ten-

sions led to their separation in 1973 and there followed a bitterly contested court battle over custody of their two children – a girl and a boy. The judge, who had the unenviable task of deciding between a mother who was in constant need of psychological counselling and a father who was a professional gambler, chose to award custody to Veronica, with Lucan allowed limited access.

The decision came as a blow to Lord Lucan and, despite the court's ruling, his efforts to gain custody of the children continued unabated. He watched Veronica and the children constantly – ostensibly in the hope of finding something he could use against his wife – and acquired an apartment near their house in Lower Belgrave Street. Veronica, who was (according to those who knew her) 'highly excitable' at the best of times, accused her husband of attempting to snatch the children and putting out 'a contract on her life'. Lord Lucan maintained that she was mentally unstable.

By the autumn of 1974, Lucan's attempts to gain custody of his children had failed. His luck at the gaming tables deserted him and he was deep in debt.

In October that year, Lucan, who it seemed had lost all faith in the courts, decided to take matters into his own hands. He borrowed an old Ford Corsair from his friend, Michael Stoop, then

began using it, instead of his own conspicuous Mercedes, to spy on his family. Whether Lucan's original intention was to kidnap his children, obtain evidence of his wife's mental instability, or to plan her murder is not clear. But on the night of 7 November 1974, matters finally came to a head.

MURDER

Early in October 1974, Veronica Lucan had acquired the services of a childrens' nanny, Sandra Rivett – a young woman who had separated from her husband. She was the latest in a long line of nannies employed by the family.

It was Veronica Lucan's habit to make herself a cup of tea every evening, but that night, Mrs Rivett offered to make one for her, and around nine o'clock went to the kitchen in the basement to put the kettle on. When she didn't return after what seemed like a long time, Veronica went to look for her. As she reached the ground floor someone attacked her, raining blows on her head with a club of some sort; she screamed and a voice she recognized as that of her husband's, told her to shut up. A fierce struggle ensued and, according to Veronica, her husband tried to suffocate her by pushing a gloved hand into her mouth, but she managed to grab him by

Sandra Rivett

the testicles. The fight apparently ended as suddenly as it had started and her husband, who Veronica later said was emotionally and physically exhausted, went upstairs with her. While he went to the bathroom to get some damp towels to wipe the blood from her face, she took the opportunity to escape. Covered in blood, she ran screaming to the Plumber's Arms, a nearby pub, where she burst into the bar screaming, 'Help me! Help me! I have just escaped from a murderer ... My children ... my children ... He's in the house ... He's murdered the nanny ... Help me!'

Despite her hysteria, no-one rushed gallantly to the house where the heinous crime had taken place.

Instead, the barman and some of the customers tried to calm her while the police and an ambulance were summoned to the scene.

At four minutes past ten, a police car arrived at the Plumber's Arms and was directed to the scene of the crime.

Two police officers went directly to the house, which they found locked and in darkness. They forced open the front door and immediately spotted fresh blood streaks on the wallpaper in the hallway. They conducted a cursory examination of the basement, discovered a large pool of blood at the bottom of the stairs, then made their way upstairs and through the house. There was a light on in a bedroom on the second floor where a bloodstained towel was found lying across one of the pillows. On the top floor the Lucans' children were found, unharmed.

Having discovered clear signs of a struggle, the two officers made a second sweep of the house. They returned to the basement and this time noticed a second pool of blood near the base of

the stairs – this one containing the remains of broken cups and saucers. The light bulb in the kitchen had, for some reason, been removed, and when they replaced it, they saw a large American canvas mailbag in the adjoining breakfast room, next to the kitchen. Blood was leaking from it and an arm was hanging out of the top.

Inside the bag they found the body of Sandra Rivett who had been savagely battered around the head with a 23 cm length of lead pipe which was found lying nearby.

But there was no sign of Lord Lucan, the alleged murderer.

The Lucan's nanny and murder victim, Sandra Rivett.

THE TRIAL

Following an unsuccessful attempt by the police to trace Lord Lucan, which lasted a period of some eight months, an inquest into the death of Sandra Rivett was opened at Westminster Coroner's Court on Monday, 16 June 1975.

Veronica Lucan, the only witness to the events that occurred on the evening of 7 November 1974, was questioned at some length by Michael Eastham QC, who had been appointed by Lord Lucan's mother to protect her son's interests. A number of interesting anomalies in Veronica's story emerged ...

In her statement to the police, for example, she did not mention the discovery of Sandra Rivett's body, although she had declared that the nanny had been murdered when she burst into the Plumber's Arms. Nor, some would argue, did she adequately explain why Lord Lucan should help her upstairs, moments after he had tried to beat her about the head with a lead pipe.

An inquest of this nature normally results in a finding of murder by 'a person or persons unknown'.

However, in this case the evidence against Lord Lucan was overwhelming. He had a motive: he wanted custody of his children; opportunity: he had keys to the house where the murder took place and was at the scene of the crime when the killing occurred. He also had method: he was carrying a lead pipe which he intended using to attack his wife. The three essential elements of a criminal act were present.

Under these circumstances, the jury had no hesitation in pronouncing Lord Lucan guilty.

The fact that the killing had occurred on a Thursday was seen as significant by those present at the inquest, as Thursday was usually Mrs Rivett's night off – a fact of which Lord Lucan would probably have been aware. That week, however, Mrs Rivett had changed her night off to Tuesday. It was speculated that Lucan had planned to murder his wife and then remove her body in the boot of the Ford Corsair which he had borrowed expressly for this purpose. It can only be surmised how Lucan intended explaining his wife's disappearance. The available evidence suggested that Lucan had waited in the dark kitchen for his wife to come down and make her nightly cup of tea. In error, he had killed Sandra Rivett, who was similar in height and build.

ON THE TRAIL OF LORD LUCAN

The movements of Lord Lucan on the night of the murder remain something of a mystery. The inquest revealed that after his wife ran from the house, to fetch help, Lucan left. Shortly afterwards, he telephoned his mother from a public call box and told her of the 'terrible catastrophe' that had befallen him when he had intervened in a fight between his wife and an unknown intruder and that he had 'panicked and fled'. He also asked that she look after the children, which she agreed to do. Lady Lucan first telephoned the police and then went to the house in Belgravia.

Lucan then drove to Uckfield in Sussex, about 50 km away, to the home of the Maxwell-Scotts. He arrived there around eleven o'clock and was let in by Mrs Maxwell-Scott – her husband was away for the night. Over a stiff whisky he repeated, with a little more detail, the story he had told his mother ...

He had been walking past the house in Lower Belgrave Street when he saw, through a basement window, a man attacking Veronica. Using his key, he had let himself into the house, but by the time he got downstairs, the intruder had vanished and Veronica, who was hysterical, accused him of hiring someone to kill her. There was blood everywhere, he said, and on the floor was a sack containing the lifeless body of Sandra Rivett.

After a brief, heated exchange Lucan said that he persuaded his wife to go upstairs with him. In the bedroom, his eldest daughter, Frances, was watching television. Lucan said that he explained to her that her mother had had a 'slight accident' then went to fetch some damp towels and tranquillizers. Veronica had run away while he was out of the room and he had panicked and fled the scene, knowing that his presence in the house would implicate him in the crime.

Well after midnight, while still at the Maxwell-Scott's house, Lucan phoned his mother at her home to check on the children. When she asked him if he wanted to speak to the police he declined, saying he would call them in the morning – but he never did. After the call, he wrote two letters to a friend, Bill Shand Kydd, about business matters and his children, adding that he intended to 'lie doggo a bit', then left the house around one o'clock, saying that he had to get back to 'clear things up'.

That, at least as far as the investigating authorities are concerned, was the last time anyone definitely saw Lord Lucan.

Three days later, the Ford Corsair he had been driving was found abandoned near a yacht marina at the town of Newhaven, close to the Newhaven-Dieppe ferry terminal. There were blood stains in the car – type A, matching Lady Lucan's, and the rare group B, matching Sandra Rivett's. These were the same blood types found at the Lucan home. The evidence suggested to the police that Lord Lucan had intended using the car as a getaway vehicle.

On the Monday following the murder, Michael Stoop was handed a letter when he arrived at the St James' Club in London, but he threw away the envelope with a postmark, without thought, which may have provided the police with an important clue as to Lord Lucan's whereabouts. This act also served to deepen police suspicion of Lucan's friends. The letter read:

My Dear Michael
I have had a traumatic night of unbelievable coincidence. However I won't bore you with anything or involve you except to say that when you come across my children, which I hope you will, please tell them that you knew me and that all I cared about was them. The fact that a crooked solicitor [whom he had employed to represent him] and a rotten psychiatrist [who had failed to condemn his wife] destroyed me between them, will be of no importance to the children.
I gave Bill Shand Kydd an account of
what really happened, but judging by my last efforts in court no-one, let alone a 67-year-old judge, would believe – and I no longer care, except that my children should be protected.

Yours ever

John

Mrs Maxwell-Scott, one of the 'Lucan set' and one of the last people to see Lord Lucan before he disappeared.

The implication of this letter is that Lucan had lost faith in the fairness of justice, evidenced by the reference he makes to his failed 'last efforts in court' when the authorities had elected to grant custody of the children to Veronica. But this hardly justifies his subsequent flight.

Warrants for Lucan's arrest on the counts of murder and attempted murder were issued and Interpol was alerted to be on the look-out for him. But the elusive Lord was never apprehended and his whereabouts became a matter of intense speculation. 'Sightings' were allegedly made in England, Las Vegas, Ireland, where he owned substantial land, the Seychelles and, on numerous occasions, South Africa.

In March 1976 an article appeared in the *Argus* which read:

> *One of the detectives leading the international hunt for Lord Lucan, Detective Chief Inspector David Gerring [said] 'I believe that he is still alive and is in South Africa'.*
> *In a telephone interview from Scotland Yard he said that the search would continue until Lord Lucan, who is wanted for the murder of his childrens' nanny in November 1974, is found dead or alive. Inspector Gerring and Detective Chief Superintendent Roy Ranson have investigated numerous reports of Lord Lucan. Lucan has friends all over the world and also his body has not been found. I personally believe that he is in South Africa and Mr Ranson also feels that this is a distinct possibility.' Asked whether Lord Lucan could support himself, Inspector Gerring said that he had $25 000 in a bank account in Bulawayo but that his financial position was very bad. He is being made bankrupt and has debts of about 70 000 (pounds). Recently detectives questioned a man in a British prison who claims he saw Lord Lucan in Mozambique but there are too many discrepancies between his story and the facts for it to be true.*

In April of the same year, another article appeared in the *Sunday Times* ...

> *Lord Lucan, 41, the British peer wanted for the murder of his childrens' nanny in 1974, is believed to have been seen again in Swaziland.*

> *A Johannesburg couple say they saw him in the bar of a hotel in Mbabane. 'I am one hundred percent sure that the man I saw drinking in the bar at the Royal Swazi Spa on March 5 was Lord Lucan,' said Mr Peter Worthington, who is the second person in the last few weeks who has claimed to have spotted Lord Lucan in Swaziland. 'I was looking at the photographs of Lord Lucan in the* Sunday Times *last week, when I realized that the touched up photograph of him without his moustache and with a slightly lower hairline was the man who I had seen at the spa.'*

A week later, Lord Lucan was reported to be seen in Cape Town – but none of these 'sightings' could be confirmed. What happened to him? Is he still alive? And where did he go after he abandoned the car in Newhaven?

WHERE IS LORD LUCAN NOW?

There are two lines of speculation as to what happened to Lord Lucan following his disappearance in November 1974. There are those who maintain he would have committed suicide, as would be expected of a 'man of honour'.

However, the problem with this theory is threefold. Firstly, his body has never been found; secondly, if this was Lord Lucan's intention then there was no need for him to drive to Newhaven; and thirdly, such an action seems decidedly out of character. He was a gambler by nature and was accustomed to taking risks. Surely, one can argue, taking on the police and making good his escape was the biggest gamble of all and must have appealed to him?

One of the problems faced by the police was that Lord Lucan's friends appeared to display a strong sense of loyalty to him. A number of policemen who investigated the case felt that their efforts were hindered by his aristocratic friends. Detective Chief Superintendent

Ranson spoke out after his retirement, castigating what he called the 'Lucan Set', claiming their code of silence hampered his investigation.

No-one knows for certain where Lucan is hiding, or even if he is still alive. But over the years there has been considerable support for the theory that he came to live in South Africa.

In an article written in the *Sunday Times* on 12 September 1982, it was indicated that Lucan had spent some time in the remote Tuli area of Botswana and that he had lived in Johannesburg.

Lucan's supposed South African connection again came under the spotlight four years later in another article in the *Sunday Times* of 14 September 1986. This time it was alleged that Lucan had become engaged to a young woman from Stellenbosch, but that the marriage plans had been aborted when his true identity had been revealed.

The same article then went on to speculate ... why did Lucan's brother, Hugh Bingham, at the time an unshaven prospector, suddenly appear on a lonely Namaqualand farm? Rumour had it that the gaunt man was a financial conduit for money coming from Lucan's friends. All he will say of the affair is, 'The world is a big place. My brother could be in any corner of it.'

The *Sunday Times* also claimed that a top Fleet Street team of journalists had arrived in Cape Town from London after a 'titled woman' claimed to have seen Lucan. According to the account, the South African police fingerprinted a beer glass he was supposed to have used on that occasion. The newspaper also claimed that 'numerous sources' maintained that he sat at the front row of the first night of Shirley Bassey's first Sun City Superbowl concert in 1981; that he had been seen playing roulette and other games at the Royal Swazi Sun, and that a Durban couple, Jack and Caroline Rosen, saw him go down R800 without batting an eyelid, playing only number 17 on the roulette table.

TOWARDS A CONCLUSION

Since the night of 7 November 1974, Richard John Bingham, the seventh Earl of Lucan and the alleged murderer of Sandra Rivett, has never been seen – at least not officially. Yet the rumours about him, and particularly those about his close ties with South Africa, continue to circulate. Those who argue his innocence ask why, if he killed his childrens' nanny by accident, did he not kill his wife when he had the chance?
A question to which his detractors argue, that he lost his nerve. Unfortunately, no-one really knows the truth of the matter.

However, the fact remains that no evidence connecting anyone else to the crime has ever been found. Despite this, Lucan has neither been tried nor convicted of the crime he allegedly committed.

But in the eyes of most people, the proof positive of Lord Lucan's guilt is the fact that he absconded after the murder. There still remains some uncertainty about the events that took place on that fateful night.

At Scotland Yard, no unsolved murder docket is ever closed so, to some extent, the investigation continues. Did Lord Lucan get away with murder? And is he now living comfortably under an assumed name somewhere in southern Africa? Perhaps this is the real mystery ...

One of the letters Lord Lucan wrote to his friend Bill Shand Kydd on the night of the murder ...

Dear Bill

The most ghastly circumstances arose tonight, which I have described briefly to my mother, when I interrupted the fight at Lower Belgrave Street and the man left.
V. accused me of having hired him. I took her upstairs and sent Frances to bed and tried to clean her up. She lay doggo for a bit. I went into the bathroom and she left the house. The circumstantial evidence against me is strong in that V. will say it was all my doing and I will lie doggo for a while, but I am only concerned about the children. If you can manage it I would like them to live with you. V. has demonstrated her hatred for me in the past and would do anything to see me accused.
For George and Frances to go through life knowing their father had been in the dock accused of attempted murder would be too much for them.
When they are old enough to understand, explain to them the dream of paranoia and look after them.

Lucky

A photo-fit drawing of Lord Lucan as he may look today.

6 SA Library **7** SA Library **8** SA Library **8/9** David Thorpe (illustration) **10** De Beers Archives **11** William Fehr Collection **12** SA Library **13** David Thorpe (illustration) **14/5** SAA **15** * **15** David Thorpe (illustration) **16** Lorreta Chegwidden (map) **17** Department of Transport, Chief Directorate Civil Aviation **18** Department of Transport, Chief Directorate Civil Aviation **19** SAA **20** SA Library **21** SA Library **22** SA Library **22** Evert Smith **23** Lorreta Chegwidden (map) **24** SA Library **25** Cultural History Museum, Cape Town, John Haigh **26** SA Library **28** SA Library **29** David Thorpe (illustration) **30** Anne Emslie **30** Shaen Adey **31** Marek Patzer **31** Ian Ballantine **32** David Thorpe (illustration) **33** Lorreta Chegwidden (map) **34** Errol M Cornish **34** Emlyn Brown **35** Emlyn Brown **35** Emlyn Brown **36** Lorreta Chegwidden (map) **37** Emlyn Brown **37** *Argus* **37** Emlyn Brown **38** Mr L Wolhüter **39** David Thorpe (illustration) **40** Lorreta Chegwidden (map) **41** * **42** * **43** David Thorpe (illustration) **44** * (illustration) **45** David Thorpe (illustration) **46** Dr M du Preez **47** Bernard O'Sullivan **48/9** Bernard O'Sullivan **49** Bernard O'Sullivan **49** Archeology Contracts Office, UCT **50/1** André Gil-Artagan **52** * **53** * **54** * **55** * **55** * **57** Henk Lor **58** WJ van Rijssen **59** SA Museum **60** Obie Oberholtzer **61** *Die Beeld* **62** *Die Beeld* **63** * **64, 65, 66, 67, 68** JLB Smith Institute **69** *Argus* **70** *Argus* **70** Courtesy Colonel Jonker, Pretoria Police **71** Republican Press **72** David Thorpe (illustration) **74** Mark van Aardt **75** Roger de la Harpe **75** African Images, James Marshall **76** Peter Steyn **77** TV Bulpin **78/9** David Thorpe (illustration) **79** John Haigh **80** *The Star* **81** University of the Witwatersrand **82** Africana

Museum **83** David Thorpe (illustration) **83** Karen Korte **84** WJ van Rijssen **85** David Thorpe (illustration) **86,87** Professor Scott-Macnab **88** Courtesy of Trish Gordon **88** Courtesy of Trish Gordon **89** Lorreta Chegwidden (map) **90** Silvermine **91** Reinhold Rau **92** Courtesy Reinhold Rau, © Zoological Society of London **93** Courtesy of the Library of Parliament, from the Mendelssohn Collection of watercolour paintings by François le Vaillant (1753-1824) **94** Karen Korte **95** Reinhold Rau **96** Jonathan Goodman **96/7** SA Library **97** Courtesy Jonathan Goodman **98** Lorreta Chegwidden (illustration) **98** Jonathan Goodman **99** Photo Access, E Nagele **100** Bruce Dyer **101** Lorreta Chegwidden (illustration) **102** Africana Museum **102** Courtesy *Fair Lady* **103** *Huisgenoot* **104** *Huisgenoot* **105** Greg Withers **105** Courtesy *Fair Lady* **106** *Argus* **107** David Thorpe (illustration) **107** Evert Smith, *Eastern Province Herald* **108** Evert Smith, *Eastern Province Herald* **109** Evert Smith, *Eastern Province Herald* **110** Knysna Museum **110** David Thorpe (illustration) **111** Knysna Museum **112** Knysna Museum **113** Artur Beddy **114** SA Library **115** Knysna Museum **116** * **117** *Huisgenoot* **118** * **119** *Rand Daily Mail* from *The Evil that Men Do* by Benjamin Bennett **120** From *Murder in High Places* by Jonathan Goodman **121** From *Murder in High Places* by Jonathan Goodman **121** From *Murder in High Places* by Jonathan Goodman **122** Republican Press **123** Solo Syndication and Literary Agency **125** Sergeant Stadler, South African Police
* *Source unknown.*

NOTES

THE MYSTIFYING DEATH OF BARNEY BARNATO
1. *Bl Barnato: a memoir.*

THE FLYING DUTCHMAN
1. *The Ghost Ship.*
2. *The Ghost Ship.*

THE KRUGER MILLIONS
1. 'The Truth about the Kruger Millions',
The South African Nation, 10 October 1925.
2. 'The Truth about the Kruger Millions',
The South African Nation, 10 October 1925.
3. 'The Missing Kruger Millions',
British South Africa Annual, December 1931.
4. 'A Last Glance at the Kruger Millions',
Something Rich and Strange.
5. 'The Truth about the Kruger Millions',
The South African Nation, 10 October 1925.
6. *Sunday Times*, 15 November 1931.

WARATAH
1. *Weekend Argus*, 1 July 1989.

THE LOST CITY OF THE KALAHARI
1. *Through the Kalahari Desert.*
2. *Through the Kalahari Desert.*
3. *Through the Kalahari Desert.*

PHOENICIAN GALLEY AT THE CAPE?
1. *History*, Book IV, Chapter 42.
2. *Travels into the Interior of South Africa in the year 1797 and 1798.*
3. Surveyor General Letterbook,
13 June 1851-31 August 1851

4. Surveyor General Letterbook:
Government Letters 1852
5. *Eastern Province Monthly Herald*: 'The Geology of South Africa', lecture delivered by AG Bain,
April 1857.
6. 'The historical succession of cultural impacts upon South Africa', *Nature* 115, March 1925.
7. 'Phoenician shipwreck on the Cape Flats',
South African Archaeological Bulletin 3 (10).
8. 'A report on drilling and trenching on the Woltemade Flats, Cape Town, in 1988 and 1989',
South African Journal of Science Volume 86,
November/December 1990.

THE STRANDLOPERS
1. *Before Van Riebeeck.*

REINCARNATION
1. *The Reincarnation of Uvashnee Rattan.*

MYSTERY FLIGHT N12062
1. *Argus*, 25 June 1991.
2. *Argus*, 2 July 1991.

THE QUAGGA
1. *Historical Mammal Incidence in the Cape Province*,
Volume 1.
2. *Historical Mammal Incidence in the Cape Province*,
Volume 1.
3. *A Voyage to the Cape of Good Hope towards the Antarctic Polar Circle Round the World and to the Country of the Hottentots and the Caffres from the year 1772-1776*, Volume 1.
4. *Travels into the interior parts of Africa.*

THE PORTHOLE MURDER
1. *The Porthole Murder Case.*
2. *The Porthole Murder Case.*

WHALE AND DOLPHIN STRANDINGS
1. *Historia Animalium.*
2. *Cerebral and Cerebellar involvement of trematode parasites in dolphins and their possible role in stranding.*
3. *Air sinus parasitism and pathology in free-ranging common dolphins* (Delphinus delphis) *in the eastern tropical Pacific.*
4. Figures supplied by Nan Rice.

UFOs
1. *Fair Lady*, 2 August 1978.
2. *UFO African Encounters.*
3. *Fair Lady*, 2 August 1978.
4. *Fair Lady*, 2 August 1978.
5. *UFO African Encounters.*
6. *UFO African Encounters.*
7. *UFO African Encounters.*
8. *UFO Afrinews* July 1992.
9. *UFO Afrinews* July 1992.

GEORGE REX OF KNYSNA
1. 'George Rex of Knysna' *In the Land of Afternoon.*
2. *George Rex of Knysna.*
3. 'George Rex of Knysna' *In the Land of Afternoon.*
4. *George Rex of Knysna.*

LORD LUCAN
1. *Cape Times*, 10 August 1975.

African Wildlife, Wildlife Society of South Africa, Volume 37, 1983.

Aristotle *Historia Animalium*, H Bohn, London, 1862.

Barrow, Sir John *Travels into the Interior of South Africa in the year 1797 and 1798*, T Cadell & W Davies, London, 1806.

Brewer's Dictionary of Phrase and Fable, Cassell Publishers, London, 1990.

British South African Annual, 1939-40.

Bronowski, J *The Ascent of Man*, London, 1974.

Bruton, Michael N and Robin E Stobbs 'The Ecology and Conservation of the Coelacanth', *Environmental Biology of Fishes*, 32: 313-39, 1991.

Bulpin, TV *Discovering Southern Africa*, TV Bulpin Publications, Cape Town, 1980.

Clark, David *Vanished!: Mysterious Disappearances*, Chivers, Bath, 1991.

Clarke, Arthur C, J Fairlye and S Welfare *World of Strange Powers*, Guild Publishing, 1985.

Clement, AJ *The Kalahari and its Lost City*, Longman, Cape Town, 1967.

Cohen, Daniel *Encyclopaedia of Unsolved Crimes*, Dodd, Mead & Co, New York, 1988.

Cory, GE *The Rise of South Africa*, Vol. VI, 1853-57, Struik, Cape Town, 1965.

Dart, Raymond A 'The Historical Succession of Cultural Impacts upon South Africa', *Nature*, 115: 425-9, March 1925.

Darwin, Charles *The Voyage of the Beagle*, Marshall-Cavendish, 1987.

Doyle, Sir Arthur Conan *The Lost World*, J Murray & J Cape, London, 1979.

Edwards, George *Gleanings of Natural History*, printed at the Royal College of Physicians, London, 1858.

Emslie, Anne *The Owl House*, Viking, London, 1991.

Farini, Gilarmi A *A Recent Journey in the Kalahari*, Royal Geographical Society, Vol. VII, 437-50, London, 1886.

Farini, Gilarmi A *Through the Kalahari Desert*, Struik, Cape Town, 1973.

Fisher, Joe *The Case for Reincarnation*, Collins, Toronto, 1984.

Garlake, Peter *The Making of the Past: Kingdoms of Africa*, Elsevier/Phaidon, Oxford, 1978.

Green, Lawrence George *In the Land of Afternoon*, Timmins, Cape Town, 1949.

Green, Lawrence George *Something Rich and Strange*, Timmins, Cape Town, 1962.

Haggard, HR *King Solomon's Mines*, 1985.

Haining, Peter (editor) *The Ghost Ship*, Kimber, London, 1985.

Herbstein, D *The Porthole Murder Case*, Hodder and Stoughton, London, 1991.

Herodotus *History* Book IV, Chapter 42 (translated by AD Godley) Heinemann, 1921.

Hind, Cynthia *UFOs: African Encounters*, Gemini, Harare, 1982.

Historical Mammal Incidence in the Cape Province, Volume 1.

Hudson, Thomson J *The Law of Psychic Phenomena*, Hudson-Cohan, Monterey, California, 1970.

ICHTHOS, Newsletter of the Friends of the JLB Smith Institute of Ichthyology.

Jackson, Stanley *The Great Barnato*, Penguin, London, 1990.

Koestler, Arthur *The Roots of Coincidence*, Hutchinson, London, 1972.

Leakey, R and R Lewin *Origins Reconsidered*, Little Brown, 1992.

Lee, DN and HC Woodhouse *Art on the Rocks of Southern Africa*, Purnell, Cape Town, 1970.

Le Vaillant *Travels into the interior parts of Africa*, GGJ & J Robinson, London, 1796.

Lewis, Roy Harley *Ghosts, Haunting and the Supernatural World*, David and Charles, 1991.

Lewis-Williams, David J *The Rock Art of Southern Africa*, Cambridge University Press, Cambridge, 1983.

Marnham, Patrick *Trail of Havoc: In the Steps of Lord Lucan*, Viking, Harmondsworth, Middlesex, 1987.

Marsh, Rob *Famous South African Crimes*, Struik Timmins, Cape Town, 1991.

Metelerkamp, Sanni *George Rex of Knysna*, Howard Timmins, Cape Town, 1955.

Moody, Raymond A and P Perry *Life Before Life: regression into past lives*, Macmillan, London, 1990.

Mostert, Noel *Frontiers*, Johnathan Cape, London, 1992.

O'Sullivan, B 'A Report on Drilling and Trenching on the Woltemade Flats, Cape Town, in 1988 and 1989', *South African Journal of Science*, Vol. 86, 487-8, 1990.

Peires, JB *The Dead will Arise*, Raven, Johannesburg, 1989.

Preller, Gustav S 'The Truth About the Kruger Millions', *The South African Nation*, 2 (79), 13-6, 10 October 1925.

Raven-Hart, R *Before Van Riebeek*, Struik, 1967.

Raymond, Harry *BI Barnato: a memoir*, Juta, Cape Town, 1897.

Reader's Digest Illustrated Guide to Southern Africa, Cape Town, 1978.

Reitz, D 'The Missing Kruger Millions' *British South Africa Annual*, 24-9, December 1931.

Ridgeway, SH and MD Dailey *Cerebral and Cerebellar involvement of trematode parasites in dolphins and their possible role in stranding* in J Wildl Dis. 8: 33-43.

Rosenthal, Eric *Gold! Gold! Gold!: the Johannesburg Gold Rush*, Macmillan, London, 1990.

Royal Geographical Journal, November 1918.

Sagan, C *Cosmos*, Macdonald, 1980.

Sampson, HF 'Phoenician Shipwreck on the Cape Flats', *South African Archaeological Bulletin*, 3 (10), 34-40, June 1948.

Smith, JLB *Old Fourlegs -The Story of the Coelacanth*, Longmans, London, 1956.

Smith, JLB 'A Living Fish of Mesozoic Type', *Nature* 143: 455-6, March 1939.

South African Archaeological Bulletin, Volume 3, 1948.

Southern Africa from the Highway, AA Publications, 1991.

Sparrman, A, *A Voyage to the Cape of Good Hope towards the Antarctic Polar Circle, round the world and to the country of the Hottentots and the Caffres from the year 1772 to 1776*, Vol. 1, Van Riebeek Society Publications, Cape Town, 1977.

Spencer, John *UFOs - The Definitive Casebook*, Hamlyn, London, 1991.

Storrar, Patricia *George Rex: Death of a Legend*, Macmillan, 1974.

Summers, Roger *Ancient Ruins and Vanished Civilisations of Southern Africa*, Bulpin, Cape Town, 1971.

Surveyor General Letter Book, 13/06/1851-31/08/1852

Targ, Russell and Harold E Puthoff *Mind Reach: Scientists Look at Psychic Ability*, Johnathan Cape, London, 1977.

Thompson, George *Travels and Adventures in Southern Africa*, Africana Connoisseurs, Cape Town, 1962.

Walker, WA *Air sinus parasitism and pathology in free-ranging common dolphins*, Rep. LJ-81-23C.

'Waratah' *Wheelhouse* (Safmarine), January 1988.

Webster's New World Encyclopedia, Prentice Hall, 1990.

Wilson, Ian *Worlds Beyond*, Wiedenfeld & Nicholson, London, 1986.

Wilson, ML 'Strandlopers', *The Phoenix*, 4 (2), 14-21, October 1991.

Wilson, ML 'Lyall Watson and the *Strandlopers*', *The Digging Stick*, 7 (1), 7-9, April 1990.

Wilson, ML 'Shell middens and *Strandlopers*', *Sagittarius*, 4 (1), 2-5, March 1989.

Wilson, ML, WJJ van Rijssen and DA Gerneke 'Coldstream Stone', *Annals of the South African Museum*, 99 (6), May 1990.

Wormser, Pam *Strandlopers and other mythical beings*, Hout Bay Museum.

Argus.
Cape Times.
East London Daily Dispatch.
Eastern Province Monthly Herald.
Fair Lady.
Johannesburg Star.
London Times, 7/1/1909.
Natal Mercury, 23/11/1974.
Saturday Star, 15/5/93, 10/6/93.
Sunday Times.
The Guardian, 18/6/1980.
UFO Afrinews.
Weekly Mail, 28/6/93.

INDEX